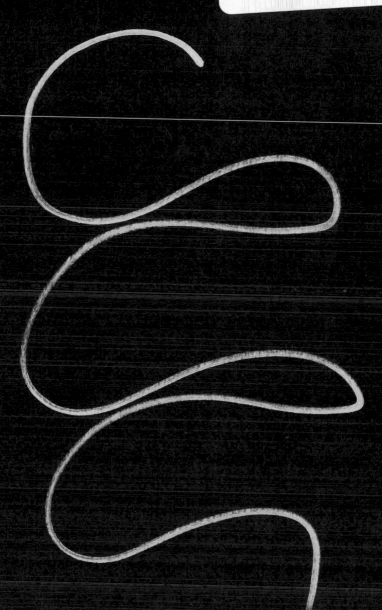

BLACK HANDS ON A WHITE FACE

From the Midnight
of Slave Time
to
Now*

BLACK HANDS

ON A

WHITE FACE

A Timepiece of Experiences
in a Black and White America

AN ANTHOLOGY EDITED BY *Whit Burnett*

DODD, MEAD & COMPANY

NEW YORK

ISBN: 0-396-06374-8

Library of Congress Catalog Card Number: 73-160860

Printed in the United States of America
by The Cornwall Press, Inc., Cornwall, N. Y.

Grateful acknowledgment is made to the following for permission to reprint
the material presented in this book:

DIAL PRESS

For "The Mud of Vietnam," from *Search for the New Land,* by Julius
Lester. Copyright © 1969 by Julius Lester.

ESTHER T. GROVER

For "The Finer Points," by Wayne Grover. Copyright © 1934 by Whit
Burnett.

HARCOURT BRACE JOVANOVICH, INC.

For "Phebe," from *All the King's Men,* by Robert Penn Warren. Copyright 1946 by Robert Penn Warren.

HARPER & ROW, INC.

For "How 'Bigger' Was Born," from *Saturday Review* and from *Native
Son,* by Richard Wright, Perennial Edition published by Harper & Row,
Inc., 1966. Copyright 1940 by Richard Wright.

HOUGHTON, MIFFLIN COMPANY

For "Black Again, White Again," from *Black Like Me,* by John Howard
Griffin. Copyright © 1960, 1961 by John Howard Griffin.

ROBERT LANTZ-CANDIDA DONADIO LITERARY AGENCY

For "Sonny's Blues," from *Going to Meet the Man,* by James Baldwin.
Copyright © 1948, 1951, 1957, 1958, 1960, 1965 by James Baldwin.

THE MACMILLAN COMPANY

For "Harlem Revisited," Chapter 18, from *Manchild in the Promised
Land,* by Claude Brown. Copyright © 1965 by Claude Brown.

MCGRAW-HILL BOOK COMPANY

For "To All Black Women," from *Soul on Ice,* by Eldridge Cleaver.
Copyright © 1968 by Eldridge Cleaver.

Preface: The Long Shadow

This is a selection of stories each of which was chosen for this volume because, whether it was written by an author whose skin was white or black, it showed a human being of its author's creation caught in a moment of significant drama. This is true especially in the many instances where over the years I or my associates at STORY had a hand in the original publication of the piece. The work chosen for STORY was not printed because it was tendentious. But looking back over the narratives and experiences in this volume—no matter from what sources they were taken *—it is evident they were all written for a message, a faint cry at first, clamorous and affirmative in the shouting of today. Hear us, see us, feel for us, the voices said at first. Then, Look, we're here. Then, *Here We ARE! No one can ignore us.* No longer a shadowy character, the black man, in fiction and in fact, stands up. And his shadow looms before him.

Common to all the stories or biographical pieces is a deep, human, often painful relationship, most meaningfully that of a black man, woman or child to the society surrounding him. At times that society takes the form of another human

* Where the material came from appears either before the story begins or on the page of Acknowledgments, often both places.

being, a black too, as often as not; but in most cases the dramatic relationship is with a white person or persons, a neighborhood or an atmosphere. At times a man's confrontation is with himself, with a code, a thing, or a drug.

In the relative time sequence of the contents, the changes in black (and white) consciousness over the years are evident in this clockwise turn of fiction and events. When I was editing a magazine of fiction some years ago I hoped, through it, to express my belief that the short story was the practically perfect American fiction medium in which could be revealed almost every imaginable aspect of the human condition. In those days stories dealing with the condition, status, plight, comedy, tragedy, submission or rebellion of the Negro in America were written by the writers of the day who then, in the main, were white. There were black writers before Richard Wright and James Baldwin. But in those days Negro writers were not publicly incautious; they seemed to be limiting themselves to poetry, private, lyrical, and nonreportorial utterances. It was not until *Uncle Tom's Children,* * *Native Son* * and *Black Boy* came from Wright that other young Negro writers—Ellison, Baldwin and the rest—began to raise their voices in fiction and to treat the black man in dramatic narratives from his own direct and personal point of view.

Twenty, thirty years later, scores of young black fiction writers, outstanding and knowledgeable in their craft and rich in authentic background, are developing their art and their lives, frankly and truthfully and, characteristically, in all the current permissive language of the day.

A dozen of the writers in this book are black, ten are unmixed white, another is a Puerto Rican living in Spanish Harlem, and still another is that white man who dyed himself black for a couple of months to experience in disguise

* Story Press books with Harper, 1938, 1940, and 1941.

the subjective reactions of a man with a black skin in the South.

Thus not all of these stories are by young black writers; nor are they simply the crafted observations of black people under stress as seen, however perceptively, by exclusively white writers. Fiction writers, black and white, write because they are concerned with human beings, the bright or dulled particularities of being. And the authors of these stories are as different, individual and personal as the people they have brought forth for our possible understanding.

The first piece is set in the Virginia of 1831 (although it was written in the very recent past). William Styron's story time was slave time, and if his controversial book *The Confessions of Nat Turner* has met with opposition by some black critics because a white man presumed to treat a black man from "inside," it cannot be unreservedly put down on that account. If Mr. Styron chose to step into a character, he had a tradition going back as far at least as the Othello of Shakespeare, and there has been no law since against it. Robert Penn Warren's story takes place in slave time, too, when Phebe was sold down the river just before the Civil War. It is interesting that both these selections have elsewhere been chosen by their authors, as writings of which they are most proud, to represent them in *This Is My Best,* a generation's assemblage of the greatest living American writers. Both, of course, are white authors and both have long been concerned with white and black relationships.

There are a few short fragments of black experience which are frankly autobiographical, such as Richard Wright's, or Claude Brown's, or Bob Teague's, or Edward Rivera's, or the short piece by John Howard Griffin, the ex-bombardier who was blinded in his World War II plane and whose moving experience of regaining sight he told about in "Is This What It Means to See?" which I anthologized in an earlier collection called *The Spirit of Man.* As hundreds of thousands of readers know, Mr. Griffin tried to find further ways of seeing when he changed the color of his skin and subjected himself to an unparalleled six weeks of black and white living in contemporary Mississippi, Alabama, Louisiana and his home state, Georgia.

In the stories of city streets, Harlem is a frequent backdrop, different in different periods, beginning in the 1920s when it was the chic thing for white visitors to slum there for drinks and jazz; later as a capital of dope, crime, and violence in the streets. But whether the locale is New York, Chicago, California, or the South of early cotton or later industry or civil-rights marches, the human problem has not essentially changed: basically, the problem seems to be how to live in this time—or any time—together, or apart, or not at all. These are black stories about that human striving. Some are dramatic, some are muted, and some are very black indeed.

—WHIT BURNETT

Contents

"A part of me hates also. Sometimes, all of me, because they
will never know, those young white kids, what it is like and
I want to drown them in their whiteness. But, because they
cannot completely know is no reason to deny them their right
to humanity. They, too, are human and those I can love, I do
and only hope that their numbers multiply with the rising of
each sun. . . ." From *Search for the New Land*

I

SLAVE TIME

WILLIAM STYRON

Hark: 1831, Virginia

From The Confessions of Nat Turner

WILLIAM STYRON was born in the Tidewater region of
Virginia in 1925 and grew up not far from the place where nearly
a century before the slave revolt led by Nat Turner began. Nat
was the protagonist of the author's Pulitzer Prize novel *The Confessions of Nat Turner*. The time of this episode was slave time,
although the novel itself is a product of contemporary sensitivities
and was published in 1967. This section was chosen by the author
to represent him in *This Is My Best* (1970, containing the greatest
living American authors and their own choices). Of it Mr. Styron
says: "I think it is as successful a fusion as I have as yet achieved of
character portrayal, narrative momentum, and a sense of environment—a combination which I believe to be an ideal in the creation
of meaningful or worthwhile fiction." Of the novel as a whole,
Eliot Fremont-Smith of *The New York Times* said: "It evokes
slavery and its continuing heritage as it has rarely been evoked
before in imaginative narrative literature . . . it resurrects and
gives meaning to an important but hitherto virtually ignored moment in our history, and thereby will help to change the teaching
of our history."

Hark always declared that he could distinguish between
good white people and bad white people—and even white
people who lay between good and bad—by their smell alone.
He was very solemn about all this; over the years he had
worked out many subtleties and refinements upon his original
philosophy, and he could talk endlessly as we worked alongside each other—advising me at the top of his voice, assigning
exact, marvelous odors to white people like Moses handing
down the law. About much of this he was deadly serious, and
as he jabbered away his broad, bold face would become fur-
rowed in the most worrisome thought; but Hark's nature was
basically humorous, outward-going, beneficent, serene, and
he could not long sustain a somber mood, even though many
horrible things had happened to him.

Finally something connected with a white person and a certain smell would tickle some interior nerve: against all re-
straint the giggles would begin to well up from his belly and
in an instant he would have broken down, clutching himself
in helpless, wheezing, rich, delirious laughter. "Now, Nat,
maybe it jes' *me*," he would begin seriously, "but dis yere nose
of mine she jes' get better ev'y day. Like I was comin' roun' de
side of de barn yestiddy evenin' and dere's ole Miss Maria
a-feedin' the chickens. She seed me afore I could take off.
'Hark!' say she. 'Hark! Come right yere!' So I come, an'
awready my nose begin twitchin' like a mushrat pokin' up
out'n de swamp. 'Hark!' say she. 'Whar de corn?' 'Why, what
corn, Miss Maria?' say I, de ole smell gittin' strong now. 'De
corn in de shed for de chickens!' de ole bitch say. 'You suppose' to have a couple bushels shelled fo' my chickens and
dere ain't a cupful lef'! Dis de fo'th time in a month! You a
shiftless black nigger scoundrel and I pray to see de day my
brother sells you off to Mississippi! *Git* dat corn shelled right

now, you shiftless nigger!' Jesus jumpin' Judas, de smell, Nat,
comin' out dat woman, if it water 'twould have drown' me in
my shoes. What it like? 'Twas like an ole catfish somebody
lef' three days up on a stump in July." And he would begin to
giggle softly, already clutching at his midriff. "Stink! Even de
buzzards fly away from ole pussy like dat!" And glorious
laughter.

But not all of them had smells like this, according to Hark.
Mr. Joseph Travis, our master, had "a right honest stench
about him," said Hark, "like a good horse what worked him
up a sweat." Joel Westbrook, the boy whom Travis employed
as an apprentice, was an uncertain, gawky lad, given to temper
fits but amiable, even generous when in the mood; hence to
Hark his smell had a changing, fitful quality; "Sometime dat
boy smell right pretty, like hay or somethin', other time he
smell up a storm." This offensive Miss Maria Pope was to
Hark, however, in every way consistent in her smell. She was
Travis's half sister, who had come down from Petersburg to
live with Travis and his family after her mother's death. A
bony, angular woman, she suffered from blocked sinuses
which caused her to breathe through her mouth; as a result
her lips were always peeling to the quick and sometimes bled,
which necessitated a poultice of lard, and this gave her ever-
parted mouth a blanched appearance altogether ghostly and
strange. Her eyes wandered distantly, and she was given to
stroking her wrists. She hated us Negroes who were at her
beck and call, with a kind of profound and pointless hatred
which was all the more burdensome to us because she was not
really of the family, and therefore her attitude had a harsh,
remote, despotic quality. On summer nights, from the windows of the upstairs room where she slept, I could hear her
sobbing hysterically and crying out for her departed mother.
She was about forty, I suspect a virgin, and she read aloud
from the Bible incessantly with a kind of hollow-eyed, mes-
meric urgency, her favorite passages being John 13, which

deals with humility and charity, and the sixth chapter of I
Timothy, beginning: *Let as many servants as are under the
yoke count their own masters worthy of all honour, that the
name of God and his doctrine be not blasphemed.* Indeed, according to Hark, she once flattened him up against the porch
wall and made him repeat this homily until he had committed
it to memory. I have no doubt that she was more than a little
cracked, but this did not diminish my intense dislike of Miss
Maria Pope, though occasionally I felt myself feeling sorry
for her against my better judgment.

But Miss Maria is, in a manner of speaking, only incidental
to a man I am trying to get at in a roundabout fashion—
namely, Mr. Jeremiah Cobb, the judge who was about to
sentence me to death, and into whose earlier acquaintance I
was led by a complicated series of transactions which I must
here try briefly to describe.

As I told Mr. Gray, I was born the property of Benjamin
Turner, about whom I remember only a little. Upon his
abrupt death when I was around eight or nine (a miller and
dealer in timber, he was killed while felling a cypress tree,
having turned his back on the monster at an improvident
moment), I passed by bequest into the possession of his
brother, Samuel Turner, whose property I remained for ten
or eleven years. These years, and those preceding them, I shall
return to in due course. Eventually Samuel Turner's fortunes
declined, and there were other problems; at any one, he was
unable to continue to operate the sawmill he inherited, along
with me, from his brother, and so for the first time I was sold,
to Mr. Thomas Moore—a sale which a weakness for irony
impels me to remark was effected at the moment I reached my
manhood, during my twenty-first year. I was the property of
Mr. Moore, who was a small farmer, for nine years until his
death (another bizarre misadventure; Moore broke his skull
while presiding at the birth of a calf. It had been a balky delivery, and he had wrapped a cord around the calf's protrud-

ing hooves in order to yank it out; as he sweated and tugged
and as the calf mused at him soulfully from the damp mem-
branes of its afterbirth, the cord snapped, catapulting him
backward and fatally against a gatepost. I had very little use
for Moore, and my grief was meager, yet at the time I could
not but help begin to wonder if ownership of me did not
presage a diminution of fortune, as does the possession, I am
told, of a certain kind of elephant in India), and upon Mr.
Moore's demise I became the property of his son, Putnam,
who was then fifteen. The following year (that is to say, last
year) Mr. Moore's widow, Miss Sarah, married Joseph Travis,
a childless widower of fifty-five desirous of offspring, who lived
in this same country region of Cross Keys, an expert wheelwright by trade and the last person so luckless as to enjoy me
in the pride of ownership. For although under law I was
Putnam's by title, I belonged also to Travis, who had the right
to exercise full control over me until Putnam reached his
majority. Thus when Miss Sarah wed Joseph Travis and became domiciled beneath his roof, I turned into a kind of two-
fold property—not an unheard-of arrangement but addition-
ally unsatisfying to property already half deranged at being
owned even once.

Travis was moderately prosperous, which is to say that like
a few of the other inhabitants of this backwater, he managed
to eke out slightly more than a living. Unlike the hapless
Moore, he was adept at that which the Lord had him cut out
to do, and it was a great relief for me to be able to help him
at his trade after the long years at Moore's and the monotony
of toting his water and sopping his feverish, languishing pigs
and alternately baking and freezing in his cornfield and his
cotton patch. In fact, because of the circumstances of my new
employment—which was to act as a general handyman around
the wheel shop—I had a sense of well being, physical at least,
such as I had not felt since leaving Samuel Turner's nearly
ten years before. Like most of the other property owners of

the region, Travis was also a small farmer, with fifteen acres or so in corn, cotton, and hay, plus an apple grove whose principal function it was to produce cider and brandy. Since the relative success of the wheel shop, however, Travis had cut back on his farm holdings, leasing out his acreage to others, and retaining just the apple orchard, and a small produce garden and patch of cotton for his own use. Besides myself, Travis owned only two Negroes—a number, however, not unusual in its smallness, inasmuch as few white people in the region could any longer afford to support more than five or six slaves, and it was rare indeed to find a citizen prosperous enough to own as many as a dozen. Travis himself had recently owned seven or eight, not counting several unserviceable children, but as his acreage diminished and his solitary craft flourished, he had no need for this obstreperous pack, indeed found so many fat mouths to feed a burden on his capital, and thus, three years before, with great moral misgivings (or so I heard) sold off the whole lot—all but one—to a trader specializing in labor for the Mississippi delta. The one left was Hark, who was my age lacking a year. Born on a vast tobacco plantation in Sussex County, he had been sold to Travis at the age of fifteen after the tobacco sucked the soil dry and the land went to rack and ruin. I had known him for years and had come to love him like a brother. The other Negro, acquired subsequent to the Mississippi sale, was Moses, a husky, tar-black, wild-eyed boy of twelve or thereabouts whom Travis, finding himself belatedy short-handed, had bought at the Richmond market several months before my arrival. He was strong and strapping for his age, and bright enough, I think; but he never quite got over the separation from his mammy; it left him bereft, stuporous, and he cried a lot and peed in his pants, sometimes even when he was at work, and all in all was a nuisance, becoming a great trial to Hark especially, who had a mother's soul in the body of a bull, and felt compelled to soothe and nurse the foundling.

This then was the population of our household at the time
when I first encountered Jeremiah Cobb, almost one year to
the day before he sentenced me to death: three Negroes—
Hark, Moses, myself—six white people—Mr. and Mrs. Travis
and Putnam, Miss Maria Pope, and two more besides. The
last were the previously mentioned Joel Westbrook, fifteen
years old, a budding wheelwright whom Travis had appren-
ticed to himself; and Travis's child by Miss Sarah, an infant
boy of two months born with a purple blemish spreading
across the center of his tiny face like the single shriveling petal
of a blighted gentian. The white people, of course, lived in
the main house, a modest, plain but comfortable two-storied
structure of six rooms which Travis had built twenty years
before. He had hewn the beams himself, planed the timbers,
made it all weather-tight with pine gum and mortar, and had
been wise enough to leave standing round it several enormous
beech trees which offered shade from any angle against the
summer sun. Adjacent to the house, separated from it only
by the pigpen and a short path through the vegetable garden,
was the wheel shop, converted from a one-time barn: here was
the center of activity on the farm, here were the stores of oak
and ashwood and iron, the forge and anvils, the bending
frames, the modeling hammers and tongs and vises and the
rows of chisels and punches and all the other equipment which
Travis employed in his demanding craft. Doubtless at least
in part because of my repute (descent albeit somewhat am-
biguous and suspect in a way I will soon explain) as a kind of
harmless, runabout, comic nigger minister of the gospel, I was
later made custodian of the shop; in fact, prompted by Miss
Sarah's avowal of my integrity, Travis gave into my keeping
one of two sets of keys. I had plenty enough to do, but I cannot honestly say that my work here was toilsome; unlike
Moore, Travis was no taskmaster, being by nature unable, I
think, to drive his servants unreasonably and already having
been well provided with willing help in the person of his

stepson and the Westbrook boy, who was an eager apprentice if there ever was one.

Thus my duties, compared to what I had been used to, were light and fairly free of strain: I kept the place clean and added my shoulder to a job when extra strength was needed, such as bending a wheel rim, and frequently I spelled Hark as he pumped at the bellows of the forge, but generally speaking (and for the first time in years) the tasks I encountered were those calculated to tax not my muscles but my ingenuity. (For instance, the loft of the shop since its conversion from the status of a barn had still been infested by bats, tolerable enough when the place was the abode of cattle but an insufferable plague of drizzling bat shit to humans laboring daily below. Travis had tried half a dozen futile measures to rid himself of the pests, including fire and smoke, which nearly burned the place down; whereupon at this point I went out into the woods to a certain nest I knew of and plucked a blacksnake out of hibernation, wrenching it from the tail-end of its winter's sleep and installing it in the eaves. When spring came a week later the bats quickly vanished, and the blacksnake continued in friendly, satisfied residence, slithering benevolently around the circumference of the shop as it gobbled up rats and field mice, its presence earning me, I know, quiet admiration in Travis's regard.) So, all things being equal, from the beginning of my stay with Travis, I was in as palmy and benign a state as I could remember in many years. Miss Maria's demands were annoying, but she was a small thorn. Instead of the nigger food I was accustomed to at Moore's, fat pork and corn pone, I got house food like the white people —a lot of lean bacon and red meat, occasionally even the leavings from a roast of beef, and often white bread made of wheat —and the lean-to shed adjoining the wheel shop where Hark and I shared housekeeping was roomy enough, with the first bed elevated above the ground that I had slept on since the old days with Samuel Turner; and I constructed, with my

owner's blessing, an ingenious wooden vent leading through
the wall from the forge, which was always banked with charcoal: the vent could be shut off in the summer, but in the
winter its constant warmth made Hark and me (the poor boy
Moses slept in the house, in a damp kitchen closet, where he
could be available for errands night and day) as snug as two
grubs beneath a log. Above all, I had quite a bit of time on
my hands. I could fish and trap and do considerable Scriptural
reading. I had for going on to several years now considered
the necessity of exterminating all the white people in South-
ampton County and as far beyond as destiny carried me, and
there was thus available to me more time than I had ever had
before to ponder the Bible and its exhortations, and to think
over the complexities of the bloody mission that was set out
before me.

The particular November day I met Jeremiah Cobb is clear
in my memory: an afternoon of low gray clouds scudding eastward on a gusty wind, cornfields brown and sere stretching
toward the distant woods, and the kind of stillness which
comes with that time of autumn, the buzz and hum of insects
having flickered out, the songbirds flown south, leaving the
fields and woods to dwell in a vast gray globe of silence; nothing stirs, minutes pass in utter quiet, then through the smoky
light comes the sound of crows cawing over some far-off cornfield, a faint raucous hullabaloo which swiftly dwindles off in
the distance, and silence again, broken only by the scratching
and scrabble of dead windblown leaves. That afternoon I
heard dogs yapping in the north, as if they were coming down
the road. It was a Saturday, Travis and Joel Westbrook had
driven that morning to Jerusalem on an errand, and only
Putnam was at work in the shop. I was outside at the corner
of my shed cleaning some rabbits from my trapline, when in
the midst of this deep and brooding silence I heard the dogs
yapping up the road. They were foxhounds, but not enough
of them for a hunt, and I recall being puzzled, my puzzlement

vanishing just as I rose and looked up the road and saw a whirlwind of dust: out of the whirlwind came a tall white man in a pale beaver hat and gray cloak, perched on the seat of a dogcart drawn by a frisky jet-black mare. Behind and below the seat were the dogs, three flop-eared hounds yapping at one of Travis's yellow cur dogs who was trying to get at them through the spokes of the wheels. It was, I think, the first time I ever saw a dogcart with dogs. From where I stood I saw the dogcart draw up to a halt in front of the house, then saw the man dismount; I thought he came down clumsily, seeming for an instant to falter or to stumble as if weak in the knees, but then, instantly regaining control of himself, he muttered something half aloud and at the same time aimed a kick at the yellow dog, missed wildly, his booted foot fetching up against the side of the carriage with a clatter.

It was comical to watch—a white man's discomfiture, observed on the sly, has always been a Negro's richest delight—but even as I felt the laughter gurgling up inside me the man turned and my laughter ceased. I was now able to observe him for the first time straight on: the face I beheld was one of the most unhappy faces I had ever seen. It was blighted, ravaged by sorrow, as if grief had laid actual hands on the face, wrenching and twisting it into an attitude of ineradicable pain. Now too I could see that the man was a little drunk. He stared somberly at the dog howling at him from the dust of the road, then raised his hollow eyes briefly to the gray clouds scudding across the heavens. I thought I heard a groan pass his lips; a spasm of coughing seized him. Then with an abrupt, clumsy gesture he drew the cloak about his gaunt and bony frame and proceeded with fumbling gloved hands to fasten the mare to the tethering post. Just then I heard Miss Sarah call from the porch. "Judge Cobb!" I heard her cry. "Sakes alive! What are you doin' down this way?" He shouted something back to her, the cadence of his words obscure, muffled against the gusty wind. The leaves whirled around him, all the dogs kept yap-

ping and howling, the pretty little mare chafed and tossed her
mane and stamped. I managed to make out the words: a hunt
in Drewrysville, he was taking his dogs there, a grinding noise
in the spindle box of his wheel. He thought the axle broke,
split, something; being nearby he had come here for repairs.
Was Mr. Joe to home? Downwind came Miss Sarah's voice
from the porch, loud, buxom, cheerful: "Mr. Joe's done gone
to Jerusalem! My boy Putnam's here, though! He'll fix that
wheel for you, Judge Cobb, straightaway! Won't you come in
and set a spell!" Thank you no ma'am, Cobb hollered back;
he was in a rush, he'd get that axle fixed and be on his way.
"Well, I 'spect you know where the cider press is," Miss Sarah
called. "Right next to the shop. They's some brandy too! Just
help yourself and drink your fill!"

I went back to the corner of the shed, attending to my rabbits, and paid no more mind to Cobb for the moment. Travis
had allowed me to have the trapline, and in fact encouraged
me in the enterprise since by arrangement he was to get two
out of every three rabbits I caught. Such an agreement was
satisfactory to me, inasmuch as this game was plentiful in the
countryside and the two or three rabbits a week left for Hark
and me were as much as we cared to eat, and more; nor did it
matter to me that Travis sold most of the rabbits in Jerusalem
and retained the money, which was clear profit, since if he was
to earn interest on the capital which, body and brain, I rep-
resented anyway, I was glad to be capitalized upon in one
small way which I myself took pleasure in. For after all of the
dull drudgery at Moore's, it was the greatest delight to me to
be able to make use of some actual indwelling talent, to
fashion the traps myself—box traps which I made out of scrap
pine from the shop, sawing and planing the wood with my
own hands, carving the pegs and the notched pins which
tripped the doors, and uniting one after another of the neat
miniature coffins into a single smoothly operating, silent,
lethal assembly. But this was not all. As much as manufactur-

ing the traps I enjoyed walking the trapline at daybreak in the silence of the countryside, when frost crackled on the ground and the hollows overflowed as if with milk in the morning mists. It was a three-mile hike through the woods along a familar pine-needled path, and I devised a sort of cloth pouch to take along with me, in which I carried my Bible and my breakfast—two apples and a piece of streak-of-lean pork already cooked the night before. On my return, the Bible shared the pouch with a couple of rabbits, which I brained bloodlessly with a hickory club. A multitude of squirrels preceded me on these walks, in rippling stop-and-go motion; with some of them I became quite familiar and I bestowed names upon them, prophetic Hebrew names like Ezra and Amos, and I numbered them among God's blest since unlike rabbits they could not by nature be easily trapped and could not by law be shot (at least by me, Negroes being denied the use of guns). It was a silent, gentle, pristine time of day, and as the sun shone pale through the dews and the mists, and the woods hovered round me gray and still in the autumnal birdless quiet, it was like the morn of Genesis with the breath of creation fresh upon it.

Near the end of my trapline there was a little knoll, surrounded on three sides by a thicket of scrub oak trees, and here I would make my breakfast. From this knoll (though hardly taller than a small tree, it was the highest point of land for miles) I could obtain a clear and secret view of the countryside, including several of the farmhouses which it had already become my purpose eventually to invade and pillage. Thus these morning trapping expeditions also served to allow me to reconnoiter and to lay plans for the great event which I knew was in the offing. For at such times it seemed that the spirit of God hovered very close to me, advising me in this fashion: *Son of man, prophesy, and say, Thus saith the Lord; Say, a sword, a sword is sharpened, and also furbished: it is sharpened to make a sore slaughter* . . . Of all the Prophets it was

Ezekiel with his divine fury to whom I felt closest by kinship, and as I sat there these mornings, the pork and apples devoured, the bag of brained cottontails at my side, I would for a long time ponder Ezekiel's words because it was through his words that the wishes of the Lord concerning my destiny (even more so than through the words of the other Prophets) seemed most clearly to be revealed: *Go through the midst of Jerusalem, and set a mark upon the foreheads of the men that sigh and that cry for all the abominations that be done in the midst thereof . . . Slay utterly old and young, both maids and little children, and women: but come not near any man upon whom is the mark . . .* Often as I brooded over these lines, I wondered why God should wish to spare the well-meaning and slay the helpless; nonetheless, it was His word. Great mornings, filled with hints, auguries, portents! I find it hard to describe the exaltation which seized me at such times when, crouched upon my secret knoll in gray momentous dawns, I saw in the unfolding future—fixed there as immutably as Saul or Gideon—myself, black as the blackest vengeance, the illimitable, devastating instrument of God's wrath. For on these mornings as I looked down upon the gray and somber and shriveling landscape it seemed as if His will and my mission could not be more plain and intelligible: to free my people I must one day only commence with the slumbering, mist-shrouded dwellings below, destroying all therein, then set forth eastward across the swamps and fields, where lay Jerusalem.

But to get back to Cobb, rather meanderingly I'm afraid, and again by way of Hark. Hark had a flair for the odd, the off-center: had he been able to read and write, been white, free, living in some Elysian time when he was anything but negotiable property worth six hundred dollars in a depressed market, he might have been a lawyer; to my disappointment, Christian teachings (my own mainly) had made only the shallowest imprint upon his spirit, so that being free of spiritual rules and

restraints he responded to the mad side of life and could laugh
with abandon, thrilling to each day's new absurdity. In short,
he had a feeling for the crazy, the unexpected; all in all, this
caused me mild envy. There was for instance the time when
our shed behind the wheel shop was still uncompleted, and
our master paid us a visit during a roaring thunderstorm, gazing skyward at the water cascading through the roof. "It's
leaking in here," he said, to which Hark replied: "Nawsuh,
Marse Joe, hit leakin' outside. Hit *rainin'* in here." Likewise,
it was Hark who gave expression to that certain inward sense
—an essence of being which is almost impossible to put into
words—that every Negro possesses when, dating from the age
of twelve or ten or even earlier, he becomes aware that he is
only merchandise, goods, in the eyes of all white people devoid
of character or moral sense or soul. This feeling Hark called
"black-assed," and it comes as close to summing up the numb-
ness and dread which dwells in every Negro's heart as any
word I have ever known. "Don' matter who dey is, Nat, good
or bad, even ol' Marse Joe, dey white folks dey gwine make
you feel *black-assed*. Never seed a white man smile at me yet
'thout I didn' feel just about twice as black-assed as I was
befo'. How come dat 'plies, Nat? Figger a white man treat you
right you gwine feel *white-assed*. Naw *suh!* Young massah, old
massah sweet-talk me, I jes' feel *black-assed* th'ough an'
th'ough. Figger when I gets to heaven like you says I is, de
good Lord hisself even *He* gwine make old Hark feel black-
assed, standin' befo' de golden throne. Dere He is, white as
snow, givin' me at lot of sweet talk and me feelin' like a
black-assed angel. 'Cause pretty soon I know His line, yas *suh!*
Yas *suh*, pretty soon I can hear Him holler out: 'Hark! You
dere, boy! Need some spick and span roun' de throne room.
Hop to, you *black-assed* scoundrel! Hop to wid de mop and de
broom!' "
    It is impossible to exaggerate the extent to which white
people dominate the conversation of Negroes, and it is with

certainty I can record that these were the words that Hark
(who had come out of the shed to help me dress and clean the
rabbits) had been speaking on this gray November day when,
like the most vaguely discernible shadow, we felt simultaneously a presence at our crouched backs and again, half startled,
looked upward to see the distressed and ravaged face of Jeremiah Cobb. I don't know whether he overheard Hark's words,
it would hardly have mattered if he had. Both Hark and I
were taken unawares by the man's magisterial, sudden, lofty figure looming above us, swaying slightly against the smoky sky;
so abruptly and silently had he come upon us that it was a long
instant before the face of him actually registered, and before
we were able to let slip from our hands the bloody rabbits and
begin to move erect into that posture of respect or deference
it is wise for any Negro to assume whenever a strange white
man—always a bundle of obscure motives—enters upon the
scene. But now, even before we had gotten up, he spoke. "Go
on," he said, "go on, go on," in a curiously rough and raspy
voice—and with a motion of his hands he bade us to continue
at our work, which we did, easing back slowly on our haunches
yet still gazing up into the unsmiling, bleak, tormented face.
Suddenly a hiccup escaped his lips, a sound incongruous and
unseemly and even faintly comical emanating from that stern
face, and there was a long moment of silence all around; he
hiccuped again, and this time I was sure I sensed Hark's huge
body beginning to shudder with—with what? Laughter? Embarrassment? Fear? But then Cobb said: "Boys, where's the
press?"

"Yondah, massah," Hark said. He pointed to the shed several yards away, directly at the side of the shop, where the
cider barrels lay in a moist and dusty rank in the shadows past
the open door. "Red bar'l, massah. Dat's de bar'l fo' a gennle-
man, massah." When the desire to play the obsequious coon
came over him, Hark's voice became so plump and sweet that

it was downright unctuous. "Marse Joe, he save dat red bar'l for de *fines'* gennlemens."

"Bother the cider," Cobb said, "where's the brandy?"

"Brandy in de bottles on de shelf," said Hark. He began to scramble to his feet. "I fix de brandy fo' you, massah." But again Cobb motioned him back with a brisk wave of his hand. "Go on, go on," he said. The voice was not pleasant, neither was it unkindly; it had rather a distant, abstracted quality, yet somehow it remained tinged with pain as if the mind which controlled it struggled with a preoccupying disquiet. He was abrupt, aloof, but there was nothing one might call arrogant about him. Nonetheless, something about the man offended me, filled me with the sharpest displeasure, and it wasn't until he limped unsteadily past us through the crackling brown patch of weeds toward the cider press, saying not another word, that I realized that it wasn't the man himself who annoyed me so much as it was Hark's manner in his presence—the unspeakable bootlicking Sambo, all giggles and smirks and oily, sniveling servility. Hark had slit open a rabbit. The body was still warm (on Saturdays I often collected my game in the afternoon), and Hark was holding it aloft by the ears to catch the blood, which we saved to bind stews. I can recall my sudden fury as we crouched there, as I looked up at Hark, at the bland, serene glistening black face with its wide brow and the grave, beautiful prominences of its cheekbones. With dumb absorption he was gazing at the stream of crimson blood flowing into the pan he held below. He had the face one might imagine to be the face of an African chieftain—soldierly, fearless, scary, and resplendent in its bold symmetry—yet there was something wrong with the eyes, and the eyes, or at least the expression they often took on, as now, reduced the face to a kind of harmless, dull, malleable docility. They were the eyes of a child, trustful and dependent, soft doe's eyes mossed over with a kind of furtive, fearful glaze, and as I looked at them now—the womanish eyes in the

massive, sovereign face mooning dumbly at the rabbit's blood
—I was seized by rage. I heard Cobb fumbling around in the
cider press, clinking and clattering. We were out of earshot.
"Black toadeater," I said. "Snivelin' black toadeatin' white
man's bootlickin' scum! You, Hark! Black *scum!*"

Hark's soft eyes rolled toward me, trusting yet fearful.
"How come—" he began in an abrupt startled voice.

"Hush your face, man!" I said. I was furious. I wanted to
let him have the back of my hand flush in the mouth. "Just
hush, man!" I began to mimic him, hoarsely, beneath my
breath. " 'Red bar'l, massah! Dat's de bar'l wid de *gennle-
men's* cidah! I fix de brandy fo' you, massah!' How come you
make with that kind of talk, bootlickin' nigger suckup? It was
enough to make me plain ordinary *sick!*"

Hark's expression grew hurt, downcast; he moped discon-
solately at the ground, saying nothing but moving his lips in
a moist, muttering, abstracted way as if filled with hopeless
self-recrimination. "Can't you see, miserable nigger?" I per-
sisted, boring in hard. "Can't you see the *difference?* The difference betwixt plain politeness and bootlickin'? He didn't
even say, 'Get me a drink.' He said just, 'Where the press?' A
question, that's all. And there *you* is, already: scramblin' and
scroungin' like a bitch pup, massah this and massah that! You
enough to make a man chuck up his dinner!" *Be not hasty in
thy spirit to be angry: for anger resteth in the bosom of fools.*
Ashamed suddenly, I calmed myself. Hark was a vision of
dejection. More gently I said: "You just got to *learn,* man.
You got to learn the difference. I don't mean you got to risk a
beatin'. I don't mean you got to be uppity and smart. But they
is some kind of limit. And you ain't a *man* when you act like
that. You ain't a man, you is a fool! And you do this all the
time, over and over again, with Travis and Miss Maria and
Lord help you even with them two *kids.* You don't learn
nothin'. You a fool! *As a dog returneth to his vomit, so a fool*

returneth to his folly. You a *fool,* Hark. How'm I goin' to teach you?"

Hark made no reply, only crouched there muttering in his hurt and dejection. I was seldom angry at Hark, but my anger when it came had the power to grieve him. Loving him as I did, I often reproved myself for my outbursts and for the misery they caused him, but in certain ways he was like a spendid dog, a young, beautiful, heedless, spirited dog who had, nonetheless, to be trained to behave with dignity. Although I had not yet told him of my great plans, it was my purpose that when the day came to obliterate the white people, Hark would be my right arm, my sword and shield; for this he was well endowed, being quick-witted and resourceful and as strong as a bear. Yet the very sight of white skin cowed him, humbled him, diminished him to his most fawning and servile abasement; and I knew that before placing my ultimate trust in him I must somehow eliminate from his character this weakling trait which I had seen before in Negroes who, like Hark, had spent most of their early lives on big plantations. Certainly it would not do to have a chief lieutenant who was at heart only an abject nigger, full of cheap grins and comic shufflings, unable to gut a white man and gut him without a blink or qualm. In short, Hark was for me a necessary and crucial experiment. Though it is a painful fact that most Negroes are hopelessly docile, many of them are filled with fury, and the unctuous coating of flattery which surrounds and encases that fury is but a form of self-preservation. With Hark, I knew I must strip away and destroy that repulsive outer guise, meanwhile encouraging him to nurture the murderous fury which lay beneath. Yet somehow I did not think it would take too much time.

"I don't know, Nat," Hark said finally. "I tries and tries. But hit seem I cain't git over dat black-assed feelin'. I tries, though." He paused, ruminating, nodding his head ever so slightly over the bloody carcass in his hands. " 'Sides, dat man

he look so sad an' mou'nful. Never seed such a sad an' mou'n-
ful man. Kind of felt sorry fo' de man. What you reckon made
him so sad-lookin' anyways?"

I heard Cobb returning from the press through the weeds,
unsteadily, stumbling slightly, with a brittle crackling sound
of underbrush being trampled underfoot. "Feel sorry for a
white man and you wastin' your sorrow," I said in a low voice.
Then even as I spoke I made a sudden connection in my
mind, remembering how a few months before I had overheard
Travis speaking to Miss Sarah about this man Cobb, and the
terrors which had beset him grisly and Job-like within the
space of a single year: a merchant and banker of property and
means, chief magistrate of the county, master of the South-
ampton Hounds, he lost his wife and two grown daughters to
typhoid fever on the coast of Carolina, whither, ironically, he
had sent his ladies to recuperate from winter attacks of the
bronchial ailments to which all three were prone. Shortly
afterward his stable, a brand-new structure on the outskirts
of Jerusalem, burned to the ground in one horrid and almost
instantaneous holocaust, incinerating all therein including
two or three prize Morgan hunters and many valuable English
saddles and harnesses, not to mention a young Negro groom.
Subsequently, the unfortunate man, having taken heavily to
the bottle to ease his affliction, fell down some stairs and
broke his leg; the limb failed to mend properly, and although
ambulatory, he was plagued by a hectic, mild, irresistible
fever and by unceasing pain. When I first heard of all this
adversity I could not help but feel a spasm of satisfaction (do
not consider me altogether heartless—I am not, as you shall
surely see; but the contentment a Negro takes in a white man's
misery, existing like a delicious tidbit among bleak and scanty
rations, can hardly be overestimated), and I must confess that
now as I heard Cobb behind me toiling back through the
noisy weeds I experienced anew the same sense of gratification.
(*For the thing which I greatly feared is come upon me, and that*

*which I was afraid of is come unto me. I was not in safety,
neither had I rest, neither was I quiet; yet trouble came . . .*)
A small thrill of pleasure coursed through my flesh.

I thought he was going to walk past us to the shop or perhaps the house. Certainly I was taken by surprise when, instead, Cobb halted next to us with his boots practically atop
one of the skinned rabbits. Again Hark and I started to rise,
again he motioned for us to continue work. "Go on, go on," he
repeated, taking a huge gulp from the bottle. I heard the
brandy vanish with a froglike croak in the back of his gullet,
then the long aspirated gasp of breath, the final wet smacking
of lips. "Ambrosia," he said. Above us the voice was self-con-
fident, sturdy, stentorian; it had an unmistakable vigor and
force, even though the tired undertone of sorrow remained,
and I felt the residue of an emotion, ever so faint, which I
must confess was only the fear I was born and brought up
with. *"Am-ba-ro-sia,"* he said. My fear receded. The yellow
cur dog came snuffling up and I hurled into his face a slippery
blue handful of rabbits' guts, which he made off with into the
cotton patch, groaning with pleasure. "A Greek word," Cobb
went on "From *ambrotos,* that is to say, immortal. For surely
the gods were conferring upon us poor humans a kind of im-
mortality, no matter how brief and illusory, when they ten-
dered us this voluptuous gift, made of the humble and omni-
present apple. Comforter to the lonely and outcast, an anodyne
for pain, a shelter against the chill wind of remorseless, on-
coming death—surely such an elixir must be touched by the
hand of something or someone divine!" Another hiccup—it
was like a species of shriek, really prodigious—racked his
frame, and again I heard him take a swig from the bottle. Intent upon my rabbits, I had not as yet looked up, but I had
caught a glimpse of Hark: transfixed, with bloody glistening
hands outstretched, he was gazing open-mouthed at Cobb with
a look of absolute attention, a kind of ignorant and paralyzed
awe affecting to behold; straining to understand, he moved his

lips silently in unison with Cobb's, chewing upon the gor-
geous syllables as if upon air; droplets of sweat had burst forth
from his black brow like a spray of quicksilver, and for an
instant I could almost have sworn that he had ceased breathing. "Aaa-h," Cobb sighed, smacking his lips. "Pure delight.
And is it not remarkable that to his already estimable endow-
ments—the finest wheelwright in the Southside of Virginia—
your master Mr. Joseph Travis should add another supreme
talent, that of being the most skillful distiller of this ineffable
potion within the span of a hundred miles? Do you not find
that truly remarkable? Do you *not* now." He was silent.
Then he said again, ambiguously, in a voice which seemed—
to me at least—touched with threat: "Do you *not* now?"

I had begun to feel uncomfortable, disturbed. Perhaps I
was oversensitive (as always) to the peculiar shading of a white
man's tone; nonetheless, there seemed to be something
pointed, oppressive, sardonic about this question, alarming
me. It has been my usual experience that when a strange white
man adopts this florid, familiar manner, and when his listener
is black, the white man is out to have a little fun at the black
man's expense. And such had been my developing mood of
tension during the recent months that I felt I must avoid at
all costs (and no matter how harmless the by-play) even the
faintest premonition of a *situation*. Now the man's wretched
question had deposited me squarely upon a dilemma. The
trouble is: a Negro, in much the same way as a dog, has constantly to interpret the *tone* of what is being said. If, as was
certainly possible, the question was merely drunken-rhetori-
cal, then I could remain humbly and decently mute and scrape
away at my rabbit. This (my mind all the while spinning and
whirling away like a water mill) was the eventuality I preferred—dumb nigger silence, perhaps a little scratching of the
old woolly skull, and an illiterate pink-lipped grin, reflecting
total incomprehension of so many beautiful Latinisms. If on
the other hand, as seemed more likely from the man's ex-

pectant silence, the question was drunken-surly-sarcastic and demanding of an answer, I would be forced to mutter the customary Yassuh—Nawsuh being impermissible in view of the simple-minded nature of the question. What was so disturbing about this moment was my fear (and these fears, one may be assured, are neither vagrant nor inconsequential) that the Yassuh might very well be followed by something like this: "Ah, you do now. You *do* find it remarkable? Am I to understand then that you consider your master a dummox? That because he can make wheels he can't make brandy? You darkies don't have much regard for your owners these days, do you? Well, I want to tell you something, Pompey, or whatever your ludicrous name is, that . . ." et cetera. The changes on this situation are endless, and do not think me overly cautious: motiveless nigger-needling is a common sport. But at this point it was not the possibility of humiliation I wanted to avoid so much as the possibility that having recently vowed that humiliation would never again be a constraint upon me, or a repression, I would be forced to surmount it by beating the man's brains out, thus completely wrecking all my great designs for the future.

I had begun to shake, and I felt a stirring, a kind of watery weakness in my bowels; just then, however, came a fortunate distraction: nearby in the woods there arose the sound of a crashing in the undergrowth, and we all three turned to see a tawny mud-streaked wild sow lumber out of a thicket, snorting and grunting, trailed by her squealing brood; now as quickly as they appeared pig and piglets seemed to dissolve back into the sere and withered forest, the space of sky above silent and gray and desolate with low-hanging, tattered, wind-driven clouds like smudged cotton through which faint sunlight seeped yellowish and wan. Distracted, our eyes lingered on the scene for a moment, and then came a slamming noise, very close, as the door of the shop opened suddenly, and caught by the wind, hurled itself on screaming hinges backward against the wall. "Hark!" a voice called. It was my boy owner, Putnam. "Where you, Hark?" The child was in a foul mood; I could tell this from the blotches on his pale white face: they grew prominent and rosy whenever he became exercised or harassed. I should add that Putnam had more or less had it in for Hark ever since the preceding year when, out hunting hickory nuts on a balmy afternoon, Hark had innocently but clumsily ambushed Putnam and Joel Westbrook in some tangled carnal union by the swimming pond, both of the boys naked as catfish on the muddy bank, writhing about and skylarking with each other in the most oblivious way. "Never seed such foolishness," Hark had said to me, "But 'twarn't like I was gwine pay it no never mind. Nigger don' care 'bout no white boys' foolishness. Now dat daggone Putnam he so mad, you'd think it was *me* dat *dey* caught playin' with de ole bird." I sympathized with Hark but in the end I couldn't take it too seriously, as it simply typified an uncorrectable condition: white people really see nothing of a Negro in his private activity, while a Negro, who must walk miles out of his path to avoid seeing everything white people do, has often to suffer for even the most guileless part of his ubiquitous presence by being called a spy and a snooping black scoundrel.

"Hark!" the boy called again. "Get in here straight away! What do you think you're doin' out there, you no-account nigger! Fire's gone plumb out! Get in here, God durn you lazy wretch!" The boy wore a leather apron; he had a coarse-featured, sullen, pouty-mouthed face with flowing dark hair and long side whiskers: as he shouted at Hark, I felt a brief, fleeting spasm of rage and I longed for the day to arrive when I might get my hands on him. Hark scrambled to his feet and made off for the shop as Putnam called out again, this time to Cobb: "I think you have someways broke a axle, Judge, sir! My stepdad will fix it! He should be here afore too long!"

"Very well," Cobb called back. Then so abruptly that for an

instant I thought he was still talking to the boy, he said: *"As a dog returneth to his vomit, so a fool returneth to his folly.* That of course is most familiar, but for the life of me I am unable to place it within the Scriptures. I suspect however that it is one of the Proverbs of King Solomon, whose delight it was to rail at fools, and to castigate human folly . . ." As he went on talking, a queasy sensation crept over me: the customary positions were reversed, the white man this time had caught the nigger at *his* gossip. How did I know that my own black blabbermouth would betray me, and that he would overhear every word I had said? Humiliated, ashamed of my humiliation, I let the sticky wet rabbit corpse fall from my fingers and braced my spirit, preparing for the worst. "Was it not Solomon who said the fool shall be the servant to the wise? Was it not he too who said a fool despiseth his father's instruction? And is not the instruction of the father, through Paul the Jew of Tarsus, manifest even to the fools of this great dominion, to wit: *Stand fast therefore in the liberty wherewith Christ hath made us free, and be not entangled again with the yoke of bondage!"* As he continued to speak I slowly stood erect, but even at my full height he towered over me, sickly, pale, and sweating, his nose, leaking slightly in the cold, like a great scimitar protruding from the stormy and anguished face, the brandy bottle clutched in one huge mottled hand against his breast as he stood there in a limping posture, swaying and perspiring, speaking not so much to me as through and past me toward the scudding clouds. "Yes, and to this comes the reply, to this mighty and manifest truth we hear the response"—he paused for an instant, hiccuping, and then his voice rose in tones of mockery—"to this irresistible and binding edict we hear the Pharisee cry out of that great institution the College of William & Mary, out of Richmond, from the learned mountebanks abroad like locusts in the Commonwealth: 'Theology must answer theology. Speak you of liberty? Speak you of the yoke of bondage? How then, country magistrate, do you answer this? Ephesians Six, Five: *Servants, be obedient to them that are your masters according to the flesh, with fear and trembling, in singleness of your heart, as unto Christ.* Or this, my hayseed colleague, how answer you to this? One Peter, Two, Eighteen: *Servants, be subject to your masters with all fear; not only to the good and gentle, but also to the froward.* There, friend—*there*—is not that divine sanction for the bondage of which you rave and prattle?' Merciful God in heaven, will such casuistry never end! Is not the handwriting on the wall?" For the first time he seemed to look at me, fixing me for a moment with his feverish eyes before upending the bottle, thrusting its neck deep into his throat, where the brandy gulped and gurgled. *"Howl ye,"* he resumed, *"Howl ye: for the day of the Lord is at hand: it shall come as a destruction from the Almighty.* You're the preacher they call Nat, are you not? Tell me then, preacher, am I not right? Is not Isaiah only a witness to the truth when he says *howl ye?* When he says the day of the Lord is at hand, and it shall come as a destruction from the Almighty? Tell me in the honesty of truth, preacher: is not the handwriting on the wall for this beloved and foolish and tragic Old Dominion?"

"Praise God, mastah," I said, "that sure is true." My words were evasively meek and humble, with a touch of ministerial sanctimony, but I uttered them mainly to cover up my sudden alarm. For now I was truly afraid that he had identified me; the fact that this strange and drunken white man knew who I was smote me like a blow between the eyes. A Negro's most cherished possession is the drab, neutral cloak of anonymity he can manage to gather around himself, allowing him to merge faceless and nameless with the common swarm: impudence and misbehavior are, for obvious reasons, unwise, but equally so is the display of an uncommon distinction, for if the former attributes can get you starved, whipped, chained, the latter may subject you to such curiosity and hostile suspicion as to ruinously impair the minute amount of freedom you possess. As for the rest, his words had spilled from his lips so rapidly and wildly that I was as yet unable to get the exact drift of his thought, which seemed nonetheless mighty precarious for a white man; and I still could not get over the sensation that he was trying to bait me, or lead me into some kind of trap. To conceal my dismay and confusion, again I mumbled, "That sure is true," and I chuckled idiotically, gazing toward the ground while I slowly wagged my head—as if to indicate that this poor darky understood precious little if indeed he understood anything.

But now, bending down slightly, his face drifted nearer to me, the skin close up not flushed and whiskey-pink as I had imagined but pale as lard, utterly bloodless and seeming to grow even whiter as I forced myself to return his gaze. "Don't play dumb with me," he said. There was no hostility in his voice, its sound was more request than command. "Your mistress pointed you out to me just now. Even so, I would have known, I could have distinguished between you two. The other Negro, what's his name?"

"Hark," I said. "That's Hark, mastah."

"Yes, I would have known you. I would have known even had I not overheard you. 'Feel sorry for a white man and the sorrow is wasted.' Is that not what you said?"

A shiver of fear, old and habitual and humiliating, passed through me, and despite myself I averted my eyes and blurted: "I'm sorry I said that, mastah. I'm dreadful sorry. I didn't mean it, mastah."

"Poppycock!" he exclaimed. "Sorry that you said you're *not* sorry for a white man? Come, come, preacher, you don't mean that. You don't mean that, do you?" He paused, waiting for an answer, but by now my distress and embarrassment had so unsettled me that I couldn't even force a reply. Worse, I had begun to despise and curse myself for my own slow-witted inability to deal with the situation. I stood there licking my lips as I gazed out toward the woods, feeling suddenly like the most squalid type of cornfield coon.

"Now don't play dumb with me," he repeated, the voice edged with a tone almost gentle, curiously ingratiating. "Your reputation precedes you, as it were. For several years now there has come to my attention wondrous bruit of a remarkable slave, owned at different times by various masters here in the vicinity of Cross Keys, who had so surpassed the paltry condition into which he had been cast by destiny that—*mirabile dictu*—he could swiftly read, if called upon to demonstrate, from a difficult and abstract work in natural philosophy, and in a fair hand inscribe page after page of random dictation, and had mastered his numbers as far as a comprehension of simple algebra, and had so attained an understanding of Holy Scripture that such of those few adepts in the science of divinity as had examined his knowledge of the Bible came away shaking their heads in wonder at the splendor of his erudition." He paused and belched. My eyes moved back again toward his, and I saw him wipe his mouth with his sleeve. "Rumor!" he resumed quickly. Now his voice had risen to a kind of impassioned runaway sing-song, his eyes were wild and obsessed. "Astounding rumor to emerge from the backwoods of Old Virginny! Astounding as those rumors which in olden times came back from the depths of Asia— that at the source of the River Indus, I believe it was, dwelt a species of mammoth rat, six feet long, which could dance a lively jig while accompanying itself on a tambourine, and when approached would sprout heretofore invisible wings and fly to the topmost branch of the nearest palm tree. Rumor almost impossible to entertain! For to believe that from this downtrodden race, the very laws governing which bind it to an ignorance more benighted and final than death, there could arise one single specimen capable of spelling *cat* is asking rational intelligence to believe that balmy King George the Third was not a dastardly tyrant or that the moon is made of clabber cheese!" He had begun to jab his finger at me as he spoke, a long bony finger with hairy joints, sending it forth into my face in quick thrusts like a snake's darting neck. "But beyond this, mind you, beyond this—to imagine this . . . this prodigy, this *paragon*, a Negro *slave*—oh, perish the vile word!—who had acquired the lineaments not just of literacy but of knowledge, who it was rumored could almost speak in the accents of a white man of breeding and cultivation; who, in short, while still one of this doomed empire's most wretched minions, had transcended his sorry state and had become not a thing but a *person*—all this is beyond the realm of one's wildest imagination. No. No! The mind boggles, refuses to accept such a grotesque image! Tell me, preacher, how do you spell *cat?* Come now, prove to me the reality of this hoax, this canard!" He kept jabbing his finger at me, the voice cajoling, amiable, the eyes still wintry-wild and obsessed. The smell of applejack was around him like a sweet vapor. "Cat!" he said. "Spell *cat*. Cat!"

I had begun to feel surely that he was not being sarcastic, that he was somehow trying to express mad, hulking, terrifying feelings beyond anyone's surmise. I felt blood pounding at my temples and the cold sweat of fear and anxiety clammy beneath my arms. "Don't mock me, mastah, I pray you," I breathed in a whisper. "Kindly please, mastah. Don't mock me." Time crept past and we were both silent, gazing at each other, and the November wind boomed behind us in the forest, crashing like giant, diminishing footfalls across the graying waste of cedar and cypress and pine; for a moment my compliant lips trembled on a broken wisp of air, faltering —"Ca-, Ca-"—and a grief-haunted sense of futility, childish, lifelong, nigger-black, welled up in me like a sigh of pain. I stood there sweating in the blustery wind, thinking: So this is the way it is. Even when they care, even when they are somehow on your side they cannot help but taunt and torment you. The palms of my hands slimy, and my mind roaring, thinking: I do not want to, but now, now if he forces me to spell the word I will have to try to kill him. I lowered my eyes again, saying more distinctly: "Don't mock me, mastah, please."

Yet now Cobb, adrift in his brandy haze, seemed to have forgotten what he had said to me and turned away, staring madly toward the forest where the wind still thrashed and flayed the distant treetops. He clutched the bottle as if with desperation at a lopsided angle against his chest, and a trickle of brandy oozed out against his cloak. With his other hand he began to massage his thigh, holding the leg so tightly that above the knuckles the flesh grew bone-white. "Almighty God," he groaned, "this everlasting mortal ache! *If a man live many years and rejoice in them all, yet let him remember the days of darkness, for they shall be many.* God, God, my poor Virginia, blighted domain! The soil wrecked and ravaged on every hand, turned to useless dust by that abominable weed. Tobacco we cannot any longer raise, nor cotton ever, save for a meager crop in these few southern counties, nor oats nor barley nor wheat. A wasteland! A plump and virginal principality, a cornucopia of riches the like of which the world has never seen, transformed within the space of a century to a withering, defeated hag! And all to satisfy the demand of ten million Englishmen for a pipeful of Virginia leaf! Now even that is gone, and all we can raise is horses! Horses!" he cried as if to himself now, stroking and kneading his thigh. "Horses and what else, *what else?* Horses and pickaninnies! *Pickaninnies!* Little black infants by the score, the hundreds, the thousands, the tens of thousands! The fairest state of them all, this tranquil and beloved domain—what has it now become? A *nursery* for Mississippi, Alabama, Arkansas. A monstrous breeding farm to supply the sinew to gratify the maw of Eli Whitney's infernal machine, cursed be that blackguard's name! In such a way is our human decency brought down, when we pander all that is in us noble and just to the false god which goes by the vile name of *Capital!* Oh, Virginia, woe

betide thee! Woe, thrice woe, and ever damned in memory be
the day when poor black men in chains first trod upon thy
sacred strand!"

Groaning in pain now, fiercely stroking his thigh with one
hand while with the other he elevated the bottle to his lips
and drained it to the dregs, Cobb seemed, for once, oblivious
of me, and I recall thinking that wisdom dictated my stealing
out of his presence, if only I could find a decent way to do it.
In scattered, disordered riot, all manner of emotions had run
through me as he had spoken; not in years having heard a
white man talk in this crazy fashion, I would not be honest
if I did not admit that what he said (or the drunken gist of it,
stealing in upon my consciousness like some unreal ghostly
light) caused me to feel a shiver of awe and something else,
dim and remote, which might have been a thrill of hope. But
for some reason I cannot explain, both awe and hope swiftly
retreated in my mind, dwindled, died, and even as I looked at
Cobb, I could only smell the musky scent of danger—flagrant,
imminent danger—and feel a sense of suspicion and mistrust
such as I had rarely ever known. Why? It is perhaps impossible to explain save by God, who knows all things. Yet I will
say this, without which you cannot understand the central
madness of nigger existence: beat a nigger, starve him, leave
him wallowing in his own shit, and he will be yours for life.
Awe him by some unforeseen hint of philanthropy, tickle him
with the idea of hope, and he will want to slice your throat.

Yet now before I could make any kind of move, a cracking
noise sounded behind us as once again the shop door opened,
swung wide, and drove itself with windy force against the
wall. And as we turned then, Hark emerged with shirttail flying, scrambling away from the shop, plunging in panicky
headlong flight toward the fields and the woods beyond. Legs
churning, his great black body moved at a furious gallop; his
eyes rolled white with alarm. Scant yards behind him now
came Putnam, his leather apron flapping as he brandished a

stick of lightwood, bawling at the top of his voice. "You, Hark, come back here! Come back here, you dad-dratted no-good an'mal! I'll get hold of you at last, black bastard!" Fleet as a deer, Hark scampered across the open lot, bare black feet sowing puffs of dust, the barnyard cat fleeing his approach, goose and gander too, cumbersomely flapping their flightless wings, emitting dismal honking sounds as they waddled from his path. On he came past us, looking neither left nor right, eyes round and white as eggshells, and we could hear the voice panting *ah-ah-ah* as he sprinted for the woods, moving now with such nimble-footed speed that he seemed whisked for-ward like a sail on the wind. Far beyond, losing ground each second, came the pimpled boy, still howling. "Stop! You, Hark! Black wretch! Stop!" But Hark's great legs were churn-ing as if propelled by steam; vaulting the pump trough, he soared through the air in a gigantic leap like something suspended by wire or wings, struck the earth with a thumping sound, and without breaking stride, bounded on toward the distant forest, the inside of his bare soles flashing splendidly pink. Then all of a sudden it was as if he had been felled by a cannon ball: his head snapped back, and the rest of him including his pinwheeling legs sailed out and forward, and he came down flat on his back with a bladdery, sacklike thud, directly beneath the clothesline which, at gullet level, had intercepted his flight. But as Cobb and I stood watching, watched him shake his head and try to rise up on his elbows, we saw now not one but two forces, though equally sinister and somber, converging on Hark from opposite directions. Putnam, still waving his lightwood stick, and Miss Maria Pope, who had appeared as if from nowhere like some augury of frustrate bitchery and vengeance, bearing down upon Hark with a hobbled spinster's gait amid black snapping yards of funereal gingham. Blown back on the wind, her voice already was hysteric with shrill malevolence. "It's up the tree for you, nigger!" she screeched. "Up the tree!"

WILLIAM STYRON   [34

"Now," I heard Cobb murmur, "now we are about to witness a ritual diversion indigenous to this Southern clime. We
are about to witness two human beings whipping another."

"No, mastah," I said. "Marse Joe don't 'low his niggers to
be beaten. But there's ways around that, as you will surely
see. You about to witness something else, mastah."

"Not a speck of charcoal in the shop!" Putnam was shouting
in a kind of wail.

"And not a drap of water in the kitchen pail!" Miss Maria
shrilled. As if vying with each other to be the chiefest victim
of Hark's enormity, they surrounded him, encompassed the
prostrate form, squawking like birds. Hark staggered to his
feet, shaking his head with the slow, stunned, dizzy bewilderment of an about-to-be-slaughtered ox that has received a
faulty glancing blow. "It's up the tree with him this time,
impudent black scoundrel!" Miss Maria cackled. "Putnam,
get the ladder!"

"Hark's most dreadful feared of heights," I found myself
explaining to Cobb. "This for him is worse than a hundred
beatings."

"A fantastic specimen!" Cobb breathed. "A regular gladi-
ator, a veritable black Apollo. And swift as a race horse!
Where did your master get him?"

"From up Sussex way," I said, "about ten, eleven years ago,
mastah, when they broke up one of the old plantations." I
paused for a moment, half wondering to myself why I was
proffering all this information. "Hark's all forlorn now," I
went on, "heartsick and forlorn. On the outside he's very
cheery, but inside he's just all torn up. He can't keep his mind
on anything. That's how come he forgets his chores, and how
come he gets punished. Poor old Hark . . ."

"Why is that, preacher?" said Cobb. Putnam had fetched
a ladder now from the barn, and we watched the procession
as it made its way across the windswept lot, bleak and gray
in the fading autumnal light—Miss Maria in the lead, grim

hands clenched, her back stiff and straight as a poker, Putnam behind with the ladder, and between them Hark in his dusty gray denim, shuffling along with his head bent in total dejection, looming over the two of them like some huge Goliath, a giant towering above a pair of vengeful, hurrying dwarfs. In Indian file, straight as an arrow, they made their way toward an ancient and enormous maple whose lowermost branch, leafless now, stretched across the pale sky like a naked arm twenty feet above the earth. I could hear Hark's bare feet scuffing across the ground, scuffing like the feet of a reluctant child. "Why is that?" Cobb said again.

"Well, mastah, I'll tell you," I said. "Couple years ago, afore I became Marse Joe's property, Marse Joe had to sell off most all of his niggers. Sell them off down to Mississippi where you know they are planting considerable cotton. Hark told me Marse Joe was in a misery about this, but he just couldn't do anything else. Well, amongst these niggers was Hark's wife and Hark's child—little boy about three or four years old he was then. Hark cared for that little boy almost more than anything."

"Yah, yah, yah," I could hear Cobb murmur, making little clucking sounds beneath his breath.

"So when that little boy was gone, Hark near about went mad with grief, couldn't think about anything else."

"Yah, yah, yah, yah."

"He wanted to run away and follow them all the way down to Mississippi, but I talked him out of it. See, he'd already run off once years ago and hadn't gotten anywhere. Besides, it's always been my idea that a nigger should follow all the rules and regulations so far as he was able."

"Yah, yah, yah."

"Anyway," I went on. "Hark ain't been quite right ever since then. You might say he's just been distracted. That's why he does things—or doesn't do things—that get him punished.

And I'll be quite truthful with you, mastah, he *doesn't* do his
chores, but I tell you he just can't help it."

"Yah, yah." Cobb muttered, "yah, great God, the logical
outcome . . . *the ultimate horror!*" He had begun to hiccup
again and the sound came forth in intermittent gasps, almost
like sobs. He started to say something else, thought better of
it, turned away, whispering over and over again: *"God, God,
God, God, God."*

"Now about this here," I explained. "Like I say, Hark's
most dreadful feared of high places. Last spring the roof
leaked and Marse Joe sent Hark and me up to fix it. But Hark
got halfway up and he just froze there. Begun to whimper
and mumble to hisself and wouldn't go an inch further. So I
had to fix that roof myself. Anyway, Marse Putnam and Miss
Maria caught ahold of this fear of Hark's—you might say they
found out his weak spot. Like I said, Marse Joe won't tolerate
anyone to mistreat his niggers, to beat them or anything like
that. So whenever Marse Joe's away, and Marse Putnam and
Miss Maria figger they can get away with it, why, they run old
Hark up a tree."

Which is what they were doing even as I spoke, their voices
muffled, remote, indistinct now on the blustery wind. Putnam
propping the long ladder against the tree trunk, then jerking
his arm furiously upward as he bade Hark to climb. And Hark
began climbing, reluctantly, at the third rung turning his
frightened face imploringly back as if to see whether they
might not have had a change of heart, but this time Miss
Maria's arms jerked upward—*up, nigger, up*—and again Hark
continued his climb, knees quaking beneath his trousers. At
last arrived at the lowermost branch, Hark swung himself off
the ladder, clutching the tree so tightly that I could see even
from this distance the veins standing out against the muscles
of his arms, then with a sort of scrounging, sliding motion of
his rump, deposited himself in the crotch formed by trunk
and branch, and sat there embracing the tree with his eyes

squeezed shut—dizzy, windy yards above the earth. Then Putnam removed the ladder and laid it flat on the ground beneath the tree.

"Five, ten minutes will go by, mastah," I said to Cobb, "and then old Hark will commence crying and moaning. Just wait and see. Then pretty soon he'll start swaying. Crying and moaning and swaying there on that branch like he's about to fall off. Then Marse Putnam and Miss Maria'll set that ladder up against the tree and Hark'll climb down. I reckon they get scared Hark will fall off and break his neck and they wouldn't want that to happen. No, they just want to give old Hark a poor time for a while."

"Yah, yah, yah," Cobb murmured, distantly now.

"And that for Hark is a poor time indeed," I said.

"Yah, yah, yah," he replied. I don't know whether he was listening to me or not. "Great God! Sometimes I think . . . sometimes . . . *it is like living in a dream!*"

Then suddenly, without another word, Cobb was gone, limping in gaunt strides toward the house, the empty brandy flask still clutched in his hand, cloak flapping, shoulders hunched against the wind. I crouched down again above my rabbits, watching Cobb limp and sway across the lot and up to the front porch, his voice faint and weary as he called out "Hallo, Miz Travis, think I'll come in and set a spell after all!" And Miss Sarah's voice way off within, high and full of cheer, and the sound of the door slamming as Cobb vanished inside the house. I stripped the white translucent inner skin from a rabbit, separating it from the pinkish flesh, and plunged the corpse into the cool water, feeling the guts squirming wet and slimy beneath my fingers. Blood mingled with the water, turning it a muddy crimson. Gusts of wind swept through the cotton patch, whistling; an army of dead withered leaves marched along the edge of the barn, rolled with a husky scrabbling noise across the vacant yard. I gazed down into the bloody water, thinking of Cobb. *Go through*

*the midst of Jerusalem, and set a mark upon the foreheads of
the men that sigh and that cry for all the abominations, that
be done in the midst thereof . . . Slay utterly old and young,
both maids and little children, and women: but come not near
any man upon whom is the mark . . .*

Suddenly I found myself thinking: It is plain, yes, plain,
plain. When I succeed in my great mission, and Jerusalem is
destroyed, this man Cobb will be among those few spared the
sword . . .

Across the roof of the woods the wind rushed in hissing,
majestic swoop and cadence, echoing in far-off hollows with
the thudding sound of footfalls. Gray and streaked, boiling,
in ponderous haste, the clouds fled eastward across the lower-
ing heavens, growing darker now in the early dusk. After a bit
I heard Hark begin to moan, a soft disconsolate wordless wail,
filled with dread. For long minutes he moaned, swaying high
in his tree. Then I heard the *tap-tap-tapping* of the ladder as
they set it against the tree trunk and let him down.

ROBERT PENN WARREN

Phebe

From the Journal of Cass Mastern

ROBERT PENN WARREN, novelist, poet, teacher, critic, essayist, won the Pulitzer Prize for fiction in 1947 for *All the King's Men*. In 1929 he won a Houghton Mifflin literary fellowship for *Night Rider*, and in 1965 he was given the Van Doren award for *Who Speaks for the Negro?*

On the literature faculty now at Yale University, he writes: "The story of Cass Mastern may need a word of background. Cass spent his childhood in a cabin in the red hills of Georgia, in dire poverty. His older brother, Gilbert, had fled that poverty, gone to Mississippi, and had found, mysteriously, perhaps criminally, his start in life. By the 1850s Gilbert reappears at the cabin, now a 'cotton snob,' a gentleman in black broadcloth, with baronial estates. Now he would take his brother Cass back to 'Valhalla,' his plantation, educate him as a gentleman, put him in politics, and make him 'great'—as an adjunct of the power of Gilbert Mastern.

"After tutoring at Valhalla, Cass is sent to Lexington, Kentucky, to Transylvania University, where he is taken up by Duncan Trice, a rich, fashionable, and somewhat dissipated friend of his brother. This section opens with the first meeting of Cass and Arabella Trice, the young wife of Duncan . . ."

The piece is a period piece—that's the way it was. It is a story of guilt. William Faulkner, who had been writing about blacks and Southerners before and concurrently with Warren, has said of this section: "Warren caught not only the pattern of their acts but the very terms they thought of in that time."

The essence of the story lies with Phebe, the maid, whose eyes saw more than perhaps they should. . . .

––––––––––––

The period of the intrigue, this phase of the story of Cass Mastern, lasted all of one academic year, part of the summer (for Cass was compelled to go back to Mississippi for his plantation affairs and to attend the wedding of his sister Lavinia, who married a well-connected young man named Willis Burden), and well through the next winter, when Cass was back in Lexington. Then, on March 19, 1850, Duncan Trice died, in his library (which was a "protected nook or angle" of his house), with a lead slug nearly the size of a man's thumb in his chest. It was quite obviously an accident.

The widow sat in church, upright and immobile. When she once raised her veil to touch at her eyes with a handkerchief, Cass Mastern saw that the cheek was "pale as marble but for a single flushed spot, like the flush of fever." But even when the veil was lowered he detected the fixed, bright eyes glittering "within that artificial shadow."

Cass Mastern, with five other young men of Lexington, cronies and boon companions of the dead man, carried the coffin. "The coffin which I carried seemed to have no weight, although my friend had been of large frame and had inclined to stoutness. As we proceeded with it, I marvelled at the fact of its lightness, and once the fancy flitted into my mind that he was not in the coffin at all, that it was empty, and that all the affair was a masquerade or mock show carried to ludicrous and blasphemous length, for no purpose, as in a dream. Or to deceive me, the fancy came. I was the object of the deception, and all the other people were in league and conspiracy against me. But when that thought came, I suddenly felt a sense of great cunning and a wild exhilaration. I had been too sharp to be caught so. I had penetrated the deception. I had the impulse to hurl the coffin to the ground and see its emptiness burst open and to laugh in triumph. But I did not, and I saw the coffin sink beneath the level of the earth on which we stood and receive the first clods upon it.

"As soon as the sound of the first clods striking the coffin came to me, I felt a great relief, and then a most overmastering desire. I looked toward her. She was kneeling at the foot of the grave, with what thoughts I could not know. Her head was inclined slightly and the veil was over her face. The bright sun poured over her black-clad figure. I could not take my eyes from the sight. The posture seemed to accentuate the charms of her person and to suggest to my inflamed senses the suppleness of her members. Even the funereal tint of her costume seemed to add to the provocation. The sunshine was hot upon my neck and could be felt through the stuff of my coat upon my shoulders. It was preternaturally bright so that I was blinded by it and my eyes were blinded and my senses swam. But all the while I could hear, as from a great distance, the scraping of the spades upon the piled earth and the muffled sound of earth falling into the excavation."

That evening Cass went to the summerhouse in the garden. It was not by appointment, simply on impulse. He waited there a long time, but she finally appeared, dressed in black "which was scarce darker than the night." He did not speak, or make any sign as she approached, "gliding like a shadow among shadows," but remained standing where he had been, in the deepest obscurity of the summerhouse. Even when she entered, he did not betray his presence. "I can not be certain that any premeditation was in my silence. It was prompted by an overpowering impulse which gripped me and sealed my throat and froze my limbs. Before that moment, and afterwards, I knew that it is dishonorable to spy upon another, but at the moment no such considerations presented themselves. I had to keep my eyes fixed upon her as she stood there thinking herself alone in the darkness of the structure. I had the fancy that since she thought herself alone I might penetrate into her being, that I might learn what change, what effect, had been wrought by the death of her husband. The passion which had seized me to the very extent of paroxysm that afternoon at the brink of my friend's grave was gone. I was perfectly cold now. But I had to know, to try to know. It was as though I might know myself by knowing her. (It is human defect—to try to know oneself by the self of another. One can only know oneself in God and in His great eye.)

"She entered the summerhouse and sank upon one of the benches, not more than a few feet from my own location. For a long time I stood there, peering at her. She sat perfectly upright and rigid. At last I whispered her name, as low as might be. If she heard it, she gave no sign. So I repeated her name, in the same fashion, and again. Upon the third utterance, she whispered, 'Yes,' but she did not change her posture or turn her head. Then I spoke more loudly, again uttering her name, and instantly, with a motion of wild alarm she rose, with a strangled cry and her hands lifted toward her face. She reeled, and it seemed that she would collapse to the floor, but she gained control of herself and stood there staring at me. Stammeringly, I made my apology, saying that I had not wanted to startle her, that I had understood her to answer yes to my whisper before I spoke, and I asked her, 'Did you not answer to my whisper?'

"She replied that she had.

" 'Then why were you distressed when I spoke again?' I asked her.

" 'Because I did not know that you were here,' she said.

" 'But,' I said, 'you say that you had just heard my whisper

and had answered to it, and now you say that you did not
know I was here.'

" 'I did not know that you were here,' she repeated, in a
low voice, and the import of what she was saying dawned
upon me.

" 'Listen,' I said, 'when you heard the whisper—did you
recognize it as my voice?'

"She stared at me, not answering.

" 'Answer me,' I demanded, for I had to know.

"She continued to stare, and finally replied hesitantly, 'I do
not know.'

" 'You thought it was—' I began, but before I could utter
the words she had flung herself upon me, clasping me in
desperation like a person frantic with drowning, and ejaculat-
ing, 'No, no, it does not matter what I thought, you are here,
you are here!' And she drew my face down and pressed her
lips against mine to stop my words. Her lips were cold, but
they hung upon mine.

"I too was perfectly cold, as of a mortal chill. And the coldness was the final horror of the act which we performed, as
though two dolls should parody the shame and filth of man
to make it doubly shameful.

"After, she said to me, 'Had I not found you here tonight,
it could never have been between us again.'

" 'Why?' I demanded.

" 'It was a sign,' she said.

" 'A sign?' I demanded.

" 'A sign that we cannot escape, that we—' and she interrupted herself, to resume, whispering fiercely in the dark—'I
do not want to escape—it is a sign—whatever I have done is
done.' She grew quiet for a moment, then she said, 'Give me
your hand.'

"I gave her my right hand. She grasped it, dropped it, and
said, 'The other, the other hand.'

"I held it out, across my own body, for I was sitting on her left. She seized it with her own left hand, bringing her hand upward from below to press my hand flat against her bosom. Then, fumblingly, she slipped a ring upon my finger, the finger next to the smallest.

" 'What is that?' I asked.

" 'A ring,' she answered, paused, and added, 'It is his ring.'

"Then I recalled that he, my friend, had always worn a wedding ring, and I felt the metal cold upon my flesh. 'Did you take it off of his finger?' I asked, and the thought shook me.

" 'No,' she said.

" 'No?' I questioned.

" 'No,' she said, 'he took it off. It was the only time he ever took it off.'

"I sat beside her, waiting for what, I did not know, while she held my hand pressed against her bosom. I could feel it rise and fall. I could say nothing.

"Then she said, 'Do you want to know how—how he took it off?'

" 'Yes,' I said in the dark, and waiting for her to speak, I moved my tongue out upon my dry lips.

" 'Listen,' she commanded me in an imperious whisper, 'that evening after—after it happened—after the house was quiet again, I sat in my room, in the little chair by the dressing table, where I always sit for Phebe to let down my hair. I had sat there out of habit, I suppose, for I was numb all over. I watched Phebe preparing the bed for the night.' (Phebe was her waiting maid, a comely yellow wench somewhat given to the fits and sulks.) 'I saw Phebe remove the bolster and then look down at a spot where the bolster had lain, on my side of the bed. She picked something up and came toward me. She stared at me—and her eyes, they are yellow, you look into them and you can't see what is in them—she stared at me—a long time—and then she held out her hand, clenched shut and she watched me—and then—slow, so slow—she opened up the fingers—and there lay the ring on the palm of her hand—and

I knew it was his ring but all I thought was, it is gold and it is lying in a gold hand. For Phebe's hand was gold—I had never noticed how her hand is the color of pure gold. Then I looked up and she was still staring at me, and her eyes were gold, too, and bright and hard like gold. And I knew that she knew.'

" 'Knew?' I echoed, like a question, but I knew, too, now. My friend had learned the truth—from the coldness of his wife, from the gossip of servants—and had drawn the gold ring from his finger and carried it to the bed where he had lain with her and had put it beneath her pillow and had gone down and shot himself but under such circumstances that no one save his wife would ever guess it to be more than an accident. But he had made one fault of calculation. The yellow wench had found the ring.

" 'She knows,' she whispered, pressing my hand hard against her bosom, which heaved and palpitated with a new wildness. 'She knows—and she looks at me—she will always look at me.' Then suddenly her voice dropped, and a wailing intonation came into it: 'She will tell. All of them will know. All of them in the house will look at me and know—when they hand me the dish—when they come into the room—and their feet don't make any noise!' She rose abruptly, dropping my hand. I remained seated, and she stood there beside me, her back toward me, the whiteness of her face and hands no longer visible, and to my sight the blackness of her costume faded into the shadow, even in such proximity. Suddenly, in a voice which I did not recognize for its hardness, she said in the darkness above me, 'I will not abide it, I will not abide it!' Then she turned, and with a swooping motion leaned to kiss me upon the mouth. Then she was gone from my side and I heard her feet running up the gravel of the path. I sat there in the darkness for a time longer, turning the ring upon my finger."

After that meeting in the summerhouse, Cass did not see Annabelle Trice for some days. He learned that she had gone to Louisville, where, he recalled, she had close friends. She

had, as was natural, taken Phebe with her. Then he heard that
she had returned, and that night, late, went to the summerhouse in the garden. She was there, sitting in the dark. She
greeted him. She seemed, he wrote later, peculiarly cut off,
remote, and vague in manner, like a somnambulist or a person drugged. He asked about her trip to Louisville, and she
replied briefly that she had been down the river to Paducah.
He remarked that he had not known that she had friends in
Paducah, and she said that she had none there. Then, all at
once, she turned on him, the vagueness changing to violence,
and burst out, "You are prying—you are prying into my affairs
—and I will not tolerate it." Cass stammered out some excuse
before she cut in to say, "But if you must know, I'll tell you.
I took her there."

For a moment Cass was genuinely confused.

"Her?" he questioned.

"Phebe," she replied, "I took her to Paducah, and she's
gone."

"Gone—gone where?"

"Down the river," she answered, repeated, "down the
river," and laughed abruptly, and added, "and she won't look
at me any more like that."

"You sold her?"

"Yes, I sold her. In Paducah, to a man who was making up
a coffle of Negroes for New Orleans. And nobody knows me
in Paducah, nobody knew I was there, nobody knows I sold
her, for I shall say she ran away into Illinois. But I sold her.
For thirteen hundred dollars."

"You got a good price," Cass said, "even for a yellow girl as
sprightly as Phebe." And, as he reports in the journal, he
laughed with some "bitterness and rudeness," though he does
not say why.

"Yes," she replied, "I got a good price. I made him pay
every penny she was worth. And then do you know what I did
with the money, do you?"

"No."

"When I came off the boat at Louisville, there was an old man, a nigger, sitting on the landing stage, and he was blind and picking on a guitar and singing 'Old Dan Tucker.' I took the money out of my bag and walked to him and laid it in his old hat."

"If you were going to give the money away—if you felt the money was defiled—why didn't you free her?" Cass asked.

"She'd stay right here, she wouldn't go away, she would stay right here and look at me. Oh, no, she wouldn't go away, for she's the wife of a man the Motley's have, their coachman. Oh, she'd stay right here and look at me and tell, tell what she knows, and I'll not abide it!"

Then Cass said, "If you had spoken to me I would have bought the man from Mr. Motley and set him free, too."

"He wouldn't have sold," she said, "the Motleys won't sell a servant."

"Even to be freed?" Cass continued, but she cut in, "I tell you I won't have you interfering with my affairs, do you understand that?" And she rose from his side and stood in the middle of the summerhouse, and he saw the glimmer of her face in the shadow and heard her agitated breathing. "I thought you were fond of her," Cass said.

"I was," she said, "until—until she looked at me like that."

"You know why you got that price for her?" Cass asked, and without waiting for an answer, went on, "Because she's yellow and comely and well-made. Oh, the drovers wouldn't take her down chained in a coffle. They wouldn't wear her down. They'll take her down the river soft. And you know why?"

"Yes, I know why," she said, "and what is it to you? Are you so charmed by her?"

"That is unfair," Cass said.

"Oh, I see, Mr. Mastern," she said, "oh, I see, you are concerned for the honor of a black coachman. It is a very delicate sentiment, Mr. Mastern. Why—" and she came to stand above him as he still sat on the bench—"why did you not show some such delicate concern for the honor of your friend? Who is now dead."

According to the journal, there was, at this moment, "a tempest of feeling" in his breast. He wrote: "Thus I heard put into words for the first time the accusation which has ever in all climes been that most calculated to make wince a man of proper nurture or natural rectitude. What the hardened man can bear to hear from the still small voice within, may yet be when spoken by an external tongue an accusation dire enough to drain his very cheeks of blood. But it was not only that accusation in itself, for in very truth I had supped full of that horror and made it my long familiar. It was not merely the betrayal of my friend. It was not merely the death of my friend, at whose breast I had levelled the weapon. I could have managed somehow to live with those facts. But I suddenly felt that the world outside of me was shifting, and the substance of things, and that the process had only begun of a general disintegration of which I was the center. At that moment of perturbation, when the cold sweat broke on my brow, I did not frame any sentence distinctly to my mind. But I have looked back and wrestled to know the truth. It was not the fact that a slave woman was being sold away from the house where she had had protection and kindness and away from the arms of her husband into debauchery. I knew that such things had happened in fact, and I was no child, for after my arrival in Lexington and my acquaintance with the looser sort of companions, the sportsmen and the followers of the races, I had myself enjoyed such diversions. It was not only the fact that the woman for whom I had sacrificed my friend's life and my honor could, in her own suffering, turn on me with a cold rage and the language of insult so that I did not recognize her. It was, instead, the fact that all of these things— the death of my friend, the betrayal of Phebe, the suffering and rage and great change of the woman I had loved—all had come from my single act of sin and perfidy, as the boughs from the bole and the leaves from the bough. Or to figure the matter differently, it was as though the vibration set up in the whole fabric of the world by my act had spread infinitely and with ever increasing power and no man could know the end. I did not put it into words in such fashion, but I stood there shaken by a tempest of feeling."

When Cass had somewhat controlled his agitation, he said, "To whom did you sell the girl?"

"What's it to you?" she answered.

"To whom did you sell the girl?" he repeated.

"I'll not tell you," she said.

"I will find out," he said. "I will go to Paducah and find out."

She grasped him by the arm, driving her fingers deep into the flesh, "like talons," and demanded, "Why—why are you going?"

"To find her," he said. "To find her and buy her and set her free." He had not premeditated this. He heard the words, he wrote in the journal, and knew that that was his intention. "To find her and buy her and set her free," he said, and felt the grasp on his arm released and then in the dark suddenly felt the rake of her nails down his cheek, and heard her voice in a kind of "wild sibilance" saying, "If you do—if you do—oh, I'll not abide it—I will not!"

She flung herself from his side and to the bench. He heard her gasp and sob, "a hard dry sob like a man's." He did not move. Then he heard her voice, "If you do—if you do—she looked at me that way, and I'll not abide it—if you do—" Then after a pause, very quietly, "If you do, I shall never see you again."

He made no reply. He stood there for some minutes, he did not know how long, then left the summerhouse, where she still sat, and walked down the alley.

The next morning he left for Paducah. He learned the

name of the trader, but he also learned that the trader had
sold Phebe (a yellow wench who answered to Phebe's descrip-
tion) to a "private party" who happened to be in Paducah at
the time but who had gone on downriver. His name was
unknown in Paducah. The trader had presumably sold Phebe
so that he would be free to accompany his coffle when it had
been made up. He had now headed, it was said, into South
Kentucky, with a few bucks and wenches, to pick up more. As
Cass had predicted, he had not wanted to wear Phebe down by
taking her in the coffle. So getting a good figure of profit in
Paducah, he had sold her there. Cass went south as far as
Bowling Green, but lost track of his man there. So rather
hopelessly, he wrote a letter to the trader, in care of the market
at New Orleans, asking for the name of the purchaser and
any information about him. Then he swung back north to
Lexington.

At Lexington he went down to West Short Street, to the
Lewis C. Robards barracoon, which Mr. Robards had converted from the old Lexington Theatre a few years earlier. He
had a notion that Mr. Robards, the leading trader of the section, might be able, through his downriver connections, to
locate Phebe, if enough of a commission was in sight. At the
barracoon there was no one in the office except a boy, who
said that Mr. Robards was downriver but that Mr. Simms was
"holding things down" and was over at the "house" at an
"inspection." So Cass went next door to the house. (When
Jack Burden was in Lexington investigating the life of Cass
Mastern, he saw the "house" still standing, a two-story brick
building of the traditional residential type, roof running
lengthwise, door in center of front, window on each side,
chimney at each end, lean-to in back. Robards had kept his
"choice stock" there and not in the coops, to wait for "inspection.")

Cass found the main door unlocked at the house, entered
the hall, saw no one, but heard laughter from above. He

mounted the stairs and discovered, at the end of the hall, a small group of men gathered at an open door. He recognized a couple of them, young hangers-on he had seen about town and at the track. He approached and asked if Mr. Simms was about. "Inside," one of the men said, "showing." Over the heads, Cass could see into the room. First he saw a short, strongly made man, a varnished-looking man, with black hair, black neckcloth, large bright black eyes, and black coat, with a crop in his hand. Cass knew immediately that he was a French "speculator," who was buying "fancies" for Louisiana. The Frenchman was staring at something beyond Cass's range of vision. Cass moved farther and could see within.

There he saw the man whom he took to be Mr. Simms, a nondescript fellow in a plug hat, and beyond him the figure of a woman. She was a very young woman, some twenty years old perhaps, rather slender, with skin slightly darker than ivory, probably an octaroon, and hair crisp rather than kinky, and deep dark liquid eyes, slightly bloodshot, which stared at a spot above and beyond the Frenchman. She did not wear the ordinary plaid Osnaburg and kerchief of the female slave up for sale, but a white, loosely cut dress, with elbow-length sleeves, and skirts to the floor and no kerchief, only a band to her hair. Beyond her, in the neatly furnished room ("quite gen-teel," the journal called it, while noting the barred windows), Cass saw a rocking chair and little table, and on the table a sew-ing basket with a piece of fancy needlework lying there with the needle stuck in it, "as though some respectable young lady or householder had dropped it casually aside upon rising to greet a guest." Cass recorded that somehow he found himself staring at the needlework.

"Yeah," Mr. Simms was saying, "yeah." And grasped the girl by the shoulder to swing her slowly around for a complete view. Then he seized one of her wrists and lifted the arm to shoulder level and worked it back and forth a couple of times to show the supple articulation, saying, "Yeah." That done, he drew the arm forward, holding it toward the Frenchman, the hand hanging limply from the wrist which he held. (The hand was, according to the journal, "well moulded, and the fingers tapered.") "Yeah," Mr. Simms said, "look at that-air hand. Ain't no lady got a littler, teensier hand. And round and soft, yeah?"

"Ain't she got nuthen else round and soft?" one of the men at the door called, and the others laughed.

"Yeah," Mr. Simms said, and leaned to take the hem of her dress, which with a delicate flirting motion he lifted higher than her waist, while he reached out with his other hand to wad the cloth and draw it into a kind of "awkward girdle" about her waist. Still holding the wad of cloth he walked around her, forcing her to turn (she turned "without resistance and as though in a trance") with his motion until her small buttocks were toward the door. "Round and soft, boys," Mr. Simms said, and gave her a good whack on the near buttock to make the flesh tremble. "Ever git yore hand on anything rounder ner softer, boys?" he demanded. "Hit's a cushion, I declare. And shake like sweet jelly."

"God-a-Mighty and got on stockings," one of the men said.

While the other men laughed, the Frenchman stepped to the side of the girl, reached out to lay the tip of his riding crop at the little depression just above the beginning of the swell of the buttocks. He held the tip delicately there for a moment, then flattened the crop across the back and moved it down slowly, evenly across each buttock, to trace the fullness of the curve. "Turn her," he said in his foreign voice.

Mr. Simms obediently carried the wad around, and the body followed in the half revolution. One of the men at the door whistled. The Frenchman laid his crop across the woman's belly as though he were a "carpenter measuring something or as to demonstrate its flatness," and moved it down as before, tracing the structure, until it came to rest across the thighs, below the triangle. Then he let his hand fall to his side, with the crop. "Open your mouth," he said to the girl.

She did so, and he peered earnestly at her teeth. Then he leaned and whiffed her breath. "It is a good breath," he admitted, as though grudgingly.

"Yeah," Mr. Simms said, "yeah, you ain't a-finden no better breath."

"Have you any others?" the Frenchman demanded. "On hand?"

"We got 'em," Mr. Simms said.

"Let me see," the Frenchman said, and moved toward the door with, apparently, the "insolent expectation" that the group there would dissolve before him. He went out into the hall, Mr. Simms following. While Mr. Simms locked the door, Cass said to him, "I wish to speak to you, if you are Mr. Simms."

"Huh?" Mr. Simms said ("grunted" according to the journal), but looking at Cass became suddenly civil for he could know from dress and bearing that Cass was not one of the casual hangers-on. So Mr. Simms admitted the Frenchman to the next room to inspect its occupant, and returned to Cass. Cass remarked in the journal that trouble might have been avoided if he had been more careful to speak in private, but he wrote that at the time the matter was so much upon his mind that the men who stood about were as shadows to him.

He explained his wish to Mr. Simms, described Phebe as well as possible, gave the name of the trader in Paducah, and offered a liberal commission. Mr. Simms seemed dubious, promised to do what he could, and then said, "But nine outa ten you won't git her, Mister. And we got sumthen here better. You done seen Delphy, and she's nigh white as airy woman, and a sight more juicy, and that gal you talk about is nuthen but yaller. Now Delphy—"

"But the young gemmun got a hankeren fer yaller," one of the hangers-on said, and laughed, and the others laughed too.

Cass struck him across the mouth. "I struck him with the side of my fist," Cass wrote, "to bring blood. I struck him without thought, and I recollect the surprise which visited me when I saw the blood on his chin and saw him draw a bowie from his shirt front. I attempted to avoid his first blow, but received it upon my left shoulder. Before he could withdraw, I had grasped his wrist in my right hand, forced it down so that I could also use my left hand, which still had some strength left at that moment, and with a turning motion of my body I broke his arm across my right hip, and then knocked him to the floor. I recovered the bowie from the floor, and with it faced the man who seemed to be the friend of the man who was now prostrate. He had a knife in his hand, but he seemed disinclined to pursue the discussion."

Cass declined the assistance of Mr. Simms, pressed a handkerchief over his wound, walked out of the building and toward his lodgings, and collapsed on West Short Street. He was carried home. The next day he was better. He learned that Mrs. Trice had left the city, presumably for Washington. A couple of days later his wound infected, and for some time he lay in delirium between life and death. His recovery was slow, presumably retarded by what he termed in the journal his "will toward darkness." But his constitution was stronger than his will, and he recovered, to know himself as the "chief of sinners and a plague spot on the body of the human world." He would have committed suicide except for the fear of damnation for that act, for though "hopeless of Grace I yet clung to the hope of Grace." But sometimes the very fact of damnation because of suicide seemed to be the very reason for suicide: he had brought his friend to suicide and the friend, by that act, was eternally damned; therefore he, Cass Mastern, should, in justice, insure his own damnation by the same act. "But the Lord preserved me from self-slaughter for ends which are His and beyond my knowledge."

Mrs. Trice did not come back to Lexington.

He returned to Mississippi. For two years he operated his plantation, read the Bible, prayed, and, strangely enough, prospered greatly, almost as though against his will. In the end he repaid Gilbert his debt, and set free his slaves. He had some notion of operating the plantation with the same force on a wage basis. "You fool," Gilbert said to him, "be a private fool if you must, but in God's name don't be a public one. Do you think you can work them and them free? One day work, one day loaf. Do you think you can have a passel of free niggers next door to a plantation with slaves? If you did have to set them free, you don't have to spend the rest of your natural life nursing them. Get them out of this country, and take up law or medicine. Or preach the Gospel and at least make a living out of all this praying." Cass tried for more than a year to operate the plantation with his free Negroes, but was compelled to confess that the project was a failure. "Get them out of the country," Gilbert said to him. "And why don't you go with them. Why don't you go North?"

"I belong here," Cass replied.

"Well, why don't you preach Abolition right here?" Gilbert demanded. "Do something, do anything, but stop making a fool of yourself trying to raise cotton with free niggers."

"Perhaps I shall preach Abolition," Cass said, "some day. Even here. But not now. I am not worthy to instruct others. Not now. But meanwhile there is my example. If it is good, it is not lost. Nothing is ever lost."

"Except your mind," Gilbert said, and flung heavily from the room.

There was a sense of trouble in the air. Only Gilbert's great wealth and prestige and scarcely concealed humorous contempt for Cass saved Cass from ostracism, or worse. ("His contempt for me is a shield," Cass wrote. "He treats me like a wayward and silly child who may learn better and who does not have to be taken seriously. Therefore my neighbors do not take me seriously.") But trouble did come. One of Cass's

Negroes had a broad-wife on a plantation near by. After she
had had some minor trouble with the overseer, the husband
stole her from the plantation and ran away. Toward the Tennessee border the pair were taken. The man, resisting officers,
was shot; the woman was brought back. "See," Gilbert said,
"all you have managed to do is get one nigger killed and one
nigger whipped. I offer my congratulations." So Cass put his
free Negroes on a boat bound upriver, and never heard of
them again.

"I saw the boat head out into the channel, and watched the
wheels churn against the strong current, and my spirit was
troubled. I knew that the Negroes were passing from one
misery to another, and that the hopes they now carried would
be blighted. They had kissed my hands and wept for joy, but
I could take no part in their rejoicing. I had not flattered myself that I had done anything for them. What I had done I
had done for myself, to relieve my spirit of a burden, the burden of their misery and their eyes upon me. The wife of my
dead friend had found the eyes of the girl Phebe upon her and
had gone wild and had ceased to be herself and had sold the
girl into misery. I had found their eyes upon me and had freed
them into misery, lest I should do worse. For many cannot
bear their eyes upon them, and enter into evil and cruel ways
in their desperation."

II

THE NOT TOO DISTANT
PAST

WILLIAM FAULKNER

That Evening Sun Go Down

In this, one of WILLIAM FAULKNER'S most famous short
stories, the Nobel Prize-winning Southern author, who spent a lifetime studying and fictionalizing human (and racial) relations in
his native Mississippi, shows the effects of fear on a black woman
—fear, in this case, of a black man—and its effects on the children
of a white family, and finally, its attrition into indifference on the
part of the elders. "Ah, damnation," Father said, "Come along,
chillen. It's bedtime. . . ."

Monday is no different from any other week day in Jefferson
now. The streets are paved now, and the telephone and the
electric companies are cutting down more and more of the
shade trees—the water oaks, the maples and locusts and elms—
to make room for iron poles bearing clusters of bloated and
ghostly and bloodless grapes, and we have a city laundry which
makes the rounds on Monday morning, gathering the bundles
of clothes into bright-colored, specially made motor-cars: the
soiled wearing of a whole week now flees apparition-like behind alert and irritable electric horns, with a long diminishing noise of rubber and asphalt like a tearing of silk, and even
the Negro women who still take in white people's washing
after the old custom, fetch and deliver it in automobiles.

But fifteen years ago, on Monday morning the quiet, dusty, shady streets would be full of Negro women with, balanced on their steady turbaned heads, bundles of clothes tied up in sheets, almost as large as cotton bales, carried so without touch of hand between the kitchen door of the white house and the blackened wash-pot beside a cabin door in Negro Hollow.

Nancy would set her bundle on the top of her head, then upon the bundle in turn she would set the black straw sailor hat which she wore Winter and Summer. She was tall, with a high, sad face sunken a little where her teeth were missing. Sometimes we would go a part of the way down the lane and across the pasture with her, to watch the balanced bundle and the hat that never bobbled nor wavered, even when she walked down into the ditch and climbed out again and stooped through the fence. She would go down on her hands and knees and crawl through the gap, her head rigid, up-tilted, the bundle steady as a rock or a balloon, and rise to her feet and go on.

Sometimes the husbands of the washing women would fetch and deliver the clothes, but Jubah never did that for Nancy, even before father told him to stay away from our house, even when Dilsey was sick and Nancy would come to cook for us.

And then about half the time we'd have to go down the lane to Nancy's house and tell her to come on and get breakfast. We would stop at the ditch, because father told us to not have anything to do with Jubah—he was a short black man, with a razor scar down his face—and we would throw rocks at Nancy's house until she came to the door, leaning her head around it without any clothes on.

"What you all mean, chunking my house?" Nancy said. "What you little devils mean?"

"Father says for you to come and get breakfast," Caddy said. "Father says it's over a half an hour now, and you've got to come this minute."

"I ain't studying no breakfast," Nancy said. "I going to get my sleep out."

"I bet you're drunk," Jason said. "Father says you're drunk. Are you drunk, Nancy?"

"Who says I is?" Nancy said. "I got to get my sleep out. I ain't studying no breakfast."

So after a while we quit chunking the house and went back home. When she finally came, it was too late for me to go to school. So we thought it was whiskey until that day when they arrested her again and they were taking her to jail and they passed Mr. Stovall. He was the cashier in the bank and a deacon in the Baptist church, and Nancy began to say:

"When you going to pay me, white man? When you going to pay me, white man? It's been three times now since you paid me a cent—" Mr. Stovall knocked her down, but she kept on saying, "When you going to pay me, white man? It's been three times now since—" until Mr. Stovall kicked her in the mouth with his heel and the marshal caught Mr. Stovall back, and Nancy lying in the street, laughing. She turned her head and spat out some blood and teeth and said, "It's been three times now since he paid me a cent."

That was how she lost her teeth, and all that day they told about Nancy and Mr. Stovall, and all that night the ones that passed the jail could hear Nancy singing and yelling. They could see her hands holding to the window bars, and a lot of them stopped along the fence, listening to her and to the jailer trying to make her shut up. She didn't shut up until just before daylight, when the jailer began to hear a bumping and scraping upstairs and he went up there and found Nancy hanging from the window bar. He said that it was cocaine and not whiskey, because no nigger would try to commit suicide unless he was full of cocaine, because a nigger full of cocaine was not a nigger any longer.

The jailer cut her down and revived her; then he beat her, whipped her. She had hung herself with her dress. She had

WILLIAM FAULKNER [62

fixed it all right, but when they arrested her she didn't have
on anything except a dress and so she didn't have anything
to tie her hands with and she couldn't make her hands let go
of the window ledge. So the jailer heard the noise and ran
up there and found Nancy hanging from the window stark
naked.

When Dilsey was sick in her cabin and Nancy was cooking
for us, we could see her apron swelling out; that was before
father told Jubah to stay away from the house. Jubah was in
the kitchen, sitting behind the stove, with his razor scar on his
black face like a piece of dirty string. He said it was a watermelon that Nancy had under her dress. And it was Winter,
too.

"Where did you get a watermelon in the Winter?" Caddy
said.

"I didn't," Jubah said. "It wasn't me that give it to her. But
I can cut it down, same as if it was."

"What makes you want to talk that way before these chillen?" Nancy said. "Whyn't you go on to work? You done et.
You want Mr. Jason to catch you hanging around his kitchen,
talking that way before these chillen?"

"Talking what way, Nancy?" Caddy said.

"I can't hang around white man's kitchen," Jubah said.
"But white man can hang around mine. White man can come
in my house, but I can't stop him. When white man want to
come in my house, I ain't got no house. I can't stop him, but
he can't kick me outen it. He can't do that."

Dilsey was still sick in her cabin. Father told Jubah to stay
off our place. Dilsey was still sick. It was a long time. We were
in the library after supper.

"Isn't Nancy through yet?" mother said. "It seems to me
that she has had plenty of time to have finished the dishes."

"Let Quentin go and see," father said. "Go and see if Nancy
is through, Quentin. Tell her she can go on home."

I went to the kitchen. Nancy was through. The dishes were

put away and the fire was out. Nancy was sitting in a chair, close to the cold stove. She looked at me.

"Mother wants to know if you are through," I said.

"Yes," Nancy said. She looked at me. "I done finished." She looked at me.

"What is it?" I said. "What is it?"

"I ain't nothing but a nigger," Nancy said. "It ain't none of my fault."

She looked at me, sitting in the chair before the cold stove, the sailor hat on her head. I went back to the library. It was the cold stove and all, when you think of a kitchen being warm and busy and cheerful. And with a cold stove and the dishes all put away, and nobody wanting to eat at that hour.

"Is she through?" mother said.

"Yessum," I said.

"What is she doing?" mother said.

"She's not doing anything. She's through."

"I'll go and see," father said.

"Maybe she's waiting for Jubah to come and take her home," Caddy said.

"Jubah is gone," I said. Nancy told us how one morning she woke up and Jubah was gone.

"He quit me," Nancy said. "Done gone to Memphis, I reckon. Dodging them city *po*-lice for a while, I reckon."

"And a good riddance," father said. "I hope he stays there."

"Nancy's scaired of the dark," Jason said.

"So are you," Caddy said.

"I'm not," Jason said.

"Scairy cat," Caddy said.

"I'm not," Jason said.

"You, Candace!" mother said. Father came back.

"I am going to walk down the lane with Nancy," he said. "She says Jubah is back."

"Has she seen him?" mother said.

"No. Some Negro sent her word that he was back in town. I won't be long."

"You'll leave me alone, to take Nancy home?" mother said. "Is her safety more precious to you than mine?"

"I won't be long," father said.

"You'll leave these children unprotected, with that Negro about?"

"I'm going too," Caddy said. "Let me go, father."

"What would he do with them, if he were unfortunate enough to have them?" father said.

"I want to go, too," Jason said.

"Jason!" mother said. She was speaking to father. You could tell that by the way she said it. Like she believed that all day father had been trying to think of doing the thing that she wouldn't like the most, and that she knew all the time that after a while he would think of it. I stayed quiet, because father and I both knew that mother would want him to make me stay with her, if she just thought of it in time. So father didn't look at me. I was the oldest. I was nine and Caddy was seven and Jason was five.

"Nonsense," father said. "We won't be long."

Nancy had her hat on. We came to the lane. "Jubah always been good to me," Nancy said. "Whenever he had two dollars, one of them was mine." We walked in the lane. "If I can just get through the lane," Nancy said, "I be all right then."

The lane was always dark. "This is where Jason got scared on Hallowe'en," Caddy said.

"I didn't," Jason said.

"Can't Aunt Rachel do anything with him?" father said. Aunt Rachel was old. She lived in a cabin beyond Nancy's, by herself. She had white hair and she smoked a pipe in the door, all day long; she didn't work any more. They said she was Jubah's mother. Sometimes she said she was and sometimes she said she wasn't any kin to Jubah.

"Yes you did," Caddy said. "You were scairder than Frony. You were scairder than T.P. even. Scairder than niggers."

"Can't nobody do nothing with him," Nancy said. "He say I done woke up the devil in him, and ain't but one thing going to lay it again."

"Well, he's gone now," father said. "There's nothing for you to be afraid of now. And if you'd just let white men alone."

"Let what white men alone?" Caddy said. "How let them alone?"

"He ain't gone nowhere," Nancy said. "I can feel him. I can feel him now, in this lane. He hearing us talk, every word, hid somewhere, waiting. I ain't seen him, and I ain't going to see him again but once more, with that razor. That razor on that string down his back, inside his shirt. And then I ain't going to be even surprised."

"I wasn't scaired," Jason said.

"If you'd behave yourself, you'd have kept out of this," father said. "But it's all right now. He's probably in St. Louis now. Probably got another wife by now and forgot all about you."

"If he has, I better not find out about it," Nancy said. "I'd stand there and every time he wropped her, I'd cut that arm off. I'd cut his head off and I'd slit her belly and I'd shove—"

"Hush," father said.

"Slit whose belly, Nancy?" Caddy said.

"I wasn't scaired," Jason said. "I'd walk right down this lane by myself."

"Yah," Caddy said. "You wouldn't dare to put your foot in it if we were not with you."

II

Dilsey was still sick, and so we took Nancy home every night until mother said, "How much longer is this going to go on?

I to be left alone in this big house while you take home a frightened Negro?"

We fixed a pallet in the kitchen for Nancy. One night we waked up, hearing the sound. It was not singing and it was not crying, coming up the dark stairs. There was a light in mother's room and we heard father going down the hall, down the back stairs, and Caddy and I went into the hall. The floor was cold. Our toes curled away from the floor while we listened to the sound. It was like singing and it wasn't like singing, like the sounds that Negroes make.

Then it stopped and we heard father going down the back stairs, and we went to the head of the stairs. Then the sound began again, in the stairway, not loud, and we could see Nancy's eyes half way up the stairs, against the wall. They looked like cat's eyes do, like a big cat against the wall, watching us. When we came down the steps to where she was she quit making the sound again, and we stood there until father came back up from the kitchen, with his pistol in his hand. He went back down with Nancy and they came back with Nancy's pallet.

We spread the pallet in our room. After the light in mother's room went off, we could see Nancy's eyes again. "Nancy," Caddy whispered, "are you asleep, Nancy?"

Nancy whispered something. It was oh or no, I don't know which. Like nobody had made it, like it came from nowhere and went nowhere, until it was like Nancy was not there at all; that I had looked so hard at her eyes on the stair that they had got printed on my eyelids, like the sun does when you have closed your eyes and there is no sun. "Jesus," Nancy whispered. "Jesus."

"Was it Jubah?" Caddy whispered. "Did he try to come into the kitchen?"

"Jesus," Nancy said. Like this: Jeeeeeeeeeeeeeeeesus, until the sound went out like a match or a candle does.

"Can you see us, Nancy?" Caddy whispered. "Can you see our eyes too?"

"I ain't nothing but a nigger," Nancy said. "God knows. God knows."

"What did you see down there in the kitchen?" Caddy whispered. "What tried to get in?"

"God knows," Nancy said. We could see her eyes. "God knows."

Dilsey got well. She cooked dinner. "You'd better stay in bed a day or two longer," father said.

"What for?" Dilsey said. "If I had been a day later, this place would be to rack and ruin. Get on out of here, now, and let me get my kitchen straight again."

Dilsey cooked supper, too. And that night, just before dark, Nancy came into the kitchen.

"How do you know he's back?" Dilsey said. "You ain't seen him."

"Jubah is a nigger," Jason said.

"I can feel him," Nancy said. "I can feel him laying yonder in the ditch."

"To-night?" Dilsey said. "Is he there to-night?"

"Dilsey's a nigger too," Jason said.

"You try to eat something," Dilsey said.

"I don't want nothing," Nancy said.

"I ain't a nigger," Jason said.

"Drink some coffee," Dilsey said. She poured a cup of coffee for Nancy. "Do you know he's out there to-night? How come you know it's to-night?"

"I know," Nancy said. "He's there, waiting. I know. I done lived with him too long. I know what he fixing to do 'fore he knows it himself."

"Drink some coffee," Dilsey said. Nancy held the cup to her mouth and blew into the cup. Her mouth pursed out like a spreading adder's, like a rubber mouth, like she had blown all the color out of her lips with blowing the coffee.

"I ain't a nigger," Jason said. "Are you a nigger, Nancy?"

"I hell-born, child," Nancy said. "I won't be nothing soon. I going back where I come from soon."

III

She began to drink the coffee. While she was drinking, holding the cup in both hands, she began to make the sound again. She made the sound into the cup and the coffee sploshed out on to her hands and her dress. Her eyes looked at us and she sat there, her elbows on her knees, holding the cup in both hands, looking at us across the wet cup, making the sound.

"Look at Nancy," Jason said. "Nancy can't cook for us now. Dilsey's got well now."

"You hush up," Dilsey said. Nancy held the cup in both hands, looking at us, making the sound, like there were two of them: one looking at us and the other making the sound. "Whyn't you let Mr. Jason telefoam the marshal?" Dilsey said. Nancy stopped then, holding the cup in her long brown hands. She tried to drink some coffee again, but it sploshed out of the cup, on to her hands and her dress, and she put the cup down. Jason watched her.

"I can't swallow it," Nancy said. "I swallows but it won't go down me."

"You go down to the cabin," Dilsey said. "Frony will fix you a pallet and I'll be there soon."

"Won't no nigger stop him," Nancy said.

"I ain't a nigger," Jason said. "Am I, Dilsey?"

"I reckon not," Dilsey said. She looked at Nancy. "I don't reckon so. What you going to do, then?"

Nancy looked at us. Her eyes went fast, like she was afraid there wasn't time to look, without hardly moving at all. She looked at us, at all three of us at one time. "You 'member that night I stayed in you all's room?" she said. She told about how we waked up early the next morning, and played. We had to play quiet, on her pallet, until father woke and it was time for her to go down and get breakfast. "Go and ask you maw to let me stay here to-night," Nancy said. "I won't need no pallet. We can play some more," she said.

Caddy asked mother. Jason went too. "I can't have Negroes sleeping in the house," mother said. Jason cried. He cried until mother said he couldn't have any desert for three days if he didn't stop. Then Jason said he would stop if Dilsey would make a chocolate cake. Father was there.

"Why don't you do something about it?" mother said. "What do we have officers for?"

"Why is Nancy afraid of Jubah?" Caddy said. "Are you afraid of father, mother?"

"What could they do?" father said. "If Nancy hasn't seen him, how could the officers find him?"

"Then why is she afraid?" mother said.

"She says he is there. She says she knows he is there to-night."

"Yet we pay taxes," mother said. "I must wait here alone in this big house while you take a Negro woman home."

"You know that I am not lying outside with a razor," father said.

"I'll stop if Dilsey will make a chocolate cake," Jason said. Mother told us to go out and father said he didn't know if Jason would get a chocolate cake or not, but he knew what Jason was going to get in about a minute. We went back to the kitchen and told Nancy.

"Father said for you to go home and lock the door, and you'll be all right," Caddy said. "All right from what, Nancy? Is Jubah mad at you?" Nancy was holding the coffee cup in her hands, her elbows on her knees and her hands holding the cup between her knees. She was looking into the cup. "What have you done that made Jubah mad?" Caddy said. Nancy let the cup go. It didn't break on the floor, but the coffee spilled out, and Nancy sat there with her hands making the shape of the cup. She began to make the sound again, not loud. Not singing and not un-singing. We watched her.

"Here," Dilsey said. "You quit that, now. You get a-holt of yourself. You wait here. I going to get Versh to walk home with you." Dilsey went out.

We looked at Nancy. Her shoulders kept shaking, but she had quit making the sound. We watched her. "What's Jubah going to do to you?" Caddy said. "He went away."

Nancy looked at us. "We had fun that night I stayed in you all's room, didn't we?"

"I didn't," Jason said. "I didn't have any fun."

"You were asleep," Caddy said. "You were not there."

"Let's go down to my house and have some more fun," Nancy said.

"Mother won't let us," I said. "It's too late now."

"Don't bother her," Nancy said. "We can tell her in the morning. She won't mind."

"She wouldn't let us," I said.

"Don't ask her now," Nancy said. "Don't bother her now."

"They didn't say we couldn't go," Caddy said.

"We didn't ask," I said.

"If you go, I'll tell," Jason said.

"We'll have fun," Nancy said. "They won't mind, just to my house. I been working for you all a long time. They won't mind."

"I'm not afraid to go," Caddy said. "Jason is the one that's afraid. He'll tell."

"I'm not," Jason said.

"Yes, you are," Caddy said. "You'll tell."

"I won't tell," Jason said. "I'm not afraid."

"Jason ain't afraid to go with me," Nancy said. "Is you, Jason?"

"Jason is going to tell," Caddy said. The lane was dark. We passed the pasture gate. "I bet if something was to jump out from behind that gate, Jason would holler."

"I wouldn't," Jason said. We walked down the lane. Nancy was talking loud.

"What are you talking so loud for, Nancy?" Caddy said.

"Who; me?" Nancy said. "Listen at Quentin and Caddy and Jason saying I'm talking loud."

"You talk like there was four of us here," Caddy said. "You talk like father was here too."

"Who; me talking loud, Mr. Jason?" Nancy said.

"Nancy called Jason 'Mister,' " Caddy said.

"Listen how Caddy and Quentin and Jason talk," Nancy said.

"We're not talking loud," Caddy said. "You're the one that's talking like father—"

"Hush," Nancy said; "hush, Mr. Jason."

"Nancy called Jason 'Mister' aguh—"

"Hush," Nancy said. She was talking loud when we crossed the ditch and stooped through the fence where she used to stoop through with the clothes on her head. Then we came to her house. We were going fast then. She opened the door. The smell of the house was like the lamp and the smell of Nancy was like the wick, like they were waiting for one another to smell. She lit the lamp and closed the door and put the bar up. Then she quit talking loud, looking at us.

"What're we going to do?" Caddy said.

"What you all want to do?" Nancy said.

"You said we would have some fun," Caddy said.

There was something about Nancy's house; something you could smell. Jason smelled it, even. "I don't want to stay here," he said. "I want to go home."

"Go home, then," Caddy said.

"I don't want to go by myself," Jason said.

"We're going to have some fun," Nancy said.

"How?" Caddy said.

Nancy stood by the door. She was looking at us, only it was like she had emptied her eyes, like she had quit using them.

"What do you want to do?" she said.

"Tell us a story," Caddy said. "Can you tell a story?"

"Yes," Nancy said.

"Tell it," Caddy said. We looked at Nancy. "You don't know any stories," Caddy said.

"Yes," Nancy said. "Yes, I do."

She came and sat down in a chair before the hearth. There was some fire there; she built it up; it was already hot. You didn't need a fire. She built a good blaze. She told a story. She talked like her eyes looked, like her eyes watching us and her voice talking to us did not belong to her. Like she was living somewhere else, waiting somewhere else. She was outside the house. Her voice was there and the shape of her, the Nancy that could stoop under the fence with the bundle of clothes balanced as though without weight, like a balloon, on her head, was there. But that was all. "And so this here queen come walking up to the ditch, where that bad man was hiding. She was walking up the ditch, and she say, 'If I can just get past this here ditch,' was what she say. . . ."

"What ditch?" Caddy said. "A ditch like that one out there? Why did the queen go into the ditch?"

"To get to her house," Nancy said. She looked at us. "She had to cross that ditch to get home."

"Why did she want to go home?" Caddy said.

IV

Nancy looked at us. She quit talking. She looked at us. Jason's legs stuck straight out of his pants, because he was little. "I don't think that's a good story," he said. "I want to go home."

"Maybe we had better," Caddy said. She got up from the floor. "I bet they are looking for us right now." She went toward the door.

"No," Nancy said. "Don't open it." She got up quick and passed Caddy. She didn't touch the door, the wooden bar.

"Why not?" Caddy said.

"Come back to the lamp," Nancy said. "We'll have fun. You don't have to go."

"We ought to go," Caddy said. "Unless we have a lot of fun." She and Nancy came back to the fire, the lamp.

"I want to go home," Jason said. "I'm going to tell."

"I know another story," Nancy said. She stood close to the lamp. She looked at Caddy, like when your eyes look up at a stick balanced on your nose. She had to look down to see Caddy, but her eyes looked like that, like when you are balancing a stick.

"I won't listen to it," Jason said. "I'll bang on the floor."

"It's a good one," Nancy said. "It's better than the other one."

"What's it about?" Caddy said. Nancy was standing by the lamp. Her hand was on the lamp, against the light, long and brown.

"Your hand is on that hot globe," Caddy said. "Don't it feel hot to your hand?"

Nancy looked at her hand on the lamp chimney. She took her hand away, slow. She stood there, looking at Caddy, wringing her long hand as though it were tied to her wrist with a string.

"Let's do something else," Caddy said.

"I want to go home," Jason said.

"I got some popcorn," Nancy said. She looked at Caddy and then at Jason and then at me and then at Caddy again. "I got some popcorn."

"I don't like popcorn," Jason said. "I'd rather have candy."

Nancy looked at Jason. "You can hold the popper." She was still wringing her hand; it was long and limp and brown.

"All right," Jason said. "I'll stay a while if I can do that. Caddy can't hold it. I'll want to go home, if Caddy holds the popper."

Nancy built up the fire. "Look at Nancy putting her hands

in the fire," Caddy said. "What's the matter with you, Nancy?"

"I got popcorn," Nancy said. "I got some." She took the popper from under the bed. It was broken. Jason began to cry. "We can't have any popcorn," he said.

"We ought to go home, anyway," Caddy said. "Come on, Quentin."

"Wait," Nancy said; "wait. I can fix it. Don't you want to help me fix it?"

"I don't think I want any," Caddy said. "It's too late now."

"You help me, Jason," Nancy said. "Don't you want to help me?"

"No," Jason said. "I want to go home."

"Hush," Nancy said; "hush. Watch. Watch me. I can fix it so Jason can hold it and pop the corn." She got a piece of wire and fixed the popper.

"It won't hold good," Caddy said.

"Yes, it will," Nancy said. "You all watch. You all help me shell the corn."

The corn was under the bed too. We shelled it into the popper and Nancy helped Jason hold the popper over the fire.

"It's not popping," Jason said. "I want to go home."

"You wait," Nancy said. "It'll begin to pop. We'll have fun then." She was sitting close to the fire. The lamp was turned up so high it was beginning to smoke.

"Why don't you turn it down some?" I said.

"It's all right," Nancy said. "I'll clean it. You all wait. The popcorn will start in a minute."

"I don't believe it's going to start," Caddy said. "We ought to go home, anyway. They'll be worried."

"No," Nancy said. "It's going to pop. Dilsey will tell um you all with me. I been working for you all long time. They won't mind if you at my house. You wait, now. It'll start popping in a minute."

Then Jason got some smoke in his eyes and he began to

cry. He dropped the popper into the fire. Nancy got a wet rag and wiped Jason's face, but he didn't stop crying.

"Hush," she said. "Hush." He didn't hush. Caddy took the popper out of the fire.

"It's burned up," she said. "You'll have to get some more popcorn, Nancy."

"Did you put all of it in?" Nancy said.

"Yes," Caddy said. Nancy looked at Caddy. Then she took the popper and opened it and poured the blackened popcorn into her apron and began to sort the grains, her hands long and brown, and we watching her.

"Haven't you got any more?" Caddy said.

"Yes," Nancy said; "yes. Look. This here ain't burnt. All we need to do is——"

"I want to go home," Jason said. "I'm going to tell."

"Hush," Caddy said. We all listened. Nancy's head was already turned toward the barred door, her eyes filled with red lamplight. "Somebody is coming," Caddy said.

Then Nancy began to make that sound again, not loud, sitting there above the fire, her long hands dangling between her knees; all of a sudden water began to come out on her face in big drops, running down her face, carrying in each one a little turning ball of firelight until it dropped off her chin.

"She's not crying," I said.

"I ain't crying," Nancy said. Her eyes were closed. "I ain't crying. Who is it?"

"I don't know," Caddy said. She went to the door and looked out. "We've got to go home now," she said. "Here comes father."

"I'm going to tell," Jason said. "You all made me come."

The water still ran down Nancy's face. She turned in her chair. "Listen. Tell him. Tell him we going to have fun. Tell him I take good care of you all until in the morning. Tell him to let me come home with you all and sleep on the floor.

Tell him I won't need no pallet. We'll have fun. You remember last time how we had so much fun?"

"I didn't have any fun," Jason said. "You hurt me. You put smoke in my eyes."

V

Father came in. He looked at us. Nancy did not get up.

"Tell him," she said.

"Caddy made us come down here," Jason said. "I didn't want to."

Father came to the fire. Nancy looked up at him. "Can't you go to Aunt Rachel's and stay?" he said. Nancy looked up at father, her hands between her knees. "He's not here," father said. "I would have seen. There wasn't a soul in sight."

"He in the ditch," Nancy said. "He waiting in the ditch yonder."

"Nonsense," father said. He looked at Nancy. "Do you know he's there?"

"I got the sign," Nancy said.

"What sign?"

"I got it. It was on the table when I come in. It was a hog bone, with blood meat still on it, laying by the lamp. He's out there. When you all walk out that door, I gone."

"Who's gone, Nancy?" Caddy said.

"I'm not a tattletale," Jason said.

"Nonsense," father said.

"He out there," Nancy said. "He looking through that window this minute, waiting for you all to go. Then I gone."

"Nonsense," father said. "Lock up your house and we'll take you on to Aunt Rachel's."

" 'Twon't do no good," Nancy said. She didn't look at father now, but he looked down at her, at her long, limp, moving hands.

"Putting it off won't do no good."

"Then what do you want to do?" father said.

"I don't know," Nancy said. "I can't do nothing. Just put it off. And that don't do no good. I reckon it belong to me. I reckon what I going to get ain't no more than mine."

"Get what?" Caddy said. "What's yours?"

"Nothing," father said. "You all must get to bed."

"Caddy made me come," Jason said.

"Go on to Aunt Rachel's," father said.

"It won't do no good," Nancy said. She sat before the fire, her elbows on her knees, her long hands between her knees. "When even your own kitchen wouldn't do no good. When even if I was sleeping on the floor in the room with your own children, and the next morning there I am, and blood all——"

"Hush," father said. "Lock the door and put the lamp out and go to bed."

"I scared of the dark," Nancy said. "I scared for it to happen in the dark."

"You mean you're going to sit right here, with the lamp lighted?" father said. Then Nancy began to make the sound again, sitting before the fire, her long hands between her knees. "Ah, damnation," father said. "Come along, chillen. It's bedtime."

"When you all go, I gone," Nancy said. "I be dead tomorrow. I done have saved up the coffin money with Mr. Lovelady——"

Mr. Lovelady was a short, dirty man who collected the Negro insurance, coming around to the cabins and the kitchens every Saturday morning, to collect fifteen cents. He and his wife lived in the hotel. One morning his wife committed suicide. They had a child, a little girl. After his wife committed suicide Mr. Lovelady and the child went away. After a while Mr. Lovelady came back. We would see him going down the lanes on Saturday morning. He went to the Baptist church.

Father carried Jason on his back. We went out Nancy's door; she was sitting before the fire. "Come and put the bar up," father said. Nancy didn't move. She didn't look at us again. We left her there, sitting before the fire with the door opened, so that it wouldn't happen in the dark.

"What, father?" Caddy said. "Why is Nancy scared of Jubah? What is Jubah going to do to her?"

"Jubah wasn't there," Jason said.

"No," father said. "He's not there. He's gone away."

"Who is it that's waiting in the ditch?" Caddy said. We looked at the ditch. We came to it, where the path went down into the thick vines and went up again.

T. R. CARSKADON

Nigger Schoolhouse

T. R. CARSKADON, native of West Virginia, is one of those one- or two-story authors in the time of the Great Depression in the United States when there were not many magazines in the country that printed the short fiction of not yet established writers. Whether Mr. Carskadon was black or white we never asked at STORY Magazine. But his story had a human poignancy and it was real. It was his first published short story.

Jake seemed a funny name for such a little fellow. Black Becky came carrying him into our back yard, and she said to Mother, "He ain't been feelin' so well for the last couple of days, so I brung him along with me."

I can still see Jake, riding there with his head against his mother's big fat shoulder, and his little black arm around her neck. On his thumb he had one of those ruby rings that used to come wrapped around a penny stick of chewing gum. You could see he wasn't feeling well, and his black skin was sort of gray.

Black Becky put him down and said to Mother, "I hope you don't mind me bringin' him, Miss Ruth. I won't let him get in the way."

Mother told Becky that would be all right, and Becky took little Jake over and set him down on a box beside the grape arbor. Then she went into the house.

Black Becky came on Fridays to help get the house cleaned up for over Sunday. You could always tell when she was around by the smell of naphtha soap. We never liked naphtha much, because it took so long to get enough wrappers for a premium, and besides, the premiums they gave away with Octagon soap were much better anyway. But Becky wanted naphtha, and Mother always got it for her.

Becky used to scare us when we were real small, because she was so big and black. She always wound a white dust rag around her head when she was working. She had a heavy woolen skirt, and when she would go to scrub the back porch, he would pin up that skirt with safety pins and kneel down on her white petticoats. Her arms got all black and shiny when she put them in the scrub bucket, but the thing I could never understand was why the insides of her hands were so kind of pink, like the color had rubbed off.

Becky didn't mind us standing around watching her, but Mother didn't like to have us inside the house on Fridays and made us play outside if the weather was all right. Johnnie and Bobbie Clark, next door, were playing with us, and my sister Julia had little M'rie Cook, from down the street, with her.

We were all trying to think of something to do when we heard the school bell ring. The school buildings were about three blocks away, and they were holding Teachers' Institute. They always held Institute just before school started in the fall, and that bell reminded us that vacation was over and we would all have to start back to school on Monday.

Julia put her fingers in her ears and pretended to groan like she was being hurt, and the rest of us did that too and we made such a racket that Mother had to come out and stop us.

Then Julia got an idea. "Let's go over to the nigger schoolhouse!" As soon as she said it, she looked around to see if Jake had heard us, but he was just sitting there on his box, looking at the kitchen door where Black Becky had gone into the house.

Johnnie Clark said, "Shame on you for sayin' nigger schoolhouse," but Julia and M'rie just giggled and Julia said it again. The girls were older than we were, and didn't pay much attention to us. Julia knew she was doing wrong, though, because that was one thing Grandma Allen was always correcting us about, and she always made us say "colored schoolhouse." She said black people had souls just the same as other people, and we mustn't be hurting their feelings.

Sometimes Johnnie and Bobbie and I would act smart when we were with older boys, especially if we were over in Grandma Allen's yard, behind her big paling fence. Sometimes we'd holler,

> *"Nigger, nigger, never die,*
> *Blackie nose and shiny eye,"*

and then run as fast as we could. Usually the black boys were afraid to come over into Grandma Allen's yard to get us. But once Pete Shafer got fooled. That was in the winter time, and two little colored girls waited until everything was quiet and he couldn't see anyone, and then jumped on him when he came out of the gate. They got him down and slapped him hard and washed his face with a snowball before he could get away from them. We teased him about that for years.

The white school buildings, where the bell was ringing, were three blocks away, but the nigger schoolhouse was right across the alley, in back of our house. Nobody ever knew why it was put there, for it was near the center of town, with white people living all around, and not a colored family within blocks and blocks of it. Most of the colored people lived out in the bottom, on Lincoln street, or down along the creek, on Water street.

M'rie Cook was telling us her father was a conductor on the railroad and he said over in Pennsylvania the niggers went to school right along with the white people. Julia said she didn't believe that because Uncle Ned once told her that down in Virginia they even had separate railroad cars for niggers, and they surely wouldn't let them *go to school* together in Pennsylvania. But M'rie said, "Well, ain't Pennsylvania different from Virginia, just like West Virginia is, and you don't know what they might have in Pennsylvania." Julia said, "I still don't believe you," and Johnnie and I told them to stop arguing and come on, if they were going.

All five of us kind of tiptoed out the back gate, because Mother never liked it very much when we played out in the alley. We walked down past the back of Mrs. McCoole's house, and the Stevens' house, and Mr. Rogers' house to the place where we thought we could get over the fence and into the nigger school yard. They had a high board fence, seven feet high, with barbed wire on the top of it, running along the alley to close in the back of the nigger school yard.

The only place we had a chance to get over the fence was right where it joined onto the coal house, in back of the school. You could get a hand hold on the corner boards of the coal house, and some boys had nailed a few blocks of wood on the outside of the fence to give you a toe hold. Also, a piece of the bottom board was broken off there, and that left a hole about the size of a rabbit that you might wriggle through on the ground.

Julia had to go first, of course, and with M'rie pushing her she finally made it on top of the coal house, but she caught her drawers on a piece of barbed wire and snagged them a little before she could get loose. She reached down and gave M'rie a hand hold and got her up, and the two of them managed to get Johnnie up, but Bobbie and I decided to wriggle through the hole on the ground and we made it, though I scraped my side a little bit doing it.

Julia and M'rie went over to the edge of the coal house roof and hung by their hands and then dropped. Johnnie didn't want to do it at first, but they shamed him into it. He hit his chin on his knees when he dropped and it hurt him a little, but he didn't cry.

Once we all got inside the nigger school yard, we were a little scared. It was so empty and quiet in there, and the summer grass was high and thick, and it was like my Christmas book, "Lion Jack in the Jungle." M'rie said, "Dare you to look in the nigger schoolhouse!" and giggled, and Julia said she wouldn't take a dare, and started over, and the rest of us finally started over with her.

We wondered what kind of desks they had for the niggers, and how they could have all the grades in just one big room, and with a man for teacher, at that. It seemed funny to have a man teacher, even though he was a black man. We went over to the schoolhouse, a one-story brick building, and climbed up the rough part of the foundation to where we could get a hold on the window sill, and peeped in.

It seemed dark inside, after the glare of the sun outside, and at first all we could see were several rows of double desks, just like a regular schoolroom, with the high desks in back, and the low ones down front. Pretty soon we saw a colored man over in the corner. It was Jim Henry, who was one of the two janitors over at the white schools, and who was now getting the colored school ready to open on Monday. As soon as she saw him, M'rie squealed, "There's Jim Henry!" and we all jumped down from the window and ran over toward the coal house.

Jim Henry heard the commotion and came out of the schoolhouse. He knew all of us kids and knew our fathers and mothers, and he said, "Looka here, children, what you doin' in this yard?" We didn't answer him, but just tried to climb up the fence onto the coal house roof. Jim Henry said, "Here, here, that's no way to get out. Come on now, and I'll let you out the front gate. Come on!" We were so scared that he would tell Mother or something that we didn't say a word, but just walked over to the gate, and when he let us out we ran as fast as we could straight up Church street.

Since we came out the front gate we had to go up around the corner of the block to get to the alley and get back home the same way we came. We went in with elaborate slowness, so Mother wouldn't think anything had happened.

Black Becky had the green carpet out of the sitting-room up on a wire and was beating it with a carpet beater. Little Jake had a stick in his hands, and he would walk solemnly up to the carpet and hit it a whack and then look up at Becky and laugh. When she moved around to the other side he couldn't see her and all he could see was some big thing poking out the carpet at him, and he was scared. Finally he figured it out, and when he got around to the other side and saw Becky, he ran up and grabbed her skirt and held on a long time before he raised his stick and hit that old carpet again.

Fortunately Mother hadn't seen us children either going out or coming in, so we stayed in the back yard awhile, and then told Mother we were going over to Grandma Allen's to play. She said all right, and I think she was glad to get rid of us.

When my father came home for dinner at noon, he saw little Jake and asked Becky who that was. She said, "That's my youngest one, Mister Bob, but he ain't feelin' so peart today." My father laughed, and told Becky to feed him a good dinner, and maybe he would feel better. Julia and I hurried up our dinner so we could go out in the kitchen and watch Becky and Jake eat, but Mother made us go on outside.

That afternoon we set up a ringing stand game over at Grandma Allen's and played with it a couple of hours and then brought our little gang back to our back yard.

By that time little Jake was getting lonesome for some

company and he came over and said to us, "Kin I play too?"
Mother never let us play with colored children, and I don't
suppose Jake had ever had much chance to play with white
children, but it seemed all right to let him play with us there
in our back yard.

We started to play hide and seek. We counted out engine,
engine, number nine, running on Chicago line, and M'rie
was the last one out and she had to be It. She hid her face
against the big pear tree. While the rest of us were running
out to find places to hide, little Jake, in his deliberate way,
just walked around to the other side of the pear tree and stood
there.

As soon as M'rie left to hunt, Jake reached around and said,
"Free." M'rie said, "No fair! No fair hidin' behind base!" and
raised such a fuss about it that she and Julia made us all go
out and hide over again. This time Jake tried to hide behind
a washtub over by the grape arbor, but his legs were sticking
out and he was the first one caught.

We played hide and seek, which we called "hidey whoop,"
several times, and then we all made mud pies. Jake paid no
special attention to us, but he was a little puzzled when Julia
wouldn't let him use her little blue shovel that she let the rest
of us us to smooth off our pies. He didn't say anything, but
went to work to smooth off his pie with his little black fist.

After we had made pies for awhile, Julia said, "Let's play
school." Jake came right along with the rest of us. Julia said
she would be the teacher, and under the pear tree would be
the schoolroom. She told us all to get pieces of boards for
slates. Jake got one end of an old grape basket, which made a
funny looking slate, but he didn't seem to know what it was
for anyway.

Jake sat down between M'rie and Johnnie. Julia started to
call her roll, and then she noticed Jake. She made him get up
and go with her over by the ash pile. She picked up a stick and

marked off a square on the ground, put a box in it for him to sit on, and told him he would have to stay there.

Jake didn't understand what that was for. I think Julia was giving him a real lesson, because Jake was too little to know what going to school was like. He must have thought that when he went to school he would go right along with the rest of us, and now Julia was showing him how it was. He had to stay over by the ash pile. That was the nigger schoolhouse.

Julia came back and called the roll and made us do some arithmetic and tried to give us a geography lesson, but we all got to laughing so, she had to stop it. Then she called for some memory gems, and she and M'rie were just showing off because they were in the fourth grade and knew some, and none of us boys did. They recited everything they knew and then tried to make up some to fool us, and marked us down for not knowing any, and we were getting tired of playing school.

Nobody was paying much attention to Jake. He was all alone over there by the ash pile, sitting on his box and dodging and blinking to keep the sun out of his eyes. He looked like something was hurting him, and every once in awhile he would wriggle just a little bit, like he was afraid to move. Pretty soon tears came in his eyes, but he just sat there, and wouldn't move.

It was biggity Julia who found out what the trouble was. She went over to Jake, and then let out a squeal and called out to M'rie, "How do you spell 'up' backwards?"

M'rie took her cue at once and yelled "PEE YEW," and started to hold her nose. Pretty soon they had all of us doing it, yelling "PEE YEW," and holding our noses and dancing around poor little Jake, who just sat there with tears running down his face.

Mother and Black Becky came hurrying out of the house to see what was the matter. As soon as Becky saw what the trouble was she pretended to be very angry, trying to impress

Mother, and slapped Jake's face. Little Jake just looked up at her like his heart would break, because it was Black Becky who slapped him.

Mother said, "Becky, don't you dare touch him again. You know it's not the child's fault. It has happened to my children, just as it happened to yours. Now get a tub of water and take him out to the wood house and change him. I'll give you an old pair of pants of Ted's to put on him."

Becky got a tub of water and some soap and a rag and put them in the wood house and then came back for Jake. When she went toward him, he pulled back like he was afraid of her. That was too much for Becky, and she grabbed him up and kissed him and chewed his ear. Jake smiled at her, with the tears still on his face, and he turned his little black head around so she could chew his other ear.

Jake wasn't afraid any more. For awhile it seemed like he had been pushed out into a strange new world of white children, and unfamiliar games, and a schoolhouse over by the ash pile. But that world was gone now, and Jake knew it would never come again. He buried his nose in a familiar shoulder. Black Becky would take care of him.

E. P. O'DONNELL

Arrangement in Black

E. P. O'DONNELL, when he wrote the following story in 1932, was living in New Orleans, writing about blacks, Cajuns, and others of his neighbors in the city and outlying farms and bayous.

Mr. Colt was inspecting his assembly plant. He stopped in the welding department and watched a workman putting a spot weld on the saddle of a corn cultivator.

Ellick also stopped, a few feet away. Mr. Colt, the plant superintendent, had observed Ellick following him about for some time. From the side of his face he saw Ellick now, standing close by with something important to say. He heard Ellick clear his throat. Mr. Colt continued to watch the goggled welder bowed over the cautious fusion of metals. Ellick waited, nonchalantly unfolding and folding a worn sheet of cleansing chamois. Ellick's presence in the Birmingham Branch of the Universal Farm Machine Company was beginning to annoy Mr. Colt.

"Well?" Mr. Colt presently asked, turning without moving from the place where he was standing.

Ellick grinned at the concrete ceiling. "I put the new Number Two Disc Harrow by the entrance, where she shows up good," he said.

"O. K.," said Mr. Colt. He drew closer to the welder. Ellick stood fingering the chamois. He was a light mulatto, hired to ply a feather duster in the showroom upstairs, where agricultural implements were displayed for visiting hardware dealers. In charge of the resplendent display room, with no designated superior to watch him, Ellick loved his job. It was reputed to be the easiest in the plant, except Mr. Colt's, and it gave him a sort of distinction among his fellows.

To insure his future security in this job, Ellick had for some time helped to make Mr. Colt's job more secure. That is, he was an informer. Discovering an infraction that had escaped more authoritative eyes, immediately Ellick would contrive casually to talk with Mr. Colt. When Ellick made such an approach, usually Mr. Colt, sensing something amiss, would invent a trivial topic as a vehicle for the pregnant hint, the real object of Ellick's overtures.

"O. K., I said, Ellick," Mr. Colt repeated over his shoulder as he turned to leave. "Keep the new model stuff to the front of the showroom."

Ellick hurriedly gained Mr. Colt's side and walked along with him, still wearing a sleazy grin. "Yes, sir. Right up front. I cleaned it up nice. I found some brown stuff on one of the wheels, like it rolled over some brown stuff downstairs on the floor. Look like chew-tobacco. I don't know. Like brown pulp. Nasty, dirty brown pulp, like. All off now, though. It wasn't much. All off now."

Mr. Colt looked at Ellick, his keen gray scrutiny shifting from one to the other of the mulatto's mournful eyes.

"I see," he prompted.

"Rolled over it downstairs," Ellick continued. "Either in the wheel assembly or after it passed the wheel assembly, because it was right fresh, like."

"Oh, fresh, eh?"

"It could be the inspection department, except nobody

there wouldn't hardly chew on the job. But that's the last place the machines go before they tote them upstairs."

"Some new man somewhere, don't know the rules."

"Yes, sir. It *could* be chew-tobacco. All off now, though. All cleaned up."

"All off, eh? Well, considering you got it all off, we'll just forget about it. Get back to your work. Wait! Better go tell the chief clerk to read Local Rule Ten to you, Ellick."

Local Rule Ten prohibited any interruption of the Superintendent by employees, for any reason whatsoever, while the Superintendent was engaged in his Daily Inspection of Equipment and Personnel.

Ellick went up to the general office and stood by the chief clerk's desk. The chief clerk was busy. Ellick waited. The chief clerk rose from his chair and hurried across the office, elbowing Ellick aside. The mulatto held his hat and waited, unnoticed, gazing around at the busy clerks and stenographers. His long face was stamped with sultry insolence.

Downstairs, Mr. Colt wrote in a note-book. Soon, the foreman of the inspection department would be summoned to the telephone. Thereafter this foreman would be especially vigilant, and very soon one of the inspectors would be told to take five days off for violating Local Rule Six against using tobacco in the plant. Mr. Colt's discipline was flawless. In the Production Manager's office at Pittsburgh, the status of Birmingham, indicated on the globe by a blue and orange tack, was A Decimal Two, the highest rating among forty assembly plants encircling the globe in a wavering multi-colored belt. Discipline had done it.

Mr. Colt leaned out of a window to blow his nose; then, walking down the unloading dock where an orderly line of truckmen were pushing wheeled burdens many times heavier than themselves, again he thought of Ellick. And his pensive cud was as gross as gravel.

A crafty yellow boy, that Ellick! Skinny and slick. Taking

everything seriously, above all himself and his easy job. Knowing that he could read and write, talk and dress, dance and
love—better than any other colored man he knew—Ellick was
rigidly aloof. But his cold disdain was studied, of a kind that
readily melted into flabby superiority or fawning servility,
according to the occasion. He was known to carry an incisive
tongue in his head, and in his pocket a knife as quick, two
weapons his world had learned to respect.

The present tacit compact between Mr. Colt and Ellick was
obviously cherished by the latter, but to Mr. Colt the thing
was getting irksome, filled with unforeseen and hence doubly
galling difficulties. There are some underlings with whom one
simply dare not get familiar, no matter how legitimate the
cause.

At first, when Mr. Colt—newly promoted from the assembly
line in one of those fell reorganizations following a personal
visit from the Manager of Production—had permitted himself
to grow receptive to Ellick's maneuvers, the mulatto had con-
ducted himself with due and unobtrusive finesse. But lately,
with Mr. Colt inextricably obligated to him, Ellick was beginning to mar the delicacy of the bond. Despite tactful warn-
ings from Mr. Colt, Ellick had even come to ignore certain
Rules, both Local and General. Smoking back of the works
during hours. Neglecting to remove his hat when passing
through the hallways between eight and five.

In this organization, where the very air was properly
charged with restraining suspicion and stimulating insecurity,
such conduct, permitted with impunity, must very soon en-
gender in Ellick's more acute fellow workers certain unthink-
able speculations. A ticklish mess, fraught with no end of
obscure risks, and imperatively awaiting adroit disposal.

Mr. Colt with tightened lips resumed his inspection. He
peered into a lavatory. He frowned and twisted his wrist-
watch into view. Twenty minutes before lunch-time, and
there were four men in the lavatory! But he was pleased to

note that the walls, today, were free from pencilled epithets concerning the foremen. The floor, too, was without blemish— a clean, square expanse of battleship gray, with the tell-tale corners painted spotless white.

Proceeding to the paint department, Mr. Colt stopped at the paint foreman's desk. He opened the drawer and found all in order, no unfinished business or personal rubbish stored away. He leaned on the desk and surveyed the department, tapping his foot and briskly crackling his wad of chewing-gum. Then his restless eyes, prowling among the busy work-ers, fell upon the broad, sweat-polished torso of Hacksaw, the floor and equipment cleaner, who was wielding a lye-soaked mop.

Hacksaw was a huge Negro, pure in blood, with tough skin that an occasional splash of lye did not seriously damage, a brass religious medal on his neck, and incredibly large mus-cles. In the discordant blur of whirling belts and stuttering riveters, the big Negro's lips moved in a song. The song was soundless, yet clearly articulated in the Negro's face, his shin-ing eyes, and his massive body that moved in perfect rhythm with the husky cough of a nearby exhaust pipe. It was as though Hacksaw were using a song to clean the floor with.

Mr. Colt tarried, fingering the unclean diamond in his immaculate shirt front. Hacksaw was another employee whom Mr. Colt resented. The Negro had been sent to Mr. Colt a few months previously by Mr. Colt's brother, who was War-den of the nearby State Quarry. Hacksaw had served a sen-tence for criminal assault on a dance-hall Negress. The Com-pany frequently hired men who had served a first prison term. They proved to be excellent workmen, only too glad to find a position and especially amenable to discipline.

Something about this Negro disturbed Mr. Colt—had al-ways disturbed him. Hacksaw was humbly industrious. His whole demeanor betokened a child-like humility. But some-how, his humility had a strange origin, for it seemed to have no bearing on his relation to his superiors. Instead of his destiny being in the capable hands of his foreman, it seemed to be in his own hands. The foreman did not seem to perceive this; but Mr. Colt did, and it vexed him.

Furthermore, Hacksaw worked cheerfully. There was no knitting of the brows, no simulation of diligence when a superior appeared. His pace was always the same—active enough, yet clearly the pace of a man whose task required but a fraction of his vitality, the remainder being withheld, husbanded for use in other spheres. That was a bit beyond Mr. Colt. Here was a man of an inferior race, miraculously reinstated to respectability, surrounded by grimy workers engaged in the precarious battle for bread—hemmed in by hoarse foremen, clanging metal being shaped to the uses of the farmer, mercury lights that turned men's faces green, the sheen of sweat on bulging muscles, the whine of wheels, the pound of pistons, the swish of steam, the roar of imprisoned fire—whose task was yet such an impersonal thing that he could lose himself in a song whose phrases not even the singer could hear. Mr. Colt was nonplussed. On some vague principle that he had never had time to identify, it nettled the very core of his life's creed.

That was not all. Hacksaw had a way of unconsciously performing amusing capers while he worked, without falling foul of any definite Rule. Saving himself a walk across the floor by squeezing a piece of soap from between his fingers, through the air and into a distant bucket. Doing a kind of grotesque dance with his feet while his arms were properly engaged in bearing a heavy burden. He never tried to be funny. He never lost his dignity. But there was always this infernal suggestion of a song or dance about everything he did. A bad influence! A subtle menace to discipline. That was it! Subtle menace!

"Having any trouble with Hacksaw?" Mr. Colt asked Collins, his Assistant.

"Him? Not a chance. He always puts out, Chief."

Puts out! Puts out! That was all they could see, these so-called assistants—the surface signs of industry. They missed the subtle menaces, the deeper forces that rot an organization from within!

On his way to his private office after lunch, Mr. Colt passed through the showroom. Ellick was wiping a window. Mr. Colt ostentatiously wet his finger in his mouth and rubbed a stain from the bright red handle of a plow.

"Well, Ellick, do you understand Local Rule Ten now?" he asked.

"Mr. Kimmel was busy," the mulatto answered. "I kept waiting by his desk until lunch time, Mr. Colt."

"I see. Lunch might get cold, eh?" Mr. Colt stood with his hands behind him, like one concealing a weapon.

"After lunch, too he was busy. I'll go—"

"Listen, Ellick. Come back here. Let me tell you something." Mr. Colt wet his lips, then changed his mind. "Never mind, Ellick. Clean your windows."

That afternoon, Mr. Colt telephoned the Assistant Superintendent.

"I want to put that yellow nigger Ellick down there working with Hacksaw in the paint," he ordered. "Ellick cleans the drip-pans and hooks. Hacksaw tends to the floors and carriages. I'll send Ellick tomorrow."

"Put Ellick with Hacksaw?"

"Yes. With Hacksaw. Your tractor wheels come in?"

"Two carloads from Memphis Branch. You want two men cleaning in the one department?"

"Yes. Two men. Ellick and Hacksaw."

"They'll be in each other's way. There ain't enough work for two men in the one shift."

"You've got a man goes on at midnight. Put him elsewhere. Let both these men work four to midnight. Christ! do I have to tell you how to do it?"

"It won't work, Chief. First place, they can't work together."

Mr. Colt, alone in his office, smiled. "How do you mean, can't work together?"

"They don't click!"

"You don't say!"

"You know Ellick. High-toned nigger, fulla education, and so on. He's always kidding Hacksaw. They don't click."

"Kidding him? In this plant?"

"Oh, I don't know. But he kids him about being so black, and so on. Calling him Snowball, they tell me, and like of that."

"And, of course, in our Units Assembled Per Man Hour, we've got to allow for such things? The color prejudices of our showroom nigger. What would you suggest? Maybe we'd better write Pittsburgh."

"O. K. I'll put him down there and see if he can do the work. They won't get along. Hacksaw's going to scare that yellow nigger away from here. I think—"

"If Hacksaw chases him away, what's wrong with chasing *him* away?"

"Sure. That's just the trouble."

"I don't get you at all, Collins. What's the idea, wasting all this time on a couple of niggers?"

"I don't want to lose Hacksaw."

"Too bad. You'd better worry about unloading those wheels."

Locked in his private lavatory with a cigarette, Mr. Colt could visualize the outcome as clearly as if he already had before him the Foreman's Statement of Employees Discharged.

At first, the two men, both puzzled yet accustomed to the sudden and unexplainable shifts in technique that characterized the Company's methods, would be wary—too bewildered to think of their mutual enmity. Especially Ellick, the crafty one, remembering the Rule Ten matter, would be wary. Docile, ostensibly resigned and wary. This truce might last for days, but it would soon pass. With their suppressed bitterness toward each other growing deeper, ultimately some trifling spark would ignite their hoarded animosity. Then Hacksaw, as Collins had foreseen, would scare the yellow nigger away, perhaps even thrash him.

What! Fighting on the job? That speaks volumes for your famous discipline, Collins, but why disturb me with these trifles? Have we run out of discharge slips?

And that was that. As sound as a sabot!

Mr. Colt disposed of his cigarette and energetically sought his private office to grapple with more pressing affairs. Pittsburgh had increased his production schedule for the coming month. Outside, a generous rain laved the parched valley, a spendid cotton-shower.

"How's your floor and fixtures look?" Mr. Colt a week later asked the foreman of the paint department.

"Fine! Clean as a whistle at quitting-time. No threads, no paint."

"Both your cleaners on the job, eh?"

"And how! Little bit hard on Ellick, but he's sure putting out. Of course Hacksaw's right on the job. That's one working nigger. Always singing. He's O. K."

"They get along all right together? You want to watch that."

"Sure. What's Collins' idea, Mr. Colt, putting Ellick down here? He wants to see which one handles the work best and then fire the other one, I guess."

Mr. Colt ceased to chew his gum. He looked at the foreman. His face brightened. "Well, how did you come to think of that?" he asked.

The foreman confided in his assistant. The next day it was gossiped around that Hacksaw and Ellick were being pitted against each other. No bets were made. Hacksaw was considered an easy winner.

The foreman, mindful of instructions, watched closely, but saw no signs of belligerence. There was little change in Hacksaw's behavior. He did not believe all this talk, although he did not mind the white men, eager for novelty, having their fun.

"You two fellows want to get together and double-cross them, like they do on the assembly line when the boss matches them up," one man advised Hacksaw. "If you break your back and win now, you gotta keep it up always, remember."

Hacksaw only chuckled. He was unruffled. As before, without additional effort and as a matter of course, he accomplished more work than Ellick did. Stealthy words of encouragement from those around him were disregarded. He maintained his pace, no slower, no faster, and continued to ignore Ellick. He mildly disliked Ellick.

Ellick now attacked his drip-pans and drying-hooks more savagely. His eyes continuously sought the leisurely figure of Hacksaw, for whom he never lacked a vicious slur. Within a week, worn to the gristle, he pretended that a muscle in his back was strained.

"You've got no muscle that I can see," said the plant surgeon. "Nothing but bones back here."

The back was bound with plaster and Ellick reassigned to his work. He was now certain that his back was in fact badly injured. At lunch time, he stood before Mr. Colt's office, looking through the glass door. Mr. Colt was in the office talking to a retail dealer. Ellick remained before the door until the nearby switchboard operator told him Mr. Colt had phoned he could not see Ellick today. Ellick returned to his job.

Later, when the two were working near each other, Hacksaw accidentally backed into Ellick's bucket, spilling part of its contents.

"Watch your goddam flatboats, Black!" said Ellick.

Hacksaw chuckled. "Take yo' time, son. What's got aholt of you today? Can't we give this job time to dygest?"

"Mind out for yours and I mind out for mine, old cockan-coffee nigger."

Hacksaw, flaying the clotted paint with a wire brush, was amused. His brush-handle described a slow, reaping motion, and he spoke gently, a suave utterance following each stroke:

"Jes take yo' time—

"Ah bin thinking bout you—

"Lemme tell you—

"You go' be callin me niggah—

"An niggah—

"Tell Ah'm go' fix you up—

"So you go' be black'n me—

"Some day you don be caffle—

"You yah me, Mistah P. I.?"

Ellick's knife was out. Hacksaw's brush fell to the floor. He stood swaying, as though on the brink of an abyss. He loomed frightfully massive, slowly toward the mulatto, shining black with much sweat. Ellick crouched into a corner, bleating, his knife forgotten, his feet pawing the concrete for a hold to help him through the wall. Hacksaw laughed at this and turned away. Ellick grasped his knife more firmly and gained his legs. Hacksaw wheeled and saw. Impatiently he approached the mulatto on firmly planted feet, blazing with quiet rage, reeling like a hungry black flame, and reached into the corner with great slow hands. He lifted the squirming yellow body above his head and tossed it through a wide gap of space, plumply into a vat of black enamel, a steaming round void whose surface opened to the impact like gulping black lips.

The Assistant Superintendent called Mr. Colt on the telephone.

"There's been a fight in the paint department," he announced.

"A fine example of your discipline, Collins, but why bother me—"

"Ellick's—"

"Sure, I know. Ellick and Hacksaw. Know all about it and I'm busy. Keep your shirt on. Fire them both. Get the department running again. I guess your men are all standing around settling the bets and—"

"Listen, Chief! Hacksaw chucked Ellick in the enamel tank!"

Holy Christ a lawsuit!

Mr. Colt hurried from his office, through the general office where neat, orderly clerks worked in long rows, and entered the plant. The walls, floors, ceilings, were spotless. The great pilasters were numbered in heavy black, indicating the proper storage place for the smallest bolt or nut. Order everywhere! Bustling figures reaching for the proper tool; workers bearing burdens to a definite place; goggled shapes hunched over sparkling emery-wheels, peering closely for accuracy; foremen lithely weaving through the din—everyone peaceably industrious. That there should be anyone with sufficient irreverence to bring disorder here! Somebody had been negligent! He'd find out! Things didn't just happen. They were permitted!

Hacksaw was lacing his street shoes. There was a policeman. Hacksaw had a cigarette behind his ear. He would put it into his mouth, then remember that he was still in the plant and replace it behind his ear.

"He pull a knife on me," Hacksaw was telling the policeman. "Git somebody take mah banjo home, up in mah clothes lockah. Clara Jeff. Fi'-fo'teen Cramberry Stree'. Somma yall try and find 'at knife. He pull a knife on me, Cap. Big, shop frawg-stickah. Ah seen it."

A lawsuit! A lawsuit!

The knife was found, months later, when the enamel vat, now called the soup tureen, was drained for cleaning. Hacksaw had been sentenced to five years. Ellick's wife had been awarded damages. Mr. Colt had received a severe reprimand from Pittsburgh for lack of discipline, and forfeited his yearly bonus. It was not until his plant took the new Waste Elimination Plaque that he forgot that reprimand.

Hacksaw, the ungrateful, he never forgot. Basking again in the good graces of the distant Manager of Production, he liked to picture Hacksaw paying his price with a twelve-pound hammer in his hands and a frown of concern on his face— humbled at last beneath the kind of discipline that, after all, only the taxpayers could exact, from certain types.

And the first fine Sunday afternoon he could spare, Mr. Colt drove out to inspect the big peach orchard of his brother, the Quarry Warden. As the two strolled through the orchard, overlooking the Quarry, Mr. Colt asked about the Negro, Hacksaw. Yes, Hacksaw had been sent to the Quarry. Why, certainly they watched him closely! But Mr. Colt had his doubts.

Later, with his own eyes he spied Hacksaw, deep in the earth, breaking rocks. To look at the Negro, one would have thought that little was changed but the rhythm of things. Obviously, he found little difference between the weight of a mop and that of a sledge hammer. The indolent guard didn't seem to mind his pausing to savor the sunshine. He worked slowly, just fast enough, thought Mr. Colt, to keep awake. Clearly, he was using but a fraction of his strength, saving the remainder for other days, no doubt. Holding out on the people. There! Singing as usual! The slow circle of his descending maul would break, driving a careless phrase into the rock. Another circle, another phrase:

> *Ah'm slow in the shoulders—*
> *But mah backbone's built for—*
> *Ah said it's built for—*
> *Ah'm talkin bout fun!—*
> *Ah'm slow in the shoulders—*

> *But mah backbone's built for fun!—*
> *Mama skin a rabbit—*
> *For yo no-count Protticle Son!*

Mr. Colt left with the feeling that the matter had not been satisfactorily disposed of.

RUDOLPH FISHER

Miss Cynthie

RUDOLPH FISHER, black writer and physician, was born in Washington, D.C., in 1897, took degrees at both Howard University and Brown, completing his medical studies at Columbia. He became a roentgenologist and lived in Jamaica, Queens, New York, writing and practicing medicine until he died in 1934. He wrote two novels and many short stories, mainly about Harlem and its people in the 1920s. The story was first published in STORY in 1933.

For the first time in her life somebody had called her "madam."

She had been standing, bewildered but unafraid, while innumerable Red Caps appropriated piece after piece of the baggage arrayed on the platform. Neither her brief seventy years' journey through life nor her long two days' travel northward had dimmed the live brightness of her eyes, which, for all their bewilderment, had accurately selected her own treasures out of the row of luggage and guarded them vigilantly.

"These yours, madam?"

The biggest Red Cap of all was smiling at her. He looked for all the world like Doc Crinshaw's oldest son back home. Her little brown face relaxed; she smiled back at him.

"They got to be. You all done took all the others."

He laughed aloud. Then—"Carry 'em in for you?"

She contemplated his bulk. "Reckon you can manage it—puny little feller like you?"

Thereupon they were friends. Still grinning broadly, he surrounded himself with her impedimenta, the enormous brown extension-case on one shoulder, the big straw suitcase in the opposite hand, the carpet-bag under one arm. She herself held fast to the umbrella.

"Always like to have sump'm in my hand when I walk. Can't never tell when you'll run across a snake."

"There aren't any snakes in the city."

"There's snakes everywhere, chile."

They began the tedious hike up the interminable platform. She was small and quick. Her carriage was surprisingly erect, her gait astonishingly spry. She said:

"You liked to took my breath back yonder, boy, callin' me 'madam.' Back home everybody call me 'Miss Cynthie.' Even my own chillun. Even their chillun. Black folks, white folks too. 'Miss Cynthie.' Well, when you come up with that 'madam' o' yourn, I say to myself, 'Now, I wonder who that chile's a-grinnin' at? 'Madam' stand for mist'ess o' the house, and I sho' ain' mist'ess o' nothin' in this hyeh New York."

"Well, you see, we call everybody 'madam.' "

"Everybody?—Hm." The bright eyes twinkled. "Seem like that'd worry me some—if I was a man."

He acknowledged his slip and observed, "I see this isn't your first trip to New York."

"First trip any place, son. First time I been over fifty mile from Waxhaw. Only travelin' I've done is in my head. Ain' seen many places, but I's seen a passel o' people. Reckon places is pretty much alike after people been in 'em awhile."

"Yes, ma'am. I guess that's right."

"You ain' no reg'lar bag-toter, is you?"

"Ma'am?"

"You talk too good."

"Well, I only do this in vacation-time. I'm still in school."

"You is. What you aimin' to be?"

"I'm studying medicine."

"You is?" She beamed. "Aimin' to be a doctor, huh? Thank the Lord for that. That's what I always wanted my David to be. My grandchile hyeh in New York. He's to meet me hyeh now."

"I bet you'll have a great time."

"Mussn't bet, chile. That's sinful. I tole him 'fo' he left home, I say, 'Son, you the only one o' the chillun what's got a chance to amount to sump'm. Don' th'ow it away. Be a preacher or a doctor. Work yo' way up and don' stop short. If the Lord don' see fit for you to doctor the soul, then doctor the body. If you don' get to be a reg'lar doctor, be a tooth-doctor. If you jes' can't make that, be a foot-doctor. And if you don' get that fur, be a undertaker. That's the least you must be. That ain' so bad. Keep you acquainted with the house o' the Lord. Always mind the house o' the Lord—whatever you do, do like a church-steeple: aim high and go straight.' "

"Did he get to be a doctor?"

"Don' b'lieve he did. Too late startin', I reckon. But he's done succeeded at sump'm. Mus' be at least a undertaker, 'cause he started sendin' the homefolks money, and he come home las' year dressed like Judge Pettiford's boy what went off to school in Virginia. Wouldn't tell none of us 'zackly what he was doin', but he said he wouldn' never be happy till I come and see for myself. So hyeh I is." Something softened her voice. "His mammy died befo' he knowed her. But he was always sech a good chile—" The something was apprehension. "Hope he *is* a undertaker."

They were mounting a flight of steep stairs leading to an exit-gate, about which clustered a few people still hoping to catch sight of arriving friends. Among these a tall young brown-skinned man in a light grey suit suddenly waved his panama and yelled, "Hey, Miss Cynthie!"

Miss Cynthie stopped, looked up, and waved back with a delighted umbrella. The Red Cap's eyes lifted too. His lower jaw sagged.

"Is that your grandson?"

"It sho' is," she said and distanced him for the rest of the climb. The grandson, with an abandonment that superbly ignored on-lookers, folded the little woman in an exultant, smothering embrace. As soon as she could, she pushed him off with breathless mock impatience.

"Go 'way, you fool, you. Aimin' to squeeze my soul out my body befo' I can get a look at this place?" She shook herself into the semblance of composure. "Well. You don' look hungry, anyhow."

"Ho-ho! Miss Cynthie in New York! Can y'imagine this? Come on. I'm parked on Eighth Avenue."

The Red Cap delivered the outlandish luggage into a robin's egg blue open Packard with scarlet wheels, accepted the grandson's dollar and smile, and stood watching the car roar away up Eighth Avenue.

Another Red Cap came up. "Got a break, hey, boy?"

"Dave Tappen himself—can you beat that?"

"The old lady hasn't seen the station yet—starin' at him."

"That's not the half of it, bozo. That's Dave Tappen's grandmother. And what do you s'pose she hopes?"

"What?"

"She hopes that Dave has turned out to be a successful undertaker!"

"Undertaker? Undertaker!"

They stared at each other a gaping moment, then doubled up with laughter.

"Look—through there—that's the Chrysler Building. Oh, hell-elujah! I meant to bring you up Broadway—"

"David—"

"Ma'am?"

"This hyeh wagon yourn?"

"Nobody else's. Sweet buggy, ain't it?"

"David—you ain't turned out to be one of them moonshiners, is you?"

"Moonshiners—? Moon—Ho! No indeed, Miss Cynthie. I got a better racket 'n that."

"Better which?"

"Game. Business. Pick-up."

"Tell me, David. What is yo' racket?"

"Can't spill it yet, Miss Cynthie. Rather show you. Tomorrow night you'll know the worst. Can't you make out till tomorrow night?"

"David, you know I always wanted you to be a doctor, even if 'twasn' nothin' but a foot-doctor. The very leas' I wanted you to be was a undertaker."

"Undertaker! Oh, Miss Cynthie!—with my sunny disposition?"

"Then you ain' even a undertaker?"

"Listen, Miss Cynthie. Just forget 'bout what I am for awhile. Just till tomorrow night. I want you to see for yourself. Tellin' you will spoil it. Now stop askin', you hear?—because I'm not answerin'—I'm surprisin' you. And don't expect anybody you meet to tell you. It'll mess up the whole works. Understand? Now give the big city a break. There's the elevated train going up Columbus Avenue. Ain't that hot stuff?"

Miss Cynthie looked. "Humph!" she said. "'Tain' half high as that trestle two mile from Waxhaw."

She thoroughly enjoyed the ride up Central Park West. The stagger lights, the extent of the park, the high, close, kingly dwellings, remarkable because their stoves cooled them in summers as well as heated them in winter, all drew nods of mild interest. But what gave her special delight was not these:

it was that David's car so effortlessly sped past the headlong drove of vehicles racing northward.

They stopped for a red light; when they started again their machine leaped forward with a triumphant eagerness that drew from her an unsuppressed "Hot you, David! That's it!"

He grinned appreciatively. "Why, you're a regular New Yorker already."

"New Yorker nothin'! I done the same thing fifty years ago —befo' I knowed they was a New York."

"What!"

"'Deed so. Didn' I use to tell you 'bout my young mare, Betty? Chile, I'd hitch Betty up to yo' grandpa's buggy and pass anything on the road. Betty never knowed what another horse's dust smelt like. No 'ndeedy. Shuh, boy, this ain' nothin' new to me. Why that broke-down Fo'd yo' uncle Jake's got ain' nothin'—nothin' but a sorry mess. Done got so slow I jes' won' ride in it—I declare I'd rather walk. But this hyeh thing, now, this is right nice." She settled back in complete, complacent comfort, and they sped on, swift and silent.

Suddenly she sat erect with abrupt discovery.

"David—well—bless my soul!"

"What's the matter, Miss Cynthie?"

Then he saw what had caught her attention. They were traveling up Seventh Avenue now, and something was miraculously different. Not the road; that was as broad as ever, wide, white gleaming in the sun. Not the houses; they were lofty still, lordly, disdainful, supercilious. Not the cars; they continued to race impatiently onward, innumerable, precipitate, tumultuous. Something else, something at once obvious and subtle, insistent, pervasive, compelling.

"David—this mus' be Harlem!"

"Good Lord, Miss Cynthie—!"

"Don' use the name of the Lord in vain, David."

"But I mean—gee!—you're no fun at all. You get everything before a guy can tell you."

"You got plenty to tell me, David. But don' nobody need to tell me this. Look a yonder."

Not just a change of complexion. A completely dissimilar atmosphere. Sidewalks teeming with leisurely strollers, at once strangely dark and bright. Boys in white trousers, berets, and green shirts, with slickened black heads and proud swagger. Bareheaded girls in crisp organdie dresses, purple, canary, gay scarlet. And laughter, abandoned strong Negro laughter, some falling full on the ear, some not heard at all, yet sensed— the warm life-breath of the tireless carnival to which Harlem's heart quickens in summer.

"This is it," admitted David. "Get a good eyeful. Here's One Hundred and Twenty-fifth Street—regular little Broadway. And here's the Alhambra, and up ahead we'll pass the Lafayette."

"What's them?"

"Theatres."

"Theatres? Theatres. Humph! Look, David—is that a colored folks church?" They were passing a fine gray-stone edifice.

"That? Oh. Sure it is. So's this one on this side."

"No! Well, ain' that fine? Splendid big church like that for colored folks."

Taking his cue from this, her first tribute to the city, he said, "You ain' seen nothing yet. Wait a minute."

They swung left through a side-street and turned right on a boulevard. "What do you think o' that?" And he pointed to the quarter-million dollar St. Mark's.

"That a colored church, too?"

" 'Tain' no white one. And they built it themselves, you know. Nobody's hand-me-down gift."

She heaved a great happy sigh. "Oh, yes, it was a gift, David. It was a gift from on high." Then, "Look a hyeh—which a one you belong to?"

"Me? Why, I don't belong to any—that is, none o' these.

Mine's over in another section. Y'see, mine's Baptist. These
are all Methodist. See?"

"M-m. Uh-huh. I see."

They circled a square and slipped into a quiet narrow street
overlooking a park, stopping before the tallest of the apart-
ment-houses in the single commanding row.

Alighting, Miss Cynthie gave this imposing structure one
sidewise, upward glance, and said, "Y'all live like bees in a
hive, don't y'?—I boun' the women does all the work, too." A
moment later, "So this is a elevator? Feel like I'm glory-bound
sho' nuff."

Along a tiled corridor and into David's apartment. Rooms
leading into rooms. Luxurious couches, easy-chairs, a brown-
walnut grand piano, gay-shaded floor lamps, panelled walls,
deep rugs, treacherous glass-wood floors—and a smiling
golden-skinned girl in a gingham house-dress, approaching
with outstretched hands.

"This is Ruth, Miss Cynthie."

"Miss Cynthie!" said Ruth.

They clasped hands. "Been wantin' to see David's girl ever
since he first wrote us 'bout her."

"Come—here's your room this way. Here's the bath. Get
out of your things and get comfy. You must be worn out with
the trip."

"Worn out? Worn out? Shuh. How you gon' get worn out
on a train? Now if 'twas a horse, maybe, or Jake's no-'count
Fo'd—but a train—didn' but one thing bother me on that
train."

"What?"

"When the man made them beds down, I jes' couldn' manage to undress same as at home. Why, s'posin' sump'm bus'
the train open—where'd you be? Naked as a jay-bird in dew-
berry time."

David took in her things and left her to get comfortable.

He returned, and Ruth, despite his reassuring embrace, whispered:

"Dave, you can't fool old folks—why don't you go ahead and tell her about yourself? Think of the shock she's going to get —at her age."

David shook his head. "She'll get over the shock if she's there looking on. If we just told her, she'd never understand. We've got to railroad her into it. Then she'll be happy."

"She's nice. But she's got the same ideas as all old folks—"

"Yea—but with her you can change 'em. Specially if everything is really all right. I know her. She's for church and all, but she believes in good times too, if they're right. Why, when I was a kid—" He broke off. "Listen!"

Miss Cynthie's voice came quite distinctly to them, singing a jaunty little rhyme:

"Oh I danced with the gal with the hole in her stockin',
And her toe kep' a-kickin' and her heel kep' a-knockin'—

Come up, Jesse, and get a drink o' gin,
'Cause you near to the heaven as you'll ever get ag'in."

"She taught me that when I wasn't knee-high to a cricket," David said.

Miss Cynthie still sang softly and merrily:

"Then I danced with the gal with the dimple in her cheek;
And if she'd a' kep' a-smilin', I'd a' danced for a week—"

"God forgive me," prayed Miss Cynthie as she discovered David's purpose the following night. She let him and Ruth lead her, like an early Christian martyr, into the Lafayette Theatre. The blinding glare of the lobby produced a merciful self-anaesthesia, and she entered the sudden dimness of the interior as involuntarily as in a dream—

Attendants outdid each other for Mr. Dave Tappen. She heard him tell them, "Fix us up till we go on," and found herself sitting between Ruth and David in the front row of a lower box. A miraculous device of the devil, a motion-picture that talked, was just ending. At her feet the orchestra was assembling. The motion-picture faded out amid a scattered round of applause. Lights blazed and the orchestra burst into an ungodly rumpus.

She looked out over the seated multitude, scanning row upon row of illumined faces, black faces, white faces, yellow, tan, brown; bald heads, bobbed heads, kinky and straight heads; and upon every countenance, expectancy,—scowling expectancy in this case, smiling in that, complacent here, amused there, commentative elsewhere, but everywhere suspense, abeyance, anticipation.

Half a dozen people were ushered down the nearer aisle to reserved seats in the second row. Some of them caught sight of David and Ruth and waved to them. The chairs immediately behind them in the box were being shifted. "Hello, Tap!" Miss Cynthie saw David turn, rise, and shake hands with two men. One of them was large, bald and pink, emanating good cheer; the other short, thin, sallow with thick black hair and a sour mien. Ruth also acknowledged their greeting. "This is my grandmother," David said proudly. "Miss Cynthie, meet my managers, Lou and Lee Goldman." "Pleased to meet you," managed Miss Cynthie. "Great lad, this boy of yours," said Lou Goldman. "Great little partner he's got, too," added Lee. They also settled back expectantly.

"Here we go!"

The curtain rose to reveal a cotton-field at dawn. Pickers in blue denim overalls, bandanas, and wide-brimmed straws, or in gingham aprons and sun-bonnets, were singing as they worked. Their voices, from clearest soprano to richest bass, blended in low concordances, first simply humming a series of harmonies, until, gradually, came words, like figures forming in mist. As the sound grew, the mist cleared, the words came round and full, and the sun rose bringing light as if in answer to the song. The chorus swelled, the radiance grew, the two, as if emanating from a single source, fused their crescendos, till at last they achieved a joint transcendence of tonal and visual brightness.

"Swell opener," said Lee Goldman.

"Ripe," agreed Lou.

David and Ruth arose. "Stay here and enjoy the show, Miss Cynthie. You'll see us again in a minute."

"Go to it, kids," said Lou Goldman.

"Yea—burn 'em up," said Lee.

Miss Cynthie hardly noted that she had been left, so absorbed was she in the spectacle. To her, the theatre had always been the antithesis of the church. As the one was the refuge of righteousness, so the other was the stronghold of transgression. But this first scene awakened memories, captured and held her attention by offering a blend of truth and novelty. Having thus baited her interest, the show now proceeded to play it like the trout through swift-flowing waters of wickedness. Resist as it might, her mind was caught and drawn into the impious subsequences.

The very music that had just rounded out so majestically now distorted itself into ragtime. The singers came forward and turned to dancers; boys, a crazy, swaying background, threw up their arms and kicked out their legs in a rhythmic jamboree; girls, an agile, brazen foreground, caught their skirts up to their hips and displayed their copper calves, knees, thighs, in shameless, incredible steps. Miss Cynthie turned dismayed eyes upon the audience, to discover that mob of sinners devouring it all with fond satisfaction. Then the dancers separated and with final abandon flung themselves off the stage in both directions.

Lee Goldman commented through the applause, "They work easy, them babies."

"Yea," said Lou. "Savin' the hot stuff for later."

Two black-faced cotton-pickers appropriated the scene, indulging in dialogue that their hearers found uproarious,

"Ah'm tired."

"Ah'm hongry."

"Dis job jes' wears me out."

"Starves me to death."

"Ah'm so tired—you know what Ah'd like to do?"

"What?"

"Ah'd like to go to sleep and dream I was sleepin'."

"What good dat do?"

"Den I could wake up and still be 'sleep."

"Well y' know what Ah'd like to do?"

"No. What?"

"Ah'd like to swaller me a hog and a hen."

"What good dat do?"

"Den Ah'd always be full o' ham and eggs."

"Ham? Shuh. Don't you know a hog has to be smoked 'fo' he's a ham?"

"Well, if I swaller him, he'll have a smoke all around him, won' he?"

Presently Miss Cynthie was smiling like everyone else, but her smile soon fled. For the comics departed, and the dancing girls returned, this time in scant travesties on their earlier voluminous costumes—tiny sunbonnets perched jauntily on one side of their glistening bobs, bandanas reduced to scarlet neck-ribbons, waists mere brassieres, skirts mere gingham sashes.

And now Miss Cynthie's whole body stiffened with a new and surpassing shock; her bright eyes first widened with unbelief, then slowly grew dull with misery. In the midst of a sudden great volley of applause her grandson had broken through that bevy of agile wantons and begun to sing.

He too was dressed as a cotton-picker, but a Beau Brummel among cotton-pickers; his hat bore a pleated green band, his bandana was silk, his overalls blue satin, his shoes black patent leather. His eyes flashed, his teeth gleamed, his body swayed, his arms waved, his words came fast and clear. As he sang, his companions danced a concerted tap, uniformly wild, ecstatic. When he stopped singing, he himself began to dance, and without sacrificing crispness of execution, seemed to absorb into himself every measure of the energy which the girls, now merely standing off and swaying, had relinquished.

"Look at that boy go," said Lee Goldman.

"He ain't started yet," said Lou.

But surrounding comment, Dave's virtuosity, the eager enthusiasm of the audience were all alike lost on Miss Cynthie. She sat with stricken eyes watching this boy whom she'd raised from a babe, taught right from wrong, brought up in the church, and endowed with her prayers, this child whom she had dreamed of seeing a preacher, a regular doctor, a tooth-doctor, a foot-doctor, at the very least an undertaker—sat watching him disport himself for the benefit of a sinsick, flesh-hungry mob of lost souls, not one of whom knew or cared to know the loving kindness of God; sat watching a David she'd never foreseen, turned tool of the devil, disciple of lust, unholy prince among sinners.

For a long time she sat there watching with wretched eyes, saw portrayed on the stage David's arrival in Harlem, his escape from "old friends" who tried to dupe him; saw him working as a trap-drummer in a night-club, where he fell in love with Ruth, a dancer; not the gentle Ruth Miss Cynthie knew, but a wild and shameless young savage who danced like seven devils—in only a girdle and breast-plates; saw the two of them join in a song-and-dance act that eventually made them Broadway headliners, an act presented *in toto* as the pre-finale of this show. And not any of the melodies, not any of the sketches, not all the comic philosophy of the tired-and-hungry duo, gave her figure a moment's relaxation or brightened the dull defeat in her staring eyes. She sat apart, alone in the box, the symbol, the epitome of supreme failure. Let the rest of the theatre be riotous, clamoring for more and more of Dave Tappen, "Tap," the greatest tapster of all time, idol of uptown and downtown New York. For her, they were lauding simply an exhibition of sin which centered about her David.

"This'll run a year on Broadway," said Lee Goldman.

"Then we'll take it to Paris."

Encores and curtains with Ruth, and at last David came out on the stage alone. The clamor dwindled. And now he did something quite unfamiliar to even the most consistent of his followers. Softly, delicately, he began to tap a routine designed to fit a particular song. When he had established the rhythm, he began to sing the song:

"Oh I danced with the gal with the hole in her stockin',
And her toe kep' a-kickin' and her heel kep' a-knockin'

Come up, Jesse, and get a drink o' gin,
'Cause you near to the heaven as you'll ever get ag'in—"

As he danced and sang this song, frequently smiling across at Miss Cynthie, a visible change transformed her. She leaned forward incredulously, listened intently, then settled back in limp wonder. Her bewildered eyes turned on the crowd, on those serried rows of shiftless sinners. And she found in their faces now an overwhelmingly curious thing: a grin, a universal grin, a gleeful and sinless grin such as not the nakedest chorus in the performance had produced. In a few seconds, with her own song, David had dwarfed into unimportance, wiped off their faces, swept out of their minds every trace of what had seemed to be sin; had reduced it all to mere trivial detail and revealed these revelers as a crowd of children, enjoying the guileless antics of another child. And Miss Cynthie whispered her discovery aloud:

"Bless my soul! They didn't mean nothin' . . . They jes' didn' see no harm in it—"

"Then I danced with the gal with the dimple in her cheek,
And if she'd a' kep' a-smilin' I'd a' danced for a week—

Come up, Jesse—"

The crowd laughed, clapped their hands, whistled. Someone threw David a bright yellow flower. "From Broadway!"
He caught the flower. A hush fell. He said:

"I'm really happy tonight, folks. Y'see this flower? Means
success, don't it? Well, listen. The one who is really responsible for my success is here tonight with me. Now what do you
think o' that?"

The hush deepened.

"Y'know folks, I'm sump'm like Adam—I never had no
mother. But I've got a grandmother. Down home everybody
calls her Miss Cynthie. And everybody loves her. Take that
song I just did for you. Miss Cynthie taught me that when I
wasn't knee-high to a cricket. But that wasn't all she taught
me. Far back as I can remember, she used to always say one
thing: 'Son, do like a church steeple—aim high and go
straight.' And for doin' it—" he grinned, contemplating the
flower—"I get this."

He strode across to the edge of the stage that touched Miss
Cynthie's box. He held up the flower.

"So y'see, folks, this isn't mine. It's really Miss Cynthie's."
He leaned over to hand it to her. Miss Cynthie's last trace of
doubt was swept away. She drew a deep breath of revelation;
her bewilderment vanished, her redoubtable composure returned, her eyes lighted up; and no one but David, still holding the flower toward her, heard her sharply whispered reprimand:

"Keep it, you fool you. Where's yo' manners—givin' 'way
what somebody give you?"

David grinned:

"Take it, tyro. What you tryin' to do—crab my act?"

Thereupon, Miss Cynthie, smiling at him with bright,

meaningful eyes, leaned over without rising from her chair, jerked a tiny twig off the stem of the flower, then sat descisively back, resolutely folding her arms, with only a leaf in her hand.

"This'll do me," she said.

The finale didn't matter. People filed out of the theatre. Miss Cynthie sat awaiting her children, her foot absently patting time to the orchestra's jazz recessional. Perhaps she was thinking, "God moves in a mysterious way," but her lips were unquestionably forming the words:

> *"—danced with the gal—hole in her stockin'—*
> *—toe kep' a-kickin'—heel kep' a-knockin'—"*

WAYNE GROVER

The Finer Points

In 1934 a Westerner first entering Washington could be surprised that the capital of the country was, in most respects, a Southern city. WAYNE GROVER was from Utah, and after this story was accepted and published, we looked him up in Washington, our first visit to the capital after an absence of seven years in Europe. He showed us Washington, and then Philadelphia and Baltimore, in a Depression-vintage automobile. Blacks were everywhere, but not in positions of any great importance. Grover settled in Washington and from 1948 to 1965 was Archivist of the United States. He died in 1970, thirty or more years after he wrote "The Finer Points." By 1970 Washington had a vastly increased black population and its own black mayor.

By the middle of June it is hot in Washington and in the House office building they turn on the fans. The fans blow spurious breezes across the smooth brows of satisfied Congressmen; blow the weary words of Congressmen's secretaries into more hopeful chants and touch with menthol coolness the white throats of pretty stenographers.

One blows also in the anteroom of the House office building post office, where the boys sit between times and wait for the mail. But this one blows for another reason, because a nigger stinks.

It was Jameson's joke.

Gaheen was clear on the point that it was Jameson's, and not his own. That he was sure of. For the rest, not any of the points were clear, although he did construe himself to be something of a coward.

The thing is that Gaheen had never known Negroes. In Greeley, Colorado, where he came from, one didn't have to study these finer points. Perhaps there was a Negro there, a Pullman porter, and you met him on the street: it was nothing. You passed him and that was all. No more Negroes for three or four months. Or forever. It didn't cross his mind. Perhaps even you heard a Roland Hayes. He had a beautiful voice, you said, a grand voice. He was a Negro? What of it? And if you heard later that this same Mr. Hayes had been turned down by Greeley's finest hotel, did it give you more than a passing thought?

No, Gaheen had never known Negroes. He was aware of that when the first point arose. As for himself, when he first saw Simson, he thought he was rather extraordinarily good looking for a Negro. A slim, boyish fellow, white teeth and friendly smile, well dressed. He spoke when he was spoken to, excellent English. Quiet and retiring, smiling and friendly.

Simson was from Illinois. Gaheen had heard that the Republicans had a corner on the Negro vote in Illinois, but Simson's father was a Negro political boss and had turned them Democratic. At least the Negro came into the post office with strong backing because there was an effort to get him out and he stayed nevertheless. Mr. Randolph, the postmaster, who was from Atlanta, Georgia, had said there would be trouble, putting a nigger to work shoulder to shoulder with the other boys. He said the Southern boys wouldn't stand for it and the nigger had better keep his place. Gaheen heard Mr. Randolph had gone to his Congressman and told the Congressman there was a bad situation there with that nigger, working with white boys. Why suh, he said, they won't stand for it, no suh.

But Simson stayed. From March until the middle of June he worked along with the other boys, tossing the mail in the racks, delivering it, shoulder to shoulder. Perhaps it would have gone on, except that Jameson made a joke of the fan.

But there were points which arose before that which Gaheen couldn't understand; of the things that made him wonder, being from Greeley and unaccustomed to the company of Negroes, the fan incident was doubtlessly the most obvious to him. Not that at any time he couldn't see through to the meaning of the point—it was clear how the Southern boys felt—but what he couldn't place, what he couldn't quite work out, was his own relation to the situation. There was the Negro on the one side. It was all right with Gaheen that he should work shoulder to shoulder with Simson. The Negro seemed, at a distance, a bright, likable fellow, certainly as good as most any of them in the post office, as well educated. On the other hand, there were the Southern boys. There was Williams, from Alabama; Roth, from Tennessee; Lee, from Florida. These were the boys he ate with, the ones he went to shows with. They were his friends. He joked with them in the office while they were racking mail; he laughed at them, borrowed their money. It was simply a matter of fact with him that they were the ones he must live with.

Yet he could not settle his own situation clearly, even on the point in relation to the chairs, which really needn't have bothered him, though it came up most frequently. It grew out of the childish fact that there were not enough chairs for the boys who wanted both to sit and to rest their feet at the same time.

Usually the anteroom was crowded between mails with the boys—Westerners and Middle Westerners and Southerners for the most part, because it was a Democratic administration—

sitting and joking among themselves. The room filled up gradually, as they came in from delivering their floors, so that the last ones had difficulty finding chairs unoccupied either by feet or bodies. If one came in late, he could grab a chair unceremoniously from under the feet of another. It was considered a joke for the boy to keep his feet on the chair as long as possible and it was also considered good for a laugh if the boy who wanted the chair could jerk it out suddenly from under propped feet while the seated boy wasn't looking, dropping the feet on the floor and the boy's head with a bang against the back of the chair. Such things will make young men laugh.

But the situation which arose when the Negro came in late and there were no vacant chairs, except those on which feet were propped, was different. Each time Gaheen felt the tenseness in the air. It was as if someone in the room were waiting for a word which would affect him tremendously, yet each knew that that one wasn't he. Or as if there were a brief moment in eternity to be gotten over, like a hole in the road, and each was watching the others steer by it. Briefly and silently, and the moment would pass and leave the air clear. It would pass because someone would finally lift his feet from a chair and the Negro would take it. Or the Negro would lay his hand on the back of a chair and smile at the boy whose feet were on it. Then the feet would be lowered slowly and he would take the chair over against the wall and sit there, leaning back like the rest.

Nothing complicated, and yet to Gaheen it seemed that there was something that should be done.

Only once when Williams, from Alabama, had his feet on a chair that was nearest the Negro as he entered the room, did anything but silence happen. Then Simson tried to pull the chair a little, smiling, because Williams was reading, and Williams looked up and said, Say there, and didn't move his feet for several seconds. It was only a look then that happened.

Williams looked hard at Simson, and Simson smiled. That was all. Then Williams slowly lowered his feet.

Even if Gaheen knew what should be done in any instance, he was not sure that he had the courage to do it.

He knew that, even on the simple point of ignoring the Negro, which should have been easy, he was afraid of himself and what he should, or should not, do. When the room was full it was of course not so much trouble, but when there were only two or three. . . . It was difficult to think of the Negro sitting there smiling, as if he were about to speak, and looking at the others, even though they did not look at him. Gaheen would leave the room if he could. There was only that one thing to do.

Gaheen knew he was afraid of what the Southern boys might think. Williams would say: Yoah an ol' niggah lovah. He could hear him.

There were many days before the middle of June and the fan incident when Gaheen went to luncheon with the Southern boys, and talked about the Negro situation in the South, trying, in a way, to vindicate himself in his own mind. But he couldn't. When he said: You guys don't give Simson much of a break, do you? Williams had said: That damned nigger better watch out.

You see the way he tried to take that chair, he said. He's a bad nigger, a bad nigger.

And Gaheen said nothing.

He did try to find out from the Southern boys how to act before Negroes, but he never understood why they couldn't treat this one in such a way and that one in another way. There was the point, they made it clear, that a nigger must be kept in his place.

But couldn't you distinguish between the intelligent Negro and the ordinary kind of low class nigger? he asked.

No, Williams said, you couldn't do that or you'd never be able to keep them in their place.

Gaheen was bold enough to say that he could think just as much of a Negro who was a great singer or actor or writer, as he could of some ignorant white person. In the face of the Southern boys, it was perhaps his most courageous action. But to himself he knew that he had failed, because he had meant to say "an ignorant person such as Jameson" and had been afraid because Jameson was on the South's side and was perhaps the worst nigger-hater in the office. Gaheen felt that the Southern boys would not consider the matter of Jameson's ignorance if it came to any kind of a decision between white and black.

As for much argument of any kind, Williams could always bring it quickly to an end with the infallible question: You wouldn't want your sister to marry a nigger, would you?

There was a finality to that which Gaheen couldn't fathom.

The fan incident was built up gradually, of course, though it was in itself an accident. Its foundations were laid by Jameson, who also brought it to the climax. Jameson was the oldest man in the post office, a married man with children. He had been born in Virginia but went to Nebraska to farm, and though he seemed no Southerner, in sectional disputes in the anteroom he was loudly for the South. He hated Simson for a personal reason too. Because Jameson was only on temporarily, he hated the Negro for holding a job.

Gaheen could partly sympathize with Jameson for that, because he had a family, but the man was ignorant, with a loud, dull-witted laugh.

He talked loudly. Pretty goddam fine situation when a nigger can work and a white man can't, he would say, and curse the Negro.

It was Jameson who was in the room one day when Simson came in and tugged at the heel of Gaheen's shoe, which inspired Jameson to start the joke that Simson wanted to play with Gaheen. Gaheen was leaning back with his feet on a table in the anteroom when Simson came in and sat down opposite. There were only the three of them in the room and Gaheen tried to avoid looking at Simson, but the Negro play-fully jogged his heel, pushing a little as if to make him fall backwards in the chair. Gaheen had not anticipated the mo-ment. To himself he said instantly, I must make a decision now, and at the same time he said aloud Don't. Then he arose hastily and went out of the room. At the door he would have turned and gone back, but even then, when he should have had time to make a decent decision, he was afraid. Between the Negro and Jameson, he would have preferred the Negro. But between the ignorance of the white and the friendliness of the black, he knew the white could do him more harm.

After that, when they were talking about the Negro in the anteroom and Jameson wanted to kid Gaheen, he would say Gaheen, Simson was just here. He wants to play with you. Yeh. Got some swell black ladies down on Georgia Avenue and he wants to take you on a party.

Then Jameson would laugh loudly and curse the Negro in the same breath. Gaheen laughed too, although not so loud.

The fan came about the middle of June. Most of the boys were in the anteroom, waiting for the second mail to come in, when Jameson noticed it. See they got a fan here now, eh? he said. By Gawd, we need it around here, turn it on when that black bastard comes in, eh Williams? Never see a nigger that don't stink, do you Williams? Then he laughed, turning in his chair toward Williams and nodding his head.

Jameson continued to laugh and repeat the joke, and Wil-liams agreed with him, laughing and saying, Yes sir, yes sir, with his Southern air of agreeing in a superior way.

Jameson said, We need two fans, by Gawd, eh Williams? and they were all laughing with him when Simson walked in.

Jameson was the one who got up and turned on the fan. Gaheen decided later that Simson could not have noticed who did it, because he couldn't have attached any particular significance to the act. Simson stood near the door, smiling boyishly, a slim athletic figure, looking around for a seat. But as Jameson turned back to his own seat he looked at Williams and together they started the laughter. It rocked through the boys as if they had just heard a shady joke, and as if Simson were a girl who had walked in too late to hear it. But the laughter was for him. They roared with the secret Simson didn't know. No one looked at the Negro but he stood grinning, looking from one to the other to see the joke. Gaheen did not laugh, but he arose, irritated because he could not keep down a smile. He thought: Now somebody is going to say something and he will catch on sure.

Gaheen stood for several seconds, smiling but not feeling like smiling. There's going to be trouble now, he thought. He felt sorry for the Negro.

Then, as he had done before when the situation was beyond his bravery, he left the room.

As if that had been a signal, they all came stringing out, laughing loudly, behind him, and the Negro was left in the anteroom alone.

Gaheen heard Jameson's voice coming up behind him. It was loud, guffawing. What's the matter, Gaheen, he said, ain't one fan enough to git the stink out?

Gaheen said nothing and Jameson turned to Williams. I believe that nigger would like to play with Gaheen, he said, wouldn't he Williams? and Williams laughed.

It might have been true that Simson heard this. At any rate he came out of the anteroom and walked straight toward Gaheen, his eyes on him. Gaheen watched him come up, wondering.

You think you're pretty smart, don't you? the Negro said. His voice was tense and shaky. Gaheen said to himself, This is the first time I have ever seen him talk to anyone without smiling.

He said aloud, What do you mean, Simson?

The Negro said, You know what I mean.

Gaheen laughed. It was the only thing he could do. . . .

The Negro struck first, and Gaheen caught the blow with his arm, striking back. With the next blow Simson dropped Gaheen, dazed, then Williams jumped Simson from behind and at the same time Jameson struck the Negro on the side of the head. When he was down they continued to beat him until the chief clerk pulled them off. The postmaster came running up. I knew there was going to be trouble, he said.

They took Simson to the House first aid station. He had a broken collar bone and his nose was broken. There was also a cut in his side, a bad, bruised-looking gash.

Williams helped Gaheen up and said, By Gawd he's a bad nigger, hitting a white man. He wouldn't do that in my state, he said. No nigger could do that and get off.

Gaheen didn't say anything.

After that there was a committee meeting, and Simson was transferred to an elevator. In a sense Gaheen became a hero in the post office and it troubled him a little.

I ought to go see him and say something, he thought.

But he didn't go see the Negro, just the same.

III

SWEET HOME

ZORA NEALE HURSTON

The Gilded Six-Bits

ZORA NEALE HURSTON was one of the first black American women fiction writers to become famous. This was her first short story. After it appeared (1934) she needed money as well as encouragement, and we recommended her for a Guggenheim Fellowship, but the application was declined. She was later to write a novel which became a Book-of-the-Month. Then, in the affluence and glory of success, she was granted a Fellowship. (Some years later, when The Story Press imprint with Harpers lost money on Richard Wright's first published book, *Uncle Tom's Children,* a collection of short stories, we recommended him for a Fellowship—and very highly. But he too was turned down. When *Native Son* became a best seller and he was widely known, he also got a grant.)

Miss Hurston was born in Eau Gallie, Florida, in 1903.

It was a Negro yard around a Negro house in a Negro settlement that looked to the payroll of the G. and G. Fertilizer works for its support.

But there was something happy about the place. The front yard was parted in the middle by a sidewalk from gate to door-step, a sidewalk edged on either side by quart bottles driven neck down into the ground on a slant. A mess of homey flowers planted without a plan but blooming cheerily from their helter-skelter places. The fence and house were whitewashed. The porch and steps scrubbed white.

The front door stood open to the sunshine so that the floor of the front room could finish drying after its weekly scouring. It was Saturday. Everything clean from the front gate to the privy house. Yard raked so that the strokes of the rake would make a pattern. Fresh newspaper cut in fancy edge on the kitchen shelves.

Missie May was bathing herself in the galvanized washtub in the bedroom. Her dark-brown skin glistened under the soapsuds that skittered down from her wash rag. Her stiff young breasts thrust forward aggressively like broad-based cones with the tips lacquered in black.

She heard men's voices in the distance and glanced at the dollar clock on the dresser.

"Humph! Ah'm way behind time t'day! Joe gointer be heah 'fore Ah git mah clothes on if Ah don't make haste."

She grabbed the clean meal sack at hand and dried herself hurriedly and began to dress. But before she could tie her slippers, there came the ring of singing metal on wood. Nine times.

Missie May grinned with delight. She had not seen the big tall man come stealing in the gate and creep up the walk grinning happily at the joyful mischief he was about to commit. But she knew that it was her husband throwing silver dollars in the door for her to pick up and pile beside her plate at dinner. It was this way every Saturday afternoon. The nine dollars hurled into the open door, he scurried to a hiding place behind the cape jasmine bush and waited.

Missie May promptly appeared at the door in mock alarm. "Who dat chunkin' money in mah do'way?" she demanded. No answer from the yard. She leaped off the porch and began to search the shrubbery. She peeped under the porch and hung over the gate to look up and down the road. While she did this, the man behind the jasmine darted to the china berry tree. She spied him and gave chase.

"Nobody ain't gointer be chunkin' money at me and Ah not do 'em nothin'," she shouted in mock anger. He ran around the house with Missie May at his heels. She overtook him at the kitchen door. He ran inside but could not close it after him before she crowded in and locked with him in a rough and tumble. For several minutes the two were a furious mass of male and female energy. Shouting, laughing, twisting, turning, tussling, tickling each other in the ribs; Missie May clutching onto Joe and Joe trying, but not too hard, to get away.

"Missie May, take yo' hand out mah pocket!" Joe shouted out between laughs.

"Ah ain't, Joe, not lessen you gwine gimme whateve' it is good you got in yo' pocket. Turn it go, Joe, do Ah'll tear yo' clothes."

"Go on tear 'em. You de one dat pushes de needles round heah. Move yo' hand, Missie May."

"Lemme git dat paper sack out yo' pocket. Ah bet its candy kisses."

"Tain't. Move yo' hand. Women ain't got no business in a man's clothes nohow. Go way."

Missie May gouged way down and gave an upward jerk and triumphed.

"Unhhunh! Ah got it. It 'tis so candy kisses. Ah knowed you had somethin' for me in yo' clothes. Now Ah got to see whut's in every pocket you got."

Joe smiled indulgently and let his wife go through all of his pockets and take out the things that he had hidden there for her to find. She bore off the chewing gum, the cake of sweet soap, the pocket handkerchief as if she had wrested them from him, as if they had not been bought for the sake of this friendly battle.

"Whew! dat play-fight done got me all warmed up." Joe exclaimed. "Got me some water in de kittle?"

"Yo' water is on de fire and yo' clean things is cross de bed. Hurry up an wash yo'self and git changed so we kin eat. Ah'm hongry." As Missie said this, she bore the steaming kettle into the bedroom.

"You ain't hongry, sugar," Joe contradicted her. "Youse jes' a little empty. Ah'm de one whut's hongry. Ah could eat up camp meetin', back off 'ssociation, and drink Jurdan dry. Have it on de table when Ah git out de tub."

"Don't you mess wid mah business, man. You git in yo' clothes. Ah'm a real wife, not no dress and breath. Ah might not look lak one, but if you burn me, you won't git a thing but wife ashes."

Joe splashed in the bedroom and Missie May fanned around in the kitchen. A fresh red and white checked cloth on the table. Big pitcher of buttermilk beaded with pale drops of butter from the churn. Hot fried mullet, crackling bread, ham hock atop a mound of string beans and new potatoes, and perched on the window-sill a pone of spicy potato pudding.

Very little talk during the meal but that little consisted of banter that pretended to deny affection but in reality flaunted it. Like when Missie May reached for a second helping of the tater pone. Joe snatched it out of her reach.

After Missie May had made two or three unsuccessful grabs at the pan, she begged, "Aw, Joe gimme some mo' dat tater pone."

"Nope, sweetenin' is for us men-folks. Y'all pritty lil frail eels don't need nothin' lak dis. You too sweet already."

"Please, Joe."

"Naw, naw. Ah don't want you to git no sweeter than whut you is already. We goin' down de road a lil piece t'night so you go put on yo' Sunday-go-to-meetin' things."

Missie May looked at her husband to see if he was playing some prank. "Sho nuff, Joe?"

"Yeah. We goin' to de ice cream parlor."

"Where de ice cream parlor at, Joe?"

"A new man done come heah from Chicago and he done got a place and took and opened it up for a ice cream parlor, and bein' as it's real swell, Ah wants you to be one de first ladies to walk in dere and have some set down."

"Do Jesus, Ah ain't knowed nothin' 'bout it. Who de man done it?"

"Mister Otis D. Slemmons, of spots and places—Memphis, Chicago, Jacksonville, Philadelphia and so on."

"Dat heavy-set man wid his mouth full of gold teethes?"

"Yeah. Where did you see 'im at?"

"Ah went down to de sto' tuh git a box of lye and Ah seen 'im standin' on de corner talkin' to some of de mens, and Ah come on back and went to scrubbin' de floor, and he passed and tipped his hat whilst Ah was scourin' de steps. Ah thought Ah never seen *him* befo'."

Joe smiled pleasantly. "Yeah, he's up to date. He got de finest clothes Ah ever seen on a colored man's back."

"Aw, he don't look no better in his clothes than you do in yourn. He got a puzzlegut on 'im and he so chuckle-headed, he got a pone behind his neck."

Joe looked down at his own abdomen and said wistfully: "Wisht Ah had a build on me lak he got. He ain't puzzle-gutted, honey. He jes' got a corperation. Dat make 'm look lak a rich white man. All rich mens is got some belly on 'em."

"Ah seen de pitchers of Henry Ford and he's a spare-built man and Rockefeller look lak he ain't got but one gut. But Ford and Rockefeller and dis Slemmons and all de rest kin be as manygutted as dey please, Ah's satisfied wid you jes' lak you is, baby. God took pattern after a pine tree and built you noble. Youse a pretty man, and if Ah knowed any way to make you mo' pretty still Ah'd take and do it."

Joe reached over gently and toyed with Missie May's ear. "You jes' say dat cause you love me, but Ah know Ah can't hold no light to Otis D. Slemmons. Ah ain't never been nowhere and Ah ain't got nothin' but you."

Missie May got on his lap and kissed him and he kissed back in kind. Then he went on. "All de womens is crazy 'bout 'im everywhere he go."

"How you know dat, Joe?"

"He tole us so hisself."

"Dat don't make it so. His mouf is cut cross-ways, ain't it? Well, he kin lie jes' lak anybody else."

"Good Lawd, Missie! You womens sho is hard to sense into things. He's got a five-dollar gold piece for a stick-pin and he got a ten-dollar gold piece on his watch chain and his mouf is jes' crammed full of gold teethes. Sho wisht it wuz mine. And whut make it so cool, he got money 'cumulated. And womens give it all to 'im."

"Ah don't see whut de womens see on 'im. Ah wouldn't give 'im a wink if de sheriff wuz after 'im."

"Well, he tole us how de white womens in Chicago give 'im all dat gold money. So he don't 'low nobody to touch it at all. Not even put dey finger on it. Dey tole 'im not to. You kin make 'miration at it, but don't tetch it."

"Whyn't he stay up dere where dey so crazy 'bout 'im?"

"Ah reckon dey done made 'im vast-rich and he wants to travel some. He says dey wouldn't leave 'im hit a lick of work. He got mo' lady people crazy 'bout him than he kin shake a stick at."

"Joe, Ah hates to see you so dumb. Dat stray nigger jes' tell y'all anything and y'all b'lieve it."

"Go 'head on now, honey and put on yo' clothes. He talkin' 'bout his pritty womens—Ah want 'im to see *mine*."

Missie May went off to dress and Joe spent the time trying to make his stomach punch out like Slemmons' middle. He tried the rolling swagger of the stranger, but found that his tall bone-and-muscle stride fitted ill with it. He just had time to drop back into his seat before Missie May came in dressed to go.

On the way home that night Joe was exultant. "Didn't Ah say ole Otis was swell? Can't he talk Chicago talk? Wuzn't dat funny whut he said when great big fat ole Ida Armstrong come in? He asted me, 'Who is dat broad wid de forte shake?' Dat's a new word. Us always thought forty was a set of figgers but he showed us where it means a whole heap of things. Sometimes he don't say forty, he jes' say thirty-eight and two and dat mean de same thing. Know whut he tole me when Ah wuz payin' for our ice cream? He say, 'Ah have to hand it to you, Joe. Dat wife of yours is jes' thirty-eight and two. Yessuh, she's forte!' Ain't he killin'?"

"He'll do in case of a rush. But he sho is got uh heap uh gold on 'im. Dat's de first time Ah ever seed gold money. It lookted good on him sho nuff, but it'd look a whole heap better on you."

"Who, me? Missie May youse crazy! Where would a po' man lak me git gold money from?"

Missie May was silent for a minute, then she said, "Us might find some goin' long de road some time. Us could."

"Who would be losin' gold money round heah? We ain't even seen none dese white folks wearin' no gold money on dey watch chain. You must be figgerin' Mister Packard or Mister Cadillac goin' pass through heah."

"You don't know whut been lost 'round heah. Maybe somebody way back in memorial times lost they gold money and went on off and it ain't never been found. And then if we wuz to find it, you could wear some 'thout havin' no gang of womens lak dat Slemmons say he got."

Joe laughed and hugged her. "Don't be so wishful 'bout me. Ah'm satisfied de way Ah is. So long as Ah be yo' husband, Ah don't keer 'bout nothin' else. Ah'd ruther all de other

womens in de world to be dead than for you to have de tooth-
ache. Less we go to bed and git our night rest."

It was Saturday night once more before Joe could parade
his wife in Slemmons' ice cream parlor again. He worked the
night shift and Saturday was his only night off. Every other
evening around six o'clock he left home, and dying dawn saw
him hustling home around the lake where the challenging
sun flung a flaming sword from east to west across the trembling water.

That was the best part of life—going home to Missie May.
Their whitewashed house, the mock battle on Saturday, the
dinner and ice cream parlor afterwards, church on Sunday
nights when Missie out-dressed any woman in town—all,
everything, was right.

One night around eleven the acid ran out at the G. and G.
The foreman knocked off the crew and let the steam die
down. As Joe rounded the lake on his way home, a lean moon
rode the lake in a silver boat. If anybody had asked Joe about
the moon on the lake, he would have said he hadn't paid it
any attention. But he saw it with his feelings. It made him
yearn painfully for Missie. Creation obsessed him. He thought
about children. They had been married more than a year
now. They had money put away. They ought to be making
little feet for shoes. A little boy child would be about right.

He saw a dim light in the bedroom and decided to come
in through the kitchen door. He could wash the fertilizer dust
off himself before presenting himself to Missie May. It would
be nice for her not to know that he was there until he slipped
into his place in bed and hugged her back. She always liked
that.

He eased the kitchen door open slowly and silently, but
when he went to set his dinner bucket on the table he bumped
it into a pile of dishes, and something crashed to the floor.
He heard his wife gasp in fright and hurried to reassure her.

"Iss me, honey. Don't git skeered."

There was a quick, large movement in the bedroom. A rustle, a thud, and a stealthy silence. The light went out.

What? Robbers? Murderers? Some varmint attacking his helpless wife, perhaps. He struck a match, threw himself on guard and stepped over the door-sill into the bedroom.

The great belt on the wheel of Time slipped and eternity stood still. By the match light he could see the man's legs fighting with his breeches in his frantic desire to get them on. He had both chance and time to kill the intruder in his helpless condition—half in and half out of his pants—but he was too weak to take action. The shapeless enemies of humanity that live in the hours of Time had waylaid Joe. He was assaulted in his weakness. Like Samson awakening after his haircut. So he just opened his mouth and laughed.

The match went out and he struck another and lit the lamp. A howling wind raced across his heart, but underneath its fury he heard his wife sobbing and Slemmons pleading for his life. Offering to buy it with all that he had. "Please, suh, don't kill me. Sixty-two dollars at de sto'. Gold money."

Joe just stood. Slemmons looked at the window, but it was screened. Joe stood out like a rough-backed mountain between him and the door. Barring him from escape, from sunrise, from life.

He considered a surprise attack upon the big clown that stood there laughing like a chessy cat. But before his fist could travel an inch, Joe's own rushed out to crush him like a battering ram. Then Joe stood over him.

"Git into yo' damn rags, Slemmons, and dat quick."

Slemmons scrambled to his feet and into his vest and coat. As he grabbed his hat, Joe's fury overrode his intentions and he grabbed at Slemmons with his left hand and struck at him with his right. The right landed. The left grazed the front of his vest. Slemmons was knocked a somersault into the kitchen and fled through the open door. Joe found himself alone with Missie May, with the golden watch charm clutched in his left fist. A short bit of broken chain dangled between his fingers.

Missie May was sobbing. Wails of weeping without words. Joe stood, and after awhile he found out that he had something in his hand. And then he stood and felt without thinking and without seeing with his natural eyes. Missie May kept on crying and Joe kept on feeling so much and not knowing what to do with all his feelings, he put Slemmons' watch charm in his pants pocket and took a good laugh and went to bed.

"Missie May, whut you cryin' for?"

"Cause Ah love you so hard and Ah know you don't love *me* no mo'."

Joe sank his face into the pillow for a spell, then he said huskily, "You don't know de feelings of dat yet, Missie May."

"Oh Joe, honey, he said he wuz gointer give me dat gold money and he jes' kept on after me—"

Joe was very still and silent for a long time. Then he said, "Well, don't cry no mo', Missie May. Ah got yo' gold piece for you."

The hours went past on their rusty ankles. Joe still and quiet on one bed-rail and Missie May wrung dry of sobs on the other. Finally the sun's tide crept upon the shore of night and drowned all its hours. Missie May with her face stiff and streaked towards the window saw the dawn come into her yard. It was day. Nothing more. Joe wouldn't be coming home as usual. No need to fling open the front door and sweep off the porch, making it nice for Joe. Never no more breakfast to cook; no more washing and starching of Joe's jumper-jackets and pants. No more nothing. So why get up?

With this strange man in her bed, she felt embarrassed to get up and dress. She decided to wait till he had dressed and gone. Then she would get up, dress quickly and be gone forever beyond reach of Joe's looks and laughs. But he never moved. Red light turned to yellow, then white.

From beyond the no-man's land between them came a voice. A strange voice that yesterday had been Joe's.

"Missie May, ain't you gonna fix me no breakfus'?"

She sprang out of bed. "Yeah, Joe. Ah didn't reckon you wuz hongry."

No need to die today. Joe needed her for a few more minutes anyhow.

Soon there was a roaring fire in the cook stove. Water bucket full and two chickens killed. Joe loved fried chicken and rice. She didn't deserve a thing and good Joe was letting her cook him some breakfast. She rushed hot biscuits to the table as Joe took his seat.

He ate with his eyes in his plate. No laughter, no banter.

"Missie May, you ain't eatin' yo' breakfus'."

"Ah don't choose none. Ah thank yuh."

His coffee cup was empty. She sprang to refill it. When she turned from the stove and bent to set the cup beside Joe's plate, she saw the yellow coin on the table between them.

She slumped into her seat and wept into her arms.

Presently Joe said calmly, "Missie May, you cry too much. Don't look back lak Lot's wife aud turn to salt."

The sun, the hero of every day, the impersonal old man that beams as brightly on death as on birth, came up every morning and raced across the blue dome and dipped into the sea of fire every evening. Water ran down hill and birds nested.

Missie knew why she didn't leave Joe. She couldn't. She loved him too much, but she could not understand why Joe didn't leave her. He was polite, even kind at times, but aloof.

There were no more Saturday romps. No ringing silver dollars to stack beside her plate. No pockets to rifle. In fact the yellow coin in his trousers was like a monster hiding in the cave of his pockets to destroy her.

She often wondered if he still had it, but nothing could have induced her to ask nor yet to explore his pockets to see for herself. Its shadow was in the house whether or no.

One night Joe came home around midnight and complained of pains in the back. He asked Missie to rub him down with liniment. It had been three months since Missie had touched his body and it all seemed strange. But she rubbed him. Grateful for the chance. Before morning, youth triumphed and Missie exulted. But the next day, as she joyfully made up their bed, beneath her pillow she found the piece of money with the bit of chain attached.

Alone to herself, she looked at the thing with loathing, but look she must. She took it into her hands with trembling and saw first thing that it was no gold piece. It was a gilded half dollar. Then she knew why Slemmons had forbidden anyone to touch his gold. He trusted village eyes at a distance not to recognize his stick-pin as a gilded quarter, and his watch charm as a four-bit piece.

She was glad at first that Joe had left it there. Perhaps he was through with her punishment. They were man and wife again. Then another thought came clawing at her. He had come home to buy from her as if she were any woman in the long house. Fifty cents for her love. As if to say that he could pay as well as Slemmons. She slid the coin into his Sunday pants pocket and dressed herself and left his house.

Half way between her house and the quarters she met her husband's mother, and after a short talk she turned and went back home. Never would she admit defeat to that woman who prayed for it nightly. If she had not the substance of marriage she had the outside show. Joe must leave *her*. She let him see she didn't want his old gold four-bits too.

She saw no more of the coin for some time though she knew that Joe could not help finding it in his pocket. But his health kept poor, and he came home at least every ten days to be rubbed.

The sun swept around the horizon, trailing its robes of weeks and days. One morning as Joe came in from work, he found Missie May chopping wood. Without a word he took the ax and chopped a huge pile before he stopped.

"You ain't got no business choppin' wood, and you know it."

"How come? Ah been choppin' it for de last longest."

"Ah ain't blind. You makin' feet for shoes."

"Won't you be glad to have a lil baby chile, Joe?"

"You know dat 'thout astin' me."

"Iss gointer be a boy chile and de very spit of you."

"You reckon, Missie May?"

"Who else could it look lak?"

Joe said nothing, but he thrust his hand deep into his pocket and fingered something there.

It was almost six months later Missie May took to bed and Joe went and got his mother to come wait on the house.

Missie May was delivered of a fine boy. Her travail was over when Joe came in from work one morning. His mother and the old women were drinking great bowls of coffee around the fire in the kitchen.

The minute Joe came into the room his mother called him aside.

"How did Missie May make out?" he asked quickly.

"Who, dat gal? She strong as a ox. She gointer have plenty mo'. We done fixed her wid de sugar and lard to sweeten her for de nex' one."

Joe stood silent awhile.

"You ain't ast 'bout de baby, Joe. You oughter be mighty proud cause he sho is de spittin' image of yuh, son. Dat's yourn all right, if you never git another one, dat un is yourn. And you know Ah'm mighty proud too, son, cause Ah never thought well of you marryin' Missie May cause her ma used tuh fan her foot round right smart and Ah been mighty skeered dat Missie May wuz gointer git misput on her road."

Joe said nothing. He fooled around the house till late in

the day, then, just before he went to work, he went and stood at the foot of the bed and asked his wife how she felt. He did this every day during the week.

On Saturday he went to Orlando to make his market. It had been a long time since he had done that.

Meat and lard, meal and flour, soap and starch. Cans of corn and tomatoes. All the staples. He fooled around town for awhile and bought bananas and apples. Way after while he went around to the candy store.

"Hello, Joe," the clerk greeted him. "Ain't seen you in a long time."

"Nope, Ah ain't been heah. Been round in spots and places."

"Want some of them molasses kisses you always buy?"

"Yessuh." He threw the gilded half dollar on the counter. "Will dat spend?"

"Whut is it, Joe? Well, I'll be doggone! A gold-plated four-bit piece. Where'd you git it, Joe?"

"Often a stray nigger dat come through Eatonville. He had it on his watch chain for a charm—goin' round making out iss gold money. Ha ha! He had a quarter on his tie pin and it wuz all golded up too. Tryin' to fool people. Makin' out he so rich and everything. Ha! Ha! Tryin' to tole off folkses wives from home."

"How did you git it, Joe? Did he fool you, too?"

"Who, me? Naw suh! He ain't fooled me none. Know whut Ah done? He come round me wid his smart talk. Ah hauled off and knocked 'im down and took his old four-bits way from 'im. Gointer buy my wife some good ole lasses kisses wid it. Gimme fifty cents worth of dem candy kisses."

"Fifty cents buys a mighty lot of candy kisses, Joe. Why don't you split it up and take some chocolate bars, too. They eat good, too."

"Yessuh, dey do, but Ah wants all dat in kisses. Ah got a lil boy chile home now. Tain't a week old yet, but he kin suck a sugar tit and maybe eat one them kisses hisself."

Joe got his candy and left the store. The clerk turned to the next customer. "Wisht I could be like these darkies. Laughin' all the time. Nothin' worries 'em."

Back in Eatonville, Joe reached his own front door. There was the ring of singing metal on wood. Fifteen times. Missie May couldn't run to the door, but she crept there as quickly as she could.

"Joe Banks, Ah hear you chunkin' money in mah do'way. You wait till Ah got mah strength back and Ah'm gointer fix you for dat."

CARL RUTHVEN OFFORD

So Peaceful in the Country

CARL RUTHVEN OFFORD, a black native of Trinidad, British West Indies, came to the United States at nineteen and went into newspaper work and free-lance writing. His first novel, *The White Face,* was published in 1943. Like Miss Hurston, Dr. Fisher, Wayne Grover and others, his story first appeared in STORY Magazine, in 1945.

———————————

Viola got up before the sun and through the kitchen window she watched the slow rolling away of mountain mist. She felt a lot better. She still thought of Jim but the thinking now wasn't as sharp as last night.

Last night was awful. Last night was the first night in two years that she'd slept without him. After they'd agreed on her taking a country job it seemed that they'd slept even tighter. Something about their having to part for the summer drew them even more tightly together. So it had seemed. Then last night . . . almost a hundred miles from Jim.

Sleeping alone was terrible. Mr. and Mrs. Christian had gone to the village and the strange place had seemed too still, the room too large, the bed too different. It wasn't like Harlem. The bed hadn't seemed like a bed at all after the

light was turned off. She woke up when it was still too dark
and turned on the light and wrote to Jim. It was a long, long
letter, very tender, about herself and him. And now the day
was coming on fast and the place was beginning to feel a
lot better.

In the grayish distance of early morning the rolling mist
peeled off the high mountains like pillars of steam. Viola
stared out in a deep quiet of feeling, her mind stretching
back to Jim. He probably wasn't awake yet, she thought. Perhaps he would oversleep, she thought. That would be bad.
She suddenly smiled. If Jim got up late for his class he'd be
tearing around the room like a crazy fool. The smile stayed in
wrinkles around her full mouth as she pictured Jim getting
up late and finding himself all alone and tearing around the
room like mad.

From the dining room came the sound of padded footsteps
and she turned in surprise. Did they get up this early? The
electric clock on the kitchen wall said ten minutes to seven.
She left the window and started to prepare coffee, then she
heard the padded steps coming toward the kitchen. Without
looking up she saw the bottom of his pyjama pants and his
bare white feet on the floor.

Mr. George Christian, Jr. stood at the kitchen door and
stretched and yawned and grumbled.

"Good morning, suh," she replied. She didn't look up. Her
eyes went back to his naked feet and she thought they were
awfully white. She noticed the long white toes and decided
to herself that black toes were much better than white ones.
That was one thing nobody could argue about, she thought.

Mr. Christian ambled into the kitchen and over to the window. The sun was just breaking over the mountains. Waves
of glorious orange splashed like a fan across the sky. Stretching and yawning at the window he said, "That coffee smells
good." He turned and sniffed, his hands comically holding
his head. "Certainly smells good."

"It'll be ready in a minute, suh."

"That's fine," he mumbled. "That's fine."

Viola thought she smelled liquor on his breath. She was almost sure of it.

Mr. Christian stuck his head out the window again, then he withdrew and ambled out of the kitchen, and as he went he began to warble, "She'll be coming round the mountain when she comes. Oh, she'll be coming round the mountain when she comes."

He was tight, Viola thought. Yes. He had a hangover from last night in the village. She wondered how people could get themselves plastered smack in the middle of the week.

When she served the coffee in the dining room she noticed that there were swollen puffs under his eyes.

"Should I fix some toast, suh?"

"No, thank you. Nothing more."

She returned to the kitchen, guessing and wondering about them. How many times a week did they get themselves plastered? Yesterday they had seemed so upright and orderly. His little freckle-faced wife had struck her as being gayish but she hadn't thought . . .

"Viola!"

She put down her coffee cup and hurried in.

"Yes, suh."

He glanced at her and sighed. He didn't look so well, she thought.

"Well," he said. He spread an arm with what appeared to be a great effort. "How do you like it out here?"

"Seems very nice," she answered softly.

He pressed his face in his hands, sighed, then he took a sip of the hot coffee. Viola waited, standing awkwardly to one side.

"I've got an awful head," he said. "I guess I tried to drink the village dry. Did you ever get drunk?"

"No," she answered shortly.

"Not even once in your life?"

"No, suh."

"That's fine. That's fine. I don't as a rule, but last night was the exception."

"Drink the coffee while it's hot," she advised. "It'll make you feel better." She remembered that Jim had had a hangover once and strong coffee had helped to straighten him out.

Mr. Christian took a couple of sips, closing his eyes with each sip as if he were taking a bitter medicine.

"What did you do in the city?"

"Work," she answered.

"At what?"

"Anything. Housework, factory work. Anything."

"Your husband's unemployed?"

"He's studying."

"Studying?"

"He's studying engineering. Electrical engineering." She emphasized the words with pride.

"That's interesting." He stared at the cup and saucer, then he suddenly burped. "I'm sorry."

Viola shifted awkwardly from one foot to the other. She looked impatiently toward the kitchen.

"You'll have it pretty easy today," he said. "So don't worry about anything. It's only me now and I'm no bother."

"Just you?" She was startled.

"My wife will be back in a couple of days. Maybe tomorrow. It's nothing too serious. Nothing at all, as a matter of fact." It appeared that he was about to burp again but he didn't. His eyes stared wide and he seemed to bite his pale lips. Abruptly he got up from the table and made for the bathroom.

Viola went to the kitchen, her eyes misty with thought. This thing of his wife's absence wasn't so good. She didn't like it at all. Evidently he and his wife had quarreled in the village. She heard Mr. Christian come out from the bathroom, then he called to her in a broken, throaty voice. "I'm going back to bed! I'll be all right later!"

Good Lord, she thought. What was this she was getting into? Could she stay in this country house with him alone? She hadn't counted on anything like that. What would Jim say? What would he think? She stood at the window looking out upon the range of mountains, now bright green in the sunlight, and for a long time she pondered just what she should do.

It was after twelve when Mr. Christian got up and he was totally sober. He came out, a blue beach robe tied loosely around his waist, and he looked a lot different. The puffs under his eyes had melted down and his face was no longer stark white. He ate hungrily, in sober silence. A sad silence, Viola thought, and she actually felt sorry for him. Love was an awful mess of a thing, she thought. In few cases did it stand up as wonderfully as with Jim and herself.

After he'd finished eating he sat there smoking a cigarette in silence. Viola gathered the dishes quietly, not looking at him directly but watching him from the corner of her eyes. The blue beach robe was opened from the neck in a long V that stopped at the waist and she couldn't help noticing the little ringlets of sandy hair on his bare chest. Jim didn't have hair on his chest. Jim's chest was broad and clean and copper-colored. Jim was so different. Except for worries over money Jim was never sad and long-faced.

She went back to the kitchen feeling sorry for Mr. Christian and feeling angry at herself for caring at all. She had made up her mind to tell him she was quitting, but she had gone back and forth without saying a word. Sorry for him or not, she couldn't stay. She had coached herself as to just the exact way she would put it to him—but she hadn't. She stood over the dishes in the sink, fighting with herself, condemning herself, then she heard him coming to the kitchen.

"Viola," he said, and now she stared at his calling her name.

"There's no need to stick to the kitchen. Take the afternoon off." His face was calm and very serious as he stood in the doorway. Watching him, she began to frame the words in her mouth. She must tell him now. And yet, she felt very foolish about it. He turned, the beach robe swishing as he went to the door.

"Skip, jump, or swim!" he called back. "Do whatever you like!"

After a second she went to the window and looked after him. He took the winding, grass-beaten trail that led to the boathouse and she kept her eyes on the back of his head and parts of his broad shoulders that showed through the high foliage until she couldn't see him any more.

Staring out on the expanse of green mountains she thought of Jim. If Jim were here they could do things, she thought. Down below the lake shimmered in the bright sunlight. If only Jim were here, she thought. They could hike up the hills and just fool around, picking flowers and just fooling. Or they could go down to the lake. Or just sit under a big tree somewhere. The place was so beautiful and so peaceful. She sighed and turned from the window. Afternoon off or not, there were the dishes.

She washed the dishes leisurely, idly soaping them over as she thought. Then there were no more dishes and only the sink. She earnestly tackled the stains on the enamel and when they were all off, the white sink made her think of Mr. Christian's feet.

Some afternoon off, she thought, going back to the window. Where could she go, what could she do? The village was miles away. And what could she do in the village? She might go down to the lake, she thought. The water down below glistened warmly in the sun. Even better, she might put on her bathing suit and go in. Why not?

She changed into her one-piece bathing suit and went to the full-length mirror in Mrs. Christian's room. She thought she looked all right. The past winter hadn't altered her waist-line any, and her breasts were holding up fine. Approvingly she eyed her long graceful legs. Only in a bathing suit did they get a decent break, she thought.

She stepped lightly through the big, empty house, and out through the door, towel and bathing cap swinging in one hand. The grass crunched softly under her feet and the taller blades nicked at her brown legs as she followed the winding, down-hill path to the lake.

Before she quite reached the lake she saw Mr. Christian in a rowboat. She couldn't see much of him at first. He was stretched out in the boat and she was thinking he might be asleep when he raised himself and shouted, "Ahoy, there!"

She didn't think she could shout back that far. She didn't think she could shout back at all. She lifted a hand in a quick, timid way and didn't look at him again. She sat down by the lake for a minute, speculating on the coldness of the water, then she kicked off her slippers and waded in.

She walked out gradually, tentatively feeling the muddy bottom of the lake with every step. The water rose like a cold band around her legs, then her thighs. When it rose to her chest she stopped. This was far enough. After all, she couldn't swim. She made sure that the bathing cap was securely adjusted, then she threw herself forward. She splashed and paddled about, feeling the water shockingly cold at first, then feeling as though the water itself grew pleasantly warmer. She didn't notice Mr. Christian paddle over in the small rowboat, and when he spoke his voice startled her. "You're swimming in mud. Why don't you swim out?"

She stopped splashing and looked at him. He was laughing. "Don't let me stop you. You're doing very well."

Self-conscious, she stood still in the water up to her waist.

"I think your stroke is really good," he said. "But your legs sink."

She liked what he said about her stroke. Jim had been working on her stroke for two summers in the public swimming pool. Suddenly Mr. Christian dived from the rowboat and swam over to her.

"This is how you should kick." He swam for her to see, his strong legs working up, down, up, down, like a pair of scissors. "Now try it."

She stood still.

"Come on, I'll help you." He lifted her easily by the waist. "Now stretch out. Not rigidly. Relax. The water here's too shallow anyway." She felt him carrying her out with giant strides.

"Please," she said. "I can't swim."

"It's all right. I'm here. I'm holding you." He laughed as he talked and she felt his warm breath on her face. "Now, do as I said. Relax."

"Not here," she pleaded. "It's too deep here."

"Don't be afraid. I'm with you."

"No," she pleaded, but just then he released her. She felt herself sink into a heavy, watery world and she tried to scream. She came up clutching frantically to his neck and spouting water.

"You didn't even try," he said. "Now just be calm."

"No," she begged, shaking her head, her eyes blinking wet. Her face brushed against his and it was like receiving a sudden shock. "Take me back," she pleaded. "Please."

He shook her gently. "You'll never learn by being afraid. Now, listen to me. Look at me."

She brought her face around fearfully and looked at him. He didn't speak. Not speaking, his deep eyes suddenly held a burning that frightened her. Suddenly she thought of Jim in a way that brought his dark face right up to the watery surface of the lake.

"Please," she begged, looking away from his eyes. "Take me back now." For a long moment he neither spoke nor moved and she waited fearfully, her gaze turned away but still feeling his eyes, feeling his warm arms, his warm body. Tears suddenly filled her eyes and her body trembled.

"Are you crying?" he said hoarsely. Then he abruptly moved and she knew he was taking her out. He set her down in shallow water and as soon as her feet touched the wet earth she began to run.

She didn't look back and she didn't stop running. Up the winding path she went and into her room, the tears streaming down her face. Hastily she dressed and packed her work things in the small suitcase. Jim, she thought. Jim. Jim. Jim. She thought of nothing in connection with Jim more than seeing him. She saw him in the room and in the suitcase and in everything she did and she wanted only to get to him.

As she started out from the house along the driveway she saw Mr. Christian coming up from the lake.

"Viola!" he called. "Say—what are you doing?"

She hurried on without answering. She couldn't stay another minute.

He came up the pathway to the house on the run. "Wait!" he called. "Wait a minute!"

She kept on, a fresh flow of tears coming to her eyes. The dirt road felt hard under her thin, high-heeled shoes and as she hurried a small cloud of dust trailed behind. Mr. Christian called to her once more, then she rounded a bend in the dirt road and was out of sight.

Her blurry eyes focused on the brown dirt road, she kept going, the suitcase swinging to her stride. Then she heard his automobile coming behind.

"Come on," he said, stopping the car just ahead of her. "I'll take you to the station."

Standing in the grass beside the road she eyed him indirectly. He was wearing his beach robe and his face was set in that serious look he had had in the kitchen.

"Don't be impractical," he urged. "The station's five miles away. Get in." He flung the rear door open.

Avoiding his eyes she got in and sat huddled in the corner of the rear seat. The car shot along on the small dirt road and neither of them spoke. Once she looked into the mirror above the steering wheel and thought she caught him looking at her. After that she avoided the mirror. In a silence that was taut he drove her to the station, but as she was getting out he pressed an envelope in her hand.

"It shouldn't be said that you worked for nothing." He tried to smile but it was a strained, awkward thing on his face as he drove away.

She opened the envelope and saw two ten-dollar bills. She stared at the money with a dazed expression. It was too much for one day's work. It was ridiculously too much.

SANDRA TAYLOR

Sweet Home

SANDRA TAYLOR, a black girl student then in George Washington High School, New York City, won first prize for this essay in the Scholastic Magazines Writing Awards of 1963. She said at the time there had been too much written about Harlem "from a negative point of view. . . . I decided therefore I was going to write from a different angle." Her ambition then was to become an elementary-school teacher and a free-lance writer. She is now taking her master's degree in education, and although Harlem has changed, her own plans to teach have not.

Harlem is the center of the Negro population of New York City. It extends north from Central Park to Harlem River Drive and east from Morningside Park to Fifth Avenue. Harlem is a city within a city; a world of uniqueness, splendor, and appeal. Harlem is my home.

Harlem is a community depicted by many people who have never seen her, and who tend to do her an injustice by the picture they hold. Some European intellectuals, for example, pictured Harlem as "a steaming pit a few blocks square, crowded with sinuous black bodies twisted in the contortions of jazz and sex; exuberant and salacious, driven by alcohol and saxophones." * In short, a "Blackboard Jungle." No one but someone who has lived in Harlem knows the fantasy of such an inaccurate picture. I know, for I live here.

My world;
That they talk of,
A social outcast she—
Wants that golden chance to belong, to the thing that they call
  humanity.

My world;
A mass of streets,
Dirty streets and—
Pungent filled smelling air—
That stinks of the garbage from overridden cans—
And, too, the odor of fried chicken and old southern chitterlings.

My world;
The place they dare not go—
For they say that it's worse than Hell below—
But, all this isn't so.

My world;
Filled with black bodies, dirt, and smell—
Is not a Satan's Hell . . .
My world is a good place.

Harlem is a changed and still changing community. Harlem was at one time provincial, her ideals narrow-minded and limited. Harlem was naïve, her people unsophisticated and simple, lacking education. Harlem was dirty. Life there was difficult and frustrating. Harlem was different. The streets were crowded with loiterers, thieves, and hoodlums.

Harlem has changed. We, her people, have matured, educated ourselves, and prospered. Gone from our world are the vendors of fried fish, sweet potatoes, and peanuts. Gone are the fruit, vegetable, and egg carts, and the men shouting:

* Simon, Kate, "The Three Harlems and What Is Happening to Them," *Harper's Magazine,* March 1960.

"Git ya wa-ter-mel-o." . . . The pushcart aspect of Harlem has been replaced by small stores.

Harlem today is different. Though people tend to degrade Harlem, making her sound like a place where no one respectable wants to live, and a place swarming with indecencies, I love Harlem. What they say is not so. I know because Harlem is my life—my world. . . .

Harlem is unique. She is a community strange and new. Perhaps that is why I love her. One of the things I love about Harlem is its center of commerce, 125th Street. On 125th Street I'm able to find everything—from woven pot-holders to diamond rings to the Apollo Theatre. Whenever I have the time and money, there is no place I'd rather spend the day than at the Apollo [where] teenagers, adults, and children enjoy the antics of rock 'n' roll, rhythm and blues, and gospel caravans.

Alongside the Apollo is a penny arcade. Directly above the arcade is the Manhattan branch of the NAACP. Here youths and adults meet and make plans for scholarship aid, freedom rides, and programs designed to further the knowledge of Negro history and heritage. . . .

As I walk up and down the bustling, picturesque sidewalks of 125th Street, a feeling of life unobtainable anywhere else in New York City is acquired. It is a happy-to-be-alive feeling mixed with a touch of sorrow and joy—sorrow for the blind woman selling shopping bags in front of the Square Deal Market, and the little beggar man, whose arms and legs are twisted about themselves, his fingers clutching a small tin cup; joy at being alive, and in Harlem.

Harlem is a world in itself. Here you find everything—from dope addicts standing on corners in front of bars, slowly descending to the ground, their bodies slanting at an angle at which they appear to be almost parallel to the ground, but never falling, to teenagers playing whist in the streets, pitching pennies, or harmonizing in hallways.

Along the streets of Harlem, especially in the summertime when everyone is outside from early morning to late at night, the people get to know one another. Perhaps the fact that we of Harlem are striving to get to know one another is most vividly displayed by the teenagers. Lately it has become popular to give what is known as a pay party or a house party. These parties are sponsored by a group or club, and admission is usually thirty-five cents and open to all. These get-togethers are well planned and chaperoned. . . .

Harlem is good. I know for I live here. Harlem is my home. Harlem has slum areas, but they are constantly being torn down and replaced by projects and renovated buildings. Then, too, there are many parts of Harlem which are pleasant to view. There is perhaps nothing as beautiful as the pale green trees of Morningside Park, against the clear sky of a summer morning.

Although Harlem is a community strange and new, and we her people are just finding ourselves, we continue to mature. Yes, Harlem is dirty and plagued with vice, sin, and corruption.

Harlem, though, is alive. We scream for new birth. We are a community struggling for truth and peace. She is not a "Blackboard Jungle," but a good place. Her people possess talent, ability, and fresh ideas. Harlem has come a long way. In the years ahead she will advance further. "Good will triumph over evil."

For me the sun is a little brighter on Lenox Avenue than it is anywhere else I have ever seen. The people are a little dearer. I want that brighter future, but I hope it won't change the Harlem I know today—too much.

LANGSTON HUGHES

On the Way Home

LANGSTON HUGHES, often called the poet laureate of Black America, was born in 1902 in Joplin, Missouri, and died in 1967. He was the author of many volumes of poems, of *I Wonder As I Wander* and *The Big Sea*, both autobiographies, and the author of several plays and many essays. He also edited anthologies of the works of black writers. He was a member of the National Institute of Letters.

Carl was not what you would call a drinking man. Not that he had any moral scruples about drinking, for he prided himself on being broad-minded. But he had always been told that his father (whom he couldn't remember) was a drunkard. So in the back of his head, he didn't really feel it was right to get drunk. Except for perhaps a glass of wine on holidays, or a mug of beer if he was out with a party and didn't want to be conspicuous, he never drank. He was almost a teetotaler.

Carl had promised his mother not to drink *at all*. He was an only child, fond of his mother, but she had raised him with almost too much kindness. To adjust himself to people who were less kind had been hard. But since there were no good jobs in Sommerville, he went away to Chicago to work. Every month he went back home for a Sunday, taking the four-o'clock bus Saturday afternoon, which put him off in front of the door of his boyhood home in time for supper—a supper with country butter, fresh milk, and homemade bread.

After supper he would go uptown with his mother in the cool of evening, if it was summer, to do her Saturday-night shopping. Or if it was winter, they might go over to a neighbor's house and pop corn or drink cider. Or friends might come to their house and sit around the parlor talking and playing old records on an old Victrola—Sousa's marches, Nora Bayes, Bert Williams, Caruso—records that most other people had long ago thrown away or forgotten. It was fun, old-fashioned, and very different from the rum parties most of his office friends gave in Chicago.

Carl had promised his mother and himself not to drink. But this particular afternoon, he stood in front of a long counter in a liquor store on Clark Street and heard himself say, strangely enough, "A bottle of wine."

"What kind of wine?" the clerk asked brusquely.

"That kind," Carl answered, pointing to a row of tall yellow bottles on the middle shelf. It just happened that his finger stopped at the yellow bottles. He did not know the names or brands of wines.

"That's sweet wine," the clerk told him.

"That's all right," Carl said, for he wanted to get the wine quickly and go.

The clerk wrapped the bottle, made change, and turned to another customer. Carl took the bottle and went out. He walked slowly, yet he could hardly wait to get to his room. He had never been so anxious to drink before. He might have stopped at a bar, since he passed many, but he was not used to drinking at bars. So he went to his room.

It was quiet in the big, dark, old rooming house. There was no one in the hall as he went up the wide creaking staircase. All the roomers were at work. It was Tuesday. He would have

been at work, too, had he not received at the office that noon
a wire that his mother was suddenly very ill, and he had better
come home. He knew there was no bus until four o'clock. It
was one now. He would get ready to go soon. But he needed
a drink. Did not men sometimes drink to steady their nerves?
In novels, they took a swig of brandy—but brandy made Carl
sick. Wine would be better—milder.

In his room he tore open the package and uncorked the
bottle, even before he hung his hat in the closet. He took his
toothbrush out of a glass on his dresser and poured the glass
a third full of amber-yellow wine. He tried to keep himself
from wondering if his mother was going to die.

"Please, no!" he prayed. He drank the wine.

He sat down on the bed to get his breath back. That climb
up the steps had never taken his breath before, but now his
heart was beating fast and sweat came out on his brow; so
he took off his coat, tie, shirt, and got ready to wash his face.

But no, he would pack his bag first. Then, he suddenly
thought, he had no present for his mother—but he caught
himself in the middle of the thought. This was not Saturday,
not one of his monthly Saturdays when he went home. This
was Tuesday and there was this telegram in his pocket that
had suddenly broken the whole rhythm of his life: YOUR
MOTHER GRAVELY ILL COME HOME AT ONCE.

John and Nellie Rossiter had been neighbors since childhood. They would not frighten him needlessly. His mother
must be very ill indeed; so he need not think of taking her
a present. He went to the closet door to pull out the suitcase,
but his hands did not move. The wine, amber-yellow in its
tall bottle, stood on the dresser beside him. Warm, sweet,
forbidden.

There was no one in the room. Nobody in the whole
house, perhaps, except the landlady. Nobody really in all
Chicago to talk to in his trouble. With a mother to take care
of on a small salary, room rent, a class at business college,

books to buy, there's not much time left to make friends, or take girls out. In a big city it's hard for a young man to know people.

Carl poured the glass full of wine again—drank it. Then he opened the top drawer, took out his toilet articles, and put them on the bed. From the second drawer he took a couple of shirts. Maybe three would be better, or four. This was not a week end. Perhaps he had better take some extra clothing— in case his mother was ill long, and he had to stay a week or more. Perhaps he'd better take his dark suit in case she—

It hit him in the stomach like a fist. A pang of fear spread over his whole body. He sat down trembling on the bed.

"Buck up, old man." The sound of his own voice comforted him. He smiled weakly at his brown face in the mirror. "Be a man."

He filled the glass full this time and drank it without stopping. He had never drunk so much wine before, and this was warm, sweet, and palatable. He stood, threw his shoulders back, and felt suddenly tall as though his head were touching the ceiling. Then, for no reason at all, he looked at himself in the mirror and began to sing. He made up a song out of nowhere that repeated itself over and over:

> *In the spring the roses*
> *In the spring begin to sing*
> *Roses in the spring.*
> *Begin to sing. . . .*

He took off his clothes, put on his bathrobe, carefully drained the bottle, then went down the hall to the bathroom, still singing. He ran a tub full of water, climbed in, and sat down. The water in the tub was warm like the wine. He felt good, remembering a dark grassy slope in a corner of his mother's yard where he played with a little peach-colored girl when he was very young at home. His mother came out, separated them, and sent the little girl away because she wasn't of a decent family. But now his mother would never dismiss another little girl be—

Carl sat up quickly in the tub, splashed water over his back and over his head. Drunk? What's the matter? What's the matter with you? Thinking of your mother that way and maybe she's dy—Say! Listen, don't you know you have to catch a four-o'clock bus? And here he was getting drunk on the way home. He trembled. His heart beat very fast, so fast that he lay down in the tub to catch his breath, covered with the warm water—all but his head.

To lie quiet that way was fine. Still and quiet. Tuesday. Everybody working at the office. And here he was, Carl Anderson, lying quiet in a deep warm tub of water. Maybe someday after the war with a little money saved up, and no expenses at home, and a car to take girls out in the spring when the roses sing in the spring. . . .

He had a good voice and the song that he had made up about the roses sounded good with that sweet wine on his breath; so he stood up in the tub, grabbed a towel, and began to sing quite loudly and lustily. Suddenly there was a knock at the door.

"What's going on in there?" It was the landlady's voice in the hall outside. She must have heard him singing downstairs.

"Nothing, Mrs. Dyer! Nothing! I just feel like singing."

"Mr. Anderson? Is that you? What're you doing in the house this time of day?"

"I'm on the way home to see my mother. She's . . ."

"You sound happier than a lark about it. I couldn't imagine—"

He heard the landlady's feet shuffling off down the stairs.

"She's . . ." His head began to go round and round. "My mother's . . ." His eyes suddenly burned. To step out of the tub, he held tightly to the sides. Drunk, that's what he was! Drunk!

He lurched down the hall, fell across the bed in his room,

and buried his head in the pillows. He stretched his arms above his head and held onto the rods of the bedstead. He felt ashamed.

With his head in the pillows all was dark. His mother dying? No! No! But he was drunk. In the dark he seemed to feel his mother's hand on his head when he was a little boy, and her voice saying, "Be sweet, Carl. Be a good boy. Keep clean. Mother loves you. She'll look out for you. Be sweet and remember what you're taught at home."

Then the roses in the song he had made up, and the wine he had drunk, began to go around and around in his head, and he felt as if he had betrayed his mother and home singing about roses and spring and dreaming of cars and pretty brown girls with that yellow telegram right there in his coat pocket on the back of the chair beside the bed that suddenly seemed to go around, too.

But when he closed his eyes, it stopped. He held his breath. He buried his head deeper in the pillows. He lay very still. It was dark and warm. And quiet, and darker than ever. A long time passed, a very long time, dark, and quiet, and peaceful, and still.

"Mr. Anderson! Hey, Mr. Anderson!"

In the darkness far off, somebody called, then nearer—but still very far away—then knocking on a distant door.

"Mr. Anderson!" The voice was quite near now, sharper. The door opened, light streamed in. A hand shook his shoulder. He opened his eyes. Mrs. Dyer stood there large and dark, looking down at him in indignant amazement. "Mr. Anderson, are you drunk?"

"No, Mrs. Dyer," he said in a daze, blinking at the landlady standing above him. The electric light bulb she had switched on hurt his eyes.

"Mr. Anderson, they's a long-distance call for you on the phone downstairs in the hall. Get up. Button up that bathrobe. Hurry on down there and get it, will you? I've been yelling for five minutes."

"What time is it?" Carl sat bolt upright. The landlady stopped in the door.

"It's way after dinner time," she said. "Must be six-thirty, seven o'clock."

"Seven o'clock?" Carl gasped. "I've missed my bus!"

"What bus?"

"The four-o'clock bus."

"I guess you have," said the landlady. "Alcohol and time-tables don't mix, young man. That must be your mother on the phone now." Disgusted, she went downstairs, leaving his door open.

The phone! Carl jumped. He felt sick and unsteady on his legs. He pulled his bathrobe together, stumbled down the stairs. The telephone! A kind of weakness rushed through his veins. The telephone! He had promised his mother not to drink. She said his father—he couldn't remember his father. He died long ago. And now, his mother was . . . anyhow, he should have been home by now, by seven o'clock, at her bedside, holding her hand. He could have been home an hour ago. Now, maybe she . . .

He picked up the receiver. His voice was hoarse, frightened. "Hello. . . . Yes, this is Carl. . . . Yes, Mrs. Rossiter. . . ."

"Carl, honey, we kept looking for you on that six-o'clock bus. My husband went out on the road a piece to meet you in his car. We thought it might be quicker. Carl, honey . . ."

"Yes, Mrs. Rossiter?"

"Your mother . . ."

"Yes, Mrs. Rossiter."

"Your mother just passed away. I thought maybe you ought to know in case you hadn't already started. I thought maybe . . ."

For a moment he couldn't hear what she said. Then he

knew that she was asking him a question—that she was repeating it.

"I could have Jerry drive to Chicago and get you tonight. Would you like to have me do that, since there's no bus now until morning?"

"I wish you would, Mrs. Rossiter. But then, no—listen! Never mind! There's two or three things I ought to do before I come home. I ought to go to the bank. I must. But I'll catch that first bus in the morning. First thing in the morning, Mrs. Rossiter, I'll be home."

"We're your neighbors and your friends. You know *this* is your home, too, so come right here."

"Yes, Mrs. Rossiter, I know. I will. I'll be home."

He ran back upstairs, jumped into his clothes. He had to get out. Had to get out! His body burned. His throat was dry. He picked up the wine bottle and read the label. Good wine! Warm and easy on the throat! Hurry before the landlady comes. Hurry! She wouldn't understand this haste. I wonder— *did she die alone?* Quickly he put on his coat and plunged down the steps. Outside it was dark. The street lights seemed dimmer than usual. *Did she die alone?* At the corner there was a bar, palely lighted. He had never stopped there before, but this time he went in. He could drink all he wanted now. *Alone, at home, alone! Did she die alone?*

The bar was dismal, like a barn. A coin machine played a raucous hit song. A brown-skinned woman stood near the machine singing to herself, her hair dark and curly under her little white cap.

Carl went up to the bar.

"What'll it be?" the bartender passed his towel over the counter in front of him.

"A drink," Carl said.

"Whiskey?"

"Yes."

"Can you make it two?" asked the curly-haired woman.

"Sure," Carl said. "Make it two."

"What's the matter? You're shivering!" she exclaimed.

"Cold," Carl said.

"You've been drinking?" the woman said, close beside him. "But it don't smell like whiskey."

"Wasn't," Carl said. "Was wine."

"Oh, so you mix your drinks, heh? O.K. But if that wine along with this whiskey knocks you out, I'll have to take you home to my house, little boy."

"Home?" he asked.

"Yes," the woman said, "home—with me. You and I alone—home."

She put her arm around his shoulders.

"Home?" Carl said.

"Home, sure, baby! Home to my house."

"Home?" Carl was about to repeat when suddenly a volley of sobs shook his body, choking the word "home." He leaned forward on the bar with his head in his arms and wept. The bartender and the woman looked at him in amazement.

Then the woman said gently, "You're drunk, kid! Come on, buck up. I'll take you home. It don't have to be my house, either, if you really want to go home."

JAMES BALDWIN

Sonny's Blues

JAMES BALDWIN, novelist, essayist, short-story writer and playwright, was born in New York City and raised in Harlem. He is the son of a minister. For several years he lived in France, where he wrote the books *Go Tell It On the Mountain, Notes of a Native Son,* and *Giovanni's Room.* His books of essays, *Nobody Knows My Name, Another Country,* and *The Fire Next Time,* were best sellers. "Sonny's Blues" (1957) is from *Going to Meet the Man,* his first collection of short stories, written between 1948 and the 1970s. In whatever literary form, James Baldwin has been widely recognized here and abroad for his "searing commentary on the American, white and black."

I read about it in the paper, in the subway, on my way to work. I read it, and I couldn't believe it, and I read it again. Then perhaps I just stared at it, at the newsprint spelling out his name, spelling out the story. I stared at it in the swinging lights of the subway car, and in the faces and bodies of the people, and in my own face, trapped in the darkness which roared outside.

It was not to be believed and I kept telling myself that, as I walked from the subway station to the high school. And at the same time I couldn't doubt it. I was scared, scared for

Sonny. He became real to me again. A great block of ice got settled in my belly and kept melting there slowly all day long, while I taught my classes algebra. It was a special kind of ice. It kept melting, sending trickles of ice water all up and down my veins, but it never got less. Sometimes it hardened and seemed to expand until I felt my guts were going to come spilling out or that I was going to choke or scream. This would always be at a moment when I was remembering some specific thing Sonny had once said or done.

When he was about as old as the boys in my classes his face had been bright and open, there was a lot of copper in it; and he'd had wonderfully direct brown eyes, and great gentleness and privacy. I wondered what he looked like now. He had been picked up, the evening before, in a raid on an apartment downtown, for peddling and using heroin.

I couldn't believe it: but what I mean by that is that I couldn't find any room for it anywhere inside me. I had kept it outside me for a long time. I hadn't wanted to know. I had had suspicions, but I didn't name them, I kept putting them away. I told myself that Sonny was wild, but he wasn't crazy. And he'd always been a good boy, he hadn't ever turned hard or evil or disrespectful, the way kids can, so quick, so quick, especially in Harlem. I didn't want to believe that I'd ever see my brother going down, coming to nothing, all that light in his face gone out, in the condition I'd already seen so many others. Yet it had happened and here I was, talking about algebra to a lot of boys who might, every one of them for all I knew, be popping off needles every time they went to the head. Maybe it did more for them than algebra could.

I was sure that the first time Sonny had ever had horse, he couldn't have been much older than these boys were now. These boys, now, were living as we'd been living then, they were growing up with a rush and their heads bumped abruptly against the low ceiling of their actual possibilities.

They were filled with rage. All they really knew were two
darknesses, the darkness of their lives, which was now closing
in on them, and the darkness of the movies, which had
blinded them to that other darkness, and in which they now,
vindictively, dreamed, at once more together than they were
at any other time, and more alone.

When the last bell rang, the last class ended, I let out my
breath. It seemed I'd been holding it for all that time. My
clothes were wet—I may have looked as though I'd been sitting in a steam bath, all dressed up, all afternoon. I sat alone
in the classroom a long time. I listened to the boys outside,
downstairs, shouting and cursing and laughing. Their laughter struck me for perhaps the first time. It was not the joyous
laughter which—God knows why—one associates with children. It was mocking and insular, its intent to denigrate. It
was disenchanted, and in this, also, lay the authority of their
curses. Perhaps I was listening to them because I was thinking
about my brother and in them I heard my brother. And
myself.

One boy was whistling a tune, at once very complicated and
very simple, it seemed to be pouring out of him as though he
were a bird, and it sounded very cool and moving through
all that harsh, bright air, only just holding its own through all
those other sounds.

I stood up and walked over to the window and looked
down into the courtyard. It was the beginning of the spring
and the sap was rising in the boys. A teacher passed through
them every now and again, quickly, as though he or she
couldn't wait to get out of that courtyard, to get those boys
out of their sight and off their minds. I started collecting my
stuff. I thought I'd better get home and talk to Isabel.

The courtyard was almost deserted by the time I got downstairs. I saw this boy standing in the shadow of a doorway,
looking just like Sonny. I almost called his name. Then I saw
that it wasn't Sonny, but somebody we used to know, a boy

from around our block. He'd been Sonny's friend. He'd never been mine, having been too young for me, and, anyway, I'd never liked him. And now, even though he was a grown-up man, he still hung around that block, still spent hours on the street corners, was always high and raggy. I used to run into him from time to time and he'd often work around to asking me for a quarter or fifty cents. He always had some real good excuse, too, and I always gave it to him, I don't know why.

But now, abruptly, I hated him. I couldn't stand the way he looked at me, partly like a dog, partly like a cunning child. I wanted to ask him what the hell he was doing in the school courtyard.

He sort of shuffled over to me, and he said, "I see you got the papers. So you already know about it."

"You mean about Sonny? Yes, I already know about it. How come they didn't get you?"

He grinned. It made him repulsive and it also brought to mind what he'd looked like as a kid. "I wasn't there. I stay away from them people."

"Good for you." I offered him a cigarette and I watched him through the smoke. "You come all the way down here just to tell me about Sonny?"

"That's right." He was sort of shaking his head and his eyes looked strange, as though they were about to cross. The bright sun deadened his damp dark brown skin and it made his eyes look yellow and showed up the dirt in his kinked hair. He smelled funky. I moved a little way from him and I said, "Well, thanks. But I already know about it and I got to get home."

"I'll walk you a little ways," he said. We started walking. There were a couple of kids still loitering in the courtyard and one of them said goodnight to me and looked strangely at the boy beside me.

"What're you going to do?" he asked me. "I mean, about Sonny?"

"Look. I haven't seen Sonny for over a year, I'm not sure I'm going to do anything. Anyway, what the hell *can* I do?"

"That's right," he said quickly, "ain't nothing you can do. Can't much help old Sonny no more, I guess."

It was what I was thinking and so it seemed to me he had no right to say it.

"I'm surprised at Sonny, though," he went on—he had a funny way of talking, he looked straight ahead as though he were talking to himself—"I thought Sonny was a smart boy, I thought he was too smart to get hung."

"I guess he thought so too," I said sharply, "and that's how he got hung. And how about you? You're pretty goddamn smart, I bet."

Then he looked directly at me, just for a minute. "I ain't smart," he said. "If I was smart, I'd have reached for a pistol a long time ago."

"Look. Don't tell *me* your sad story, if it was up to me, I'd give you one." Then I felt guilty—guilty, probably, for never having supposed that the poor bastard *had* a story of his own, much less a sad one, and I asked, quickly, "What's going to happen to him now?"

He didn't answer this. He was off by himself some place. "Funny thing," he said, and from his tone we might have been discussing the quickest way to get to Brooklyn, "when I saw the papers this morning, the first thing I asked myself was if I had anything to do with it. I felt sort of responsible."

I began to listen more carefully. The subway station was on the corner, just before us, and I stopped. He stopped, too. We were in front of a bar and he ducked slightly, peering in, but whoever he was looking for didn't seem to be there. The juke box was blasting away with something black and bouncy and I half watched the barmaid as she danced her way from the juke box to her place behind the bar. And I watched her face as she laughingly responded to something someone said to her, still keeping time to the music. When she smiled one saw the little girl, one sensed the doomed, still-struggling woman beneath the battered face of the semi-whore.

"I never *give* Sonny nothing," the boy said finally, "but a long time ago I come to school high and Sonny asked me how it felt." He paused, I couldn't bear to watch him, I watched the barmaid, and I listened to the music which seemed to be causing the pavement to shake. "I told him it felt great." The music stopped, the barmaid paused and watched the juke box until the music began again. "It did."

All this was carrying me some place I didn't want to go. I certainly didn't want to know how it felt. It filled everything, the people, the houses, the music, the dark, quicksilver barmaid, with menace; and this menace was their reality.

"What's going to happen to him now?" I asked again.

"They'll send him away some place and they'll try to cure him." He shook his head. "Maybe he'll even think he's kicked the habit. Then they'll let him loose"—he gestured, throwing his cigarette into the gutter. "That's all."

"What do you mean, that's *all?*"

But I knew what he meant.

"I *mean,* that's *all.*" He turned his head and looked at me, pulling down the corners of his mouth. "Don't you know what I mean?" he asked, softly.

"How the hell *would* I know what you mean?" I almost whispered it, I don't know why.

"That's right," he said to the air, "how would *he* know what I mean?" He turned toward me again, patient and calm, and yet I somehow felt him shaking, shaking as though he were going to fall apart. I felt that ice in my guts again, the dread I'd felt all afternoon; and again I watched the barmaid, moving about the bar, washing glasses, and singing. "Listen. They'll let him out and then it'll just start all over again. That's what I mean."

"You mean—they'll let him out. And then he'll just start

working his way back in again. You mean he'll never kick the habit. Is that what you mean?"

"That's right," he said, cheerfully. "*You* see what I mean."

"Tell me," I said at last, "why does he want to die? He must want to die, he's killing himself, why does he want to die?"

He looked at me in surprise. He licked his lips. "He don't want to die. He wants to live. Don't nobody want to die, ever."

Then I wanted to ask him—too many things. He could not have answered, or if he had, I could not have borne the answers. I started walking. "Well, I guess it's none of my business."

"It's going to be rough on old Sonny," he said. We reached the subway station. "This is your station?" he asked. I nodded. I took one step down. "Damn!" he said, suddenly. I looked up at him. He grinned again. "Damn it if I didn't leave all my money home. You ain't got a dollar on you, have you? Just for a couple of days, is all."

All at once something inside gave and threatened to come pouring out of me. I didn't hate him any more. I felt that in another moment I'd start crying like a child.

"Sure," I said. "Don't sweat." I looked in my wallet and didn't have a dollar, I only had a five. "Here," I said. "That hold you?"

He didn't look at it—he didn't want to look at it. A terrible closed look came over his face, as though he were keeping the number on the bill a secret from him and me. "Thanks," he said, and now he was dying to see me go. "Don't worry about Sonny. Maybe I'll write him or something."

"Sure," I said. "You do that. So long."

"Be seeing you," he said. I went on down the steps.

And I didn't write Sonny or send him anything for a long time. When I finally did, it was just after my little girl died, he wrote me back a letter which made me feel like a bastard.

Here's what he said:

Dear brother,

You don't know how much I needed to hear from you. I wanted to write you many a time but I dug how much I must have hurt you and so I didn't write. But now I feel like a man who's been trying to climb up out of some deep, real deep and funky hole and just saw the sun up there, outside. I got to get outside.

I can't tell you much about how I got here. I mean I don't know how to tell you. I guess I was afraid of something or I was trying to escape from something and you know I have never been very strong in the head (smile). I'm glad Mama and Daddy are dead and can't see what's happened to their son and I swear if I'd known what I was doing I would never have hurt you so, you and a lot of other fine people who were nice to me and who believed in me.

I don't want you to think it had anything to do with me being a musician. It's more than that. Or maybe less than that. I can't get anything straight in my head down here and I try not to think about what's going to happen to me when I get outside again. Sometime I think I'm going to flip and *never* get outside and sometime I think I'll come straight back. I tell you one thing, though, I'd rather blow my brains out than go through this again. But that's what they all say, so they tell me. If I tell you when I'm coming to New York and if you could meet me, I sure would appreciate it. Give my love to Isabel and the kids and I was sure sorry to hear about little Gracie. I wish I could be like Mama and say the Lord's will be done, but I don't know it seems to me that trouble is the one thing that never does get stopped and I don't know what good it does to blame it on the Lord. But maybe it does some good if you believe it.

Your brother,
Sonny

Then I kept in constant touch with him and I sent him whatever I could and I went to meet him when he came back to New York. When I saw him many things I thought I had forgotten came flooding back to me. This was because I had begun, finally, to wonder about Sonny, about the life that Sonny lived inside. This life, whatever it was, had made him older and thinner and it had deepened the distant stillness in which he had always moved. He looked very unlike my baby brother. Yet, when he smiled, when we shook hands, the baby brother I'd never known looked out from the depths of his private life, like an animal waiting to be coaxed into the light.

"How you been keeping?" he asked me.

"All right. And you?"

"Just fine." He was smiling all over his face. "It's good to see you again."

"It's good to see you."

The seven years' difference in our ages lay between us like a chasm: I wondered if these years would ever operate between us as a bridge. I was remembering, and it made it hard to catch my breath, that I had been there when he was born; and I had heard the first words he had ever spoken. When he started to walk, he walked from our mother straight to me. I caught him just before he fell when he took the first steps he ever took in this world.

"How's Isabel?"

"Just fine. She's dying to see you."

"And the boys?"

"They're fine, too. They're anxious to see their uncle."

"Oh, come on. You know they don't remember me."

"Are you kidding? Of course they remember you."

He grinned again. We got into a taxi. We had a lot to say to each other, far too much to know how to begin.

As the taxi began to move, I asked, "You still want to go to India?"

He laughed. "You still remember that. Hell, no. This place is Indian enough for me."

"It used to belong to them," I said.

And he laughed again. "They damn sure knew what they were doing when they got rid of it."

Years ago, when he was around fourteen, he'd been all hipped on the idea of going to India. He read books about people sitting on rocks, naked, in all kinds of weather, but mostly bad, naturally, and walking barefoot through hot coals and arriving at wisdom. I used to say that it sounded to me as though they were getting away from wisdom as fast as they could. I think he sort of looked down on me for that.

"Do you mind," he asked, "if we have the driver drive alongside the park? On the west side—I haven't seen the city in so long."

"Of course not," I said. I was afraid that I might sound as though I were humoring him, but I hoped he wouldn't take it that way.

So we drove along, between the green of the park and the stony, lifeless elegance of hotels and apartment buildings, toward the vivid, killing streets of our childhood. These streets hadn't changed, though housing projects jutted up out of them now like rocks in the middle of a boiling sea. Most of the houses in which we had grown up had vanished, as had the stores from which we had stolen, the basements in which we had first tried sex, the rooftops from which we had hurled tin cans and bricks. But houses exactly like the houses of our past yet dominated the landscape, boys exactly like the boys we once had been found themselves smothering in these houses, came down into the streets for light and air and found themselves encircled by disaster. Some escaped the trap, most didn't. Those who got out always left something of themselves behind, as some animals amputate a leg and leave it in the trap. It might be said, perhaps, that I had escaped, after all, I was a school teacher; or that Sonny had, he hadn't lived in Harlem for years. Yet, as the cab moved uptown through streets which seemed, with a rush, to darken with dark people, and as I covertly studied Sonny's face, it came to me that what

we both were seeking through our separate cab windows was
that part of ourselves which had been left behind. It's always
at the hour of trouble and confrontation that the missing
member aches.

We hit 110th Street and started rolling up Lenox Avenue.
And I'd known this avenue all my life, but it seemed to me
again, as it had seemed on the day I'd first heard about Sonny's
trouble, filled with a hidden menace which was its very breath
of life.

"We almost there," said Sonny.

"Almost." We were both too nervous to say anything more.

We live in a housing project. It hasn't been up long. A few
days after it was up it seemed uninhabitably new, now, of
course, it's already rundown. It looks like a parody of the
good, clean, faceless life—God knows the people who live in
it do their best to make it a parody. The beat-looking grass
lying around isn't enough to make their lives green, the
hedges will never hold out the streets, and they know it. The
big windows fool no one, they aren't big enough to make
space out of no space. They don't bother with the windows,
they watch the TV screen instead. The playground is most
popular with the children who don't play at jacks, or skip
rope, or roller skate, or swing, and they can be found in it
after dark. We moved in partly because it's not too far from
where I teach, and partly for the kids; but it's really just like
the houses in which Sonny and I grew up. The same things
happen, they'll have the same things to remember. The moment Sonny and I started into the house I had the feeling that
I was simply bringing him back into the danger he had almost
died trying to escape.

Sonny has never been talkative. So I don't know why I was
sure he'd be dying to talk to me when supper was over the first
night. Everything went fine, the oldest boy remembered him,
and the youngest boy liked him, and Sonny had remembered
to bring something for each of them; and Isabel, who is really

much nicer than I am, more open and giving, had gone to a lot of trouble about dinner and was genuinely glad to see him. And she's always been able to tease Sonny in a way that I haven't. It was nice to see her face so vivid again and to hear her laugh and watch her make Sonny laugh. She wasn't, or, anyway, she didn't seem to be, at all uneasy or embarrassed. She chatted as though there were no subject which had to be avoided and she got Sonny past his first, faint stiffness. And thank God she was there, for I was filled with that icy dread again. Everything I did seemed awkward to me, and everything I said sounded freighted with hidden meaning. I was trying to remember everything I'd heard about dope addiction and I couldn't help watching Sonny for signs. I wasn't doing it out of malice. I was trying to find out something about my brother. I was dying to hear him tell me he was safe.

"Safe!" my father grunted, whenever Mama suggested trying to move to a neighborhood which might be safer for children. "Safe, hell! Ain't no place safe for kids, nor nobody."

He always went on like this, but he wasn't, ever, really as bad as he sounded, not even on weekends, when he got drunk. As a matter of fact, he was always on the lookout for "something a little better," but he died before he found it. He died suddenly, during a drunken weekend in the middle of the war, when Sonny was fifteen. He and Sonny hadn't ever got on too well. And this was partly because Sonny was the apple of his father's eye. It was because he loved Sonny so much and was frightened for him, that he was always fighting with him. It doesn't do any good to fight with Sonny. Sonny just moves back, inside himself, where he can't be reached. But the principal reason that they never hit it off is that they were so much alike. Daddy was big and rough and loud-talking, just the opposite of Sonny, but they both had—that same privacy.

Mama tried to tell me something about this, just after Daddy died. I was home on leave from the army.

This was the last time I ever saw my mother alive. Just the same, this picture gets all mixed up in my mind with pictures I had of her when she was younger. The way I always see her is the way she used to be on a Sunday afternoon, say, when the old folks were talking after the big Sunday dinner. I always see her wearing pale blue. She'd be sitting on the sofa. And my father would be sitting in the easy chair, not far from her. And the living room would be full of church folks and relatives. There they sit, in chairs all around the living room, and the night is creeping up outside, but nobody knows it yet. You can see the darkness growing against the windowpanes and you hear the street noises every now and again, or maybe the jangling beat of a tambourine from one of the churches close by, but it's real quiet in the room. For a moment nobody's talking, but every face looks darkening, like the sky outside. And my mother rocks a little from the waist, and my father's eyes are closed. Everyone is looking at something a child can't see. For a minute they've forgotten the children. Maybe a kid is lying on the rug, half asleep. Maybe somebody's got a kid in his lap and is absent-mindedly stroking the kid's head. Maybe there's a kid, quiet and big-eyed, curled up in a big chair in the corner. The silence, the darkness coming, and the darkness in the faces frightens the child obscurely. He hopes that the hand which strokes his forehead will never stop—will never die. He hopes that there will never come a time when the old folks won't be sitting around the living room, talking about where they've come from, and what they've seen, and what's happened to them and their kinfolk.

But something deep and watchful in the child knows that this is bound to end, is already ending. In a moment someone will get up and turn on the light. Then the old folks will remember the children and they won't talk any more that day. And when light fills the room, the child is filled with darkness. He knows that everytime this happens he's moved just a little closer to that darkness outside. The darkness outside is what.

the old folks have been talking about. It's what they've come from. It's what they endure. The child knows that they won't talk any more because if he knows too much about what's happened to *them,* he'll know too much too soon, about what's going to happen to *him.*

The last time I talked to my mother, I remember I was restless. I wanted to get out and see Isabel. We weren't married then and we had a lot to straighten out between us.

There Mama sat, in black, by the window. She was humming an old church song, *Lord, you brought me from a long ways off.* Sonny was out somewhere. Mama kept watching the streets.

"I don't know," she said, "if I'll ever see you again, after you go off from here. But I hope you'll remember the things I tried to teach you."

"Don't talk like that," I said, and smiled. "You'll be here a long time yet."

She smiled, too, but she said nothing. She was quiet for a long time. And I said, "Mama, don't you worry about nothing. I'll be writing all the time, and you be getting the checks. . . ."

"I want to talk to you about your brother," she said, suddenly. "If anything happens to me he ain't going to have nobody to look out for him."

"Mama," I said, "ain't nothing going to happen to you *or* Sonny. Sonny's all right. He's a good boy and he's got good sense."

"It ain't a question of his being a good boy," Mama said, "nor of his having good sense. It ain't only the bad ones, nor yet the dumb ones that gets sucked under." She stopped, looking at me. "Your Daddy once had a brother," she said, and she smiled in a way that made me feel she was in pain. "You didn't never know that, did you?"

"No," I said, "I never knew that," and I watched her face.

"Oh, yes," she said, "your Daddy had a brother." She looked out of the window again. "I know you never saw your

Daddy cry. But *I* did—many a time, through all these years."

I asked her, "What happened to his brother? How come nobody's ever talked about him?"

This was the first time I ever saw my mother look old.

"His brother got killed," she said, "when he was just a little younger than you are now. I knew him. He was a fine boy. He was maybe a little full of the devil, but he didn't mean nobody no harm."

Then she stopped and the room was silent, exactly as it had sometimes been on those Sunday afternoons. Mama kept looking out into the streets.

"He used to have a job in the mill," she said, "and, like all young folks, he just liked to perform on Saturday nights. Saturday nights, him and your father would drift around to different places, go to dances and things like that, or just sit around with people they knew, and your father's brother would sing, he had a fine voice, and play along with himself on his guitar. Well, this particular Saturday night, him and your father was coming home from some place, and they were both a little drunk and there was a moon that night, it was bright like day. Your father's brother was feeling kind of good, and he was whistling to himself, and he had his guitar slung over his shoulder. They was coming down a hill and beneath them was a road that turned off from the highway. Well, your father's brother, being always kind of frisky, decided to run down this hill, and he did, with that guitar banging and clanging behind him, and he ran across the road, and he was making water behind a tree. And your father was sort of amused at him and he was still coming down the hill, kind of slow. Then he heard a car motor and that same minute his brother stepped from behind the tree, into the road, in the moonlight. And he started to cross the road. And your father started to run down the hill, he says he don't know why. This car was full of white men. They was all drunk, and when they seen your father's brother they let out a great whoop and holler and they aimed the car straight at him. They was having fun, they just wanted to scare him, the way they do sometimes, you know. But they was drunk. And I guess the boy, being drunk, too, and scared, kind of lost his head. By the time he jumped it was too late. Your father says he heard his brother scream when the car rolled over him, and he heard the wood of that guitar when it give, and he heard them strings go flying, and he heard them white men shouting, and the car kept on a-going and it ain't stopped till this day. And, time your father got down the hill, his brother weren't nothing but blood and pulp."

Tears were gleaming on my mother's face. There wasn't anything I could say.

"He never mentioned it," she said, "because I never let him mention it before you children. Your Daddy was like a crazy man that night and for many a night thereafter. He says he never in his life seen anything as dark as that road after the lights of that car had gone away. Weren't nothing, weren't nobody on that road, just your Daddy and his brother and that busted guitar. Oh, yes. Your Daddy never did really get right again. Till the day he died he weren't sure but that every white man he saw was the man that killed his brother."

She stopped and took out her handkerchief and dried her eyes and looked at me.

"I ain't telling you all this," she said, "to make you scared or bitter or to make you hate nobody. I'm telling you this because you got a brother. And the world ain't changed."

I guess I didn't want to believe this. I guess she saw this in my face. She turned away from me, toward the window again, searching those streets.

"But I praise my Redeemer," she said at last, "that He called your Daddy home before me. I ain't saying it to throw no flowers at myself, but, I declare, it keeps me from feeling too cast down to know I helped your father get safely through this world. Your father always acted like he was the roughest, strongest man on earth. And everybody took him to be like that. But if he hadn't had *me* there—to see his tears!"

She was crying again. Still, I couldn't move. I said, "Lord, Lord, Mama, I didn't know it was like that."

"Oh, honey," she said, "there's a lot that you don't know. But you are going to find it out." She stood up from the window and came over to me. "You got to hold on to your brother," she said, "and don't let him fall, no matter what it looks like is happening to him and no matter how evil you gets with him. You going to be evil with him many a time. But don't you forget what I told you, you hear?"

"I won't forget," I said. "Don't you worry, I won't forget. I won't let nothing happen to Sonny."

My mother smiled as though she were amused at something she saw in my face. Then, "You may not be able to stop nothing from happening. But you got to let him know you's *there*."

Two days later I was married, and then I was gone. And I had a lot of things on my mind and I pretty well forgot my promise to Mama until I got shipped home on a special furlough for her funeral.

And, after the funeral, with just Sonny and me alone in the empty kitchen, I tried to find out something about him.

"What do you want to do?" I asked him.

"I'm going to be a musician," he said.

For he had graduated, in the time I had been away, from dancing to the juke box to finding out who was playing what, and what they were doing with it, and he had bought himself a set of drums.

"You mean, you want to be a drummer?" I somehow had the feeling that being a drummer might be all right for other people but not for my brother Sonny.

"I don't think," he said, looking at me very gravely, "that I'll ever be a good drummer. But I think I can play a piano."

I frowned. I'd never played the role of the older brother quite so seriously before, had scarcely ever, in fact, *asked* Sonny a damn thing. I sensed myself in the presence of something I didn't really know how to handle, didn't understand. So I made my frown a little deeper as I asked: "What kind of musician do you want to be?"

He grinned. "How many kinds do you think there are?"

"Be *serious*," I said.

He laughed, throwing his head back, and then looked at me. "I *am* serious."

"Well, then, for Christ's sake, stop kidding around and answer a serious question. I mean, do you want to be a concert pianist, you want to play classical music and all that, or—or what?" Long before I finished he was laughing again. "For Christ's *sake*, Sonny!"

He sobered, but with difficulty. "I'm sorry. But you sound so—*scared*!" and he was off again.

"Well, you think it's funny now, baby, but it's not going to be so funny when you have to make your living at it, let me tell you *that*." I was furious because I knew he was laughing at me and I didn't know why.

"No," he said, very sober now, and afraid, perhaps, that he'd hurt me, "I don't want to be a classical pianist. That isn't what interests me. I mean——" he paused, looking hard at me, as though his eyes would help me to understand, and then gestured helplessly, as though perhaps his hand would help—"I mean, I'll have a lot of studying to do, and I'll have to study *everything*, but, I mean, I want to play *with*—jazz musicians." He stopped. "I want to play jazz," he said.

Well, the word had never before sounded as heavy, as real, as it sounded that afternoon in Sonny's mouth. I just looked at him and I was probably frowning a real frown by this time. I simply couldn't see why on earth he'd want to spend his time hanging around nightclubs, clowning around on bandstands, while people pushed each other around a dance floor. It seemed—beneath him, somehow. I had never thought about it before, had never been forced to, but I suppose I had always put jazz musicians in a class with what Daddy called "good-time people."

"Are you *serious?*"

"Hell, *yes,* I'm serious."

He looked more helpless than ever, and annoyed, and deeply hurt.

I suggested, helpfully: "You mean—like Louis Armstrong?"

His face closed as though I'd struck him. "No. I'm not talking about none of that old-time, down home crap."

"Well, look, Sonny, I'm sorry, don't get mad. I just don't altogether get it, that's all. Name somebody—you know. a jazz musician you admire."

"Bird."

"Who?"

"Bird! Charlie Parker! Don't they teach you nothing in the goddamn army?"

I lit a cigarette. I was surprised and then a little amused to discover that I was trembling. "I've been out of touch," I said. "You'll have to be patient with me. Now. Who's this Parker character?"

"He's just one of the greatest jazz musicians alive," said Sonny, sullenly, his hands in his pockets, his back to me. "Maybe *the* greatest," he added, bitterly, "that's probably why *you* never heard of him."

"All right," I said, "I'm ignorant. I'm sorry. I'll go out and buy all the cat's records right away, all right?"

"It don't," said Sonny, with dignity, "make any difference to me. I don't care what you listen to. Don't do me no favors."

I was beginning to realize that I'd never seen him so upset before. With another part of my mind I was thinking that this would probably turn out to be one of those things kids go through and that I shouldn't make it seem important by pushing it too hard. Still, I didn't think it would do any harm to ask: "Doesn't all this take a lot of time? Can you make a living at it?"

He turned back to me and half leaned, half sat, on the kitchen table. "Everything takes time," he said, "and—well, yes, sure, I can make a living at it. But what I don't seem to be able to make you understand is that it's the only thing I want to do."

"Well, Sonny," I said, gently, "you know people can't always do exactly what they *want* to do—"

"No, I don't know that," said Sonny, surprising me. "I think people *ought* to do what they want to do, what else are they alive for?"

"You getting to be a big boy," I said desperately, "it's time you started thinking about your future."

"I'm thinking about my future," said Sonny, grimly. "I think about it all the time."

I gave up. I decided, if he didn't change his mind, that we could always talk about it later. "In the meantime," I said, "you got to finish school." We had already decided that he'd have to move in with Isabel and her folks. I knew this wasn't the ideal arrangement because Isabel's folks are inclined to be dicty and they hadn't especially wanted Isabel to marry me. But I didn't know what else to do. "And we have to get you fixed up at Isabel's."

There was a long silence. He moved from the kitchen table to the window. "That's a terrible idea. You know it yourself."

"Do you have a *better* idea?"

He just walked up and down the kitchen for a minute. He was as tall as I was. He had started to shave. I suddenly had the feeling that I didn't know him at all.

He stopped at the kitchen table and picked up my cigarettes. Looking at me with a kind of mocking, amused defiance, he put one between his lips. "You mind?"

"You smoking already?"

He lit the cigarette and nodded, watching me through the

smoke. "I just wanted to see if I'd have the courage to smoke in front of you." He grinned and blew a great cloud of smoke to the ceiling. "It was easy." He looked at my face. "Come on, now. I bet you was smoking at my age, tell the truth."

I didn't say anything but the truth was on my face, and he laughed. But now there was something very strained in his laugh. "Sure. And I bet that ain't all you was doing."

He was frightening me a little. "Cut the crap," I said. "We already decided that you was going to go and live at Isabel's. Now what's got into you all of a sudden?"

"*You* decided it," he pointed out. "*I* didn't decide nothing." He stopped in front of me, leaning against the stove, arms loosely folded. "Look, brother. I don't want to stay in Harlem no more, I really don't." He was very earnest. He looked at me, then over toward the kitchen window. There was something in his eyes I'd never seen before, some thoughtfulness, some worry all his own. He rubbed the muscle of one arm. "It's time I was getting out of here."

"Where do you want to *go*, Sonny?"

"I want to join the army. Or the navy, I don't care. If I say I'm old enough, they'll believe me."

Then I got mad. It was because I was so scared. "You must be crazy. You goddamn fool, what the hell do you want to go and join the *army* for?"

"I just told you. To get out of Harlem."

"Sonny, you haven't even finished *school*. And if you really want to be a musician, how do you expect to study if you're in the *army?*"

He looked at me, trapped, and in anguish. "There's ways. I might be able to work out some kind of deal. Anyway, I'll have the G.I. Bill when I come out."

"*If* you come out." We stared at each other. "Sonny, please. Be reasonable. I know the setup is far from perfect. But we got to do the best we can."

"I ain't learning nothing in school," he said. "Even when I

go." He turned away from me and opened the window and threw his cigarette out into the narrow alley. I watched his back. "At least, I ain't learning nothing you'd want me to learn." He slammed the window so hard I thought the glass would fly out, and turned back to me. "And I'm sick of the stink of these garbage cans!"

"Sonny," I said, "I know how you feel. But if you don't finish school now, you're going to be sorry later that you didn't." I grabbed him by the shoulders. "And you only got another year. It ain't so bad. And I'll come back and I swear I'll help you do *whatever* you want to do. Just try to put up with it till I come back. Will you please do that? For me?"

He didn't answer and he wouldn't look at me.

"Sonny. You hear me?"

He pulled away. "I hear you. But you never hear anything *I* say."

I didn't know what to say to that. He looked out of the window and then back at me. "OK," he said, and sighed. "I'll try."

Then I said, trying to cheer him up a little, "They got a piano at Isabel's. You can practice on it."

And as a matter of fact, it did cheer him up for a minute. "That's right," he said to himself. "I forgot that." His face relaxed a little. But the worry, the thoughtfulness, played on it still, the way shadows play on a face which is staring into the fire.

But I thought I'd never hear the end of that piano. At first, Isabel would write me, saying how nice it was that Sonny was so serious about his music and how, as soon as he came in from school, or wherever he had been when he was supposed to be at school, he went straight to that piano and stayed there until suppertime. And, after supper, he went back to that piano and stayed there until everybody went to bed. He was at the piano all day Saturday and all day Sunday. Then he bought a record player and started playing records. He'd play one record over and over again, all day long sometimes, and he'd improvise along with it on the piano. Or he'd play one section of the record, one chord, one change, one progression, then he'd do it on the piano. Then back to the record. Then back to the piano.

Well, I really don't know how they stood it. Isabel finally confessed that it wasn't like living with a person at all, it was like living with sound. And the sound didn't make any sense to her, didn't make any sense to any of them—naturally. They began, in a way, to be afflicted by this presence that was living in their home. It was as though Sonny were some sort of god, or monster. He moved in an atmosphere which wasn't like theirs at all. They fed him and he ate, he washed himself, he walked in and out of their door; he certainly wasn't nasty or unpleasant or rude, Sonny isn't any of those things; but it was as though he were all wrapped up in some cloud, some fire, some vision all his own; and there wasn't any way to reach him.

At the same time, he wasn't really a man yet, he was still a child, and they had to watch out for him in all kinds of ways. They certainly couldn't throw him out. Neither did they dare to make a great scene about that piano because even they dimly sensed, as I sensed, from so many thousands of miles away, that Sonny was at that piano playing for his life.

But he hadn't been going to school. One day a letter came from the school board and Isabel's mother got it—there had, apparently, been other letters but Sonny had torn them up. This day, when Sonny came in, Isabel's mother showed him the letter and asked where he'd been spending his time. And she finally got it out of him that he'd been down in Greenwich Village, with musicians and other characters, in a white girl's apartment. And this scared her and she started to scream at him and what came up, once she began—though she denies it to this day—was what sacrifices they were making to give Sonny a decent home and how little he appreciated it.

Sonny didn't play the piano that day. By evening, Isabel's mother had calmed down but then there was the old man to deal with, and Isabel herself. Isabel says she did her best to be calm but she broke down and started crying. She says she just watched Sonny's face. She could tell, by watching him, what was happening with him. And what was happening was that they penetrated his cloud, they had reached him. Even if their fingers had been a thousand times more gentle than human fingers ever are, he could hardly help feeling that they had stripped him naked and were spitting on that nakedness. For he also had to see that his presence, that music, which was life or death to him, had been torture for them and that they had endured it, not at all for his sake, but only for mine. And Sonny couldn't take that. He can take it a little better today than he could then but he's still not very good at it and, frankly, I don't know anybody who is.

The silence of the next few days must have been louder than the sound of all the music ever played since time began. One morning, before she went to work, Isabel was in his room for something and she suddenly realized that all of his records were gone. And she knew for certain that he was gone. And he was. He went as far as the navy would carry him. He finally sent me a postcard from some place in Greece and that was the first I knew that Sonny was still alive. I didn't see him any more until we were both back in New York and the war had long been over.

He was a man by then, of course, but I wasn't willing to see it. He came by the house from time to time, but we fought almost every time we met. I didn't like the way he carried himself, loose and dreamlike all the time, and I didn't like his friends, and his music seemed to be merely an excuse for the life he led. It sounded just that weird and disordered.

Then we had a fight, a pretty awful fight, and I didn't see

him for months. By and by I looked him up, where he was living, in a furnished room in the Village, and I tried to make it up. But there were lots of people in the room and Sonny just lay on his bed, and he wouldn't come downstairs with me, and he treated these other people as though they were his family and I weren't. So I got mad and then he got mad, and then I told him that he might just as well be dead as live the way he was living. Then he stood up and he told me not to worry about him any more in life, that he *was* dead as far as I was concerned. Then he pushed me to the door and the other people looked on as though nothing were happening, and he slammed the door behind me. I stood in the hallway, staring at the door. I heard somebody laugh in the room and then the tears came to my eyes. I started down the steps, whistling to keep from crying, I kept whistling to myself, *You going to need me, baby, one of these cold, rainy days.*

I read about Sonny's trouble in the spring. Little Grace died in the fall. She was a beautiful little girl. But she only lived a little over two years. She died of polio and she suffered. She had a slight fever for a couple of days, but it didn't seem like anything and we just kept her in bed. And we would certainly have called the doctor, but the fever dropped, she seemed to be all right. So we thought it had just been a cold. Then, one day, she was up, playing, Isabel was in the kitchen fixing lunch for the two boys when they'd come in from school, and she heard Grace fall down in the living room. When you have a lot of children you don't always start running when one of them falls, unless they start screaming or something. And, this time, Grace was quiet. Yet, Isabel says that when she heard that *thump* and then that silence, something happened in her to make her afraid. And she ran to the living room and there was little Grace on the floor, all twisted up, and the reason she hadn't screamed was that she couldn't get her breath. And when she did scream, it was the worst sound, Isabel says, that she'd ever heard in all her life, and she still hears it sometimes in her dreams. Isabel will sometimes wake me up with a low, moaning, strangled sound and I have to be quick to awaken her and hold her to me and where Isabel is weeping against me seems a mortal wound.

I think I may have written Sonny the very day that little Grace was buried. I was sitting in the living room in the dark, by myself, and I suddenly thought of Sonny. My trouble made his real.

One Saturday afternoon, when Sonny had been living with us, or, anyway, been in our house, for nearly two weeks, I found myself wandering aimlessly about the living room, drinking from a can of beer, and trying to work up the courage to search Sonny's room. He was out, he was usually out whenever I was home, and Isabel had taken the children to see their grandparents. Suddenly I was standing still in front of the living room window, watching Seventh Avenue. The idea of searching Sonny's room made me still. I scarcely dared to admit to myself what I'd be searching for. I didn't know what I'd do if I found it. Or if I didn't.

On the sidewalk across from me, near the entrance to a barbecue joint, some people were holding an old-fashioned revival meeting. The barbecue cook, wearing a dirty white apron, his conked hair reddish and metallic in the pale sun, and a cigarette between his lips, stood in the doorway, watching them. Kids and older people paused in their errands and stood there, along with some older men and a couple of very tough-looking women who watched everything that happened on the avenue, as though they owned it, or were maybe owned by it. Well, they were watching this, too. The revival was being carried on by three sisters in black, and a brother. All they had were their voices and their Bibles and a tambourine. The brother was testifying and while he testified two of the sisters stood together, seeming to say, amen, and the third sister walked around with the tambourine outstretched and a

couple of people dropped coins into it. Then the brother's
testimony ended and the sister who had been taking up the
collection dumped the coins into her palm and transferred
them to the pocket of her long black robe. Then she raised
both hands, striking the tambourine against the air, and then
against one hand, and she started to sing. And the two other
sisters and the brother joined in.

It was strange, suddenly, to watch, though I had been seeing
these street meetings all my life. So, of course, had everybody
else down there. Yet, they paused and watched and listened
and I stood still at the window. *"Tis the old ship of Zion,"*
they sang, and the sister with the tambourine kept a steady,
jangling beat, *"it has rescued many a thousand!"* Not a soul
under the sound of their voices was hearing this song for the
first time, not one of them had been rescued. Nor had they
seen much in the way of rescue work being done around them.
Neither did they especially believe in the holiness of the three
sisters and the brother, they knew too much about them, knew
where they lived, and how. The woman with the tambourine,
whose voice dominated the air, whose face was bright with
joy, was divided by very little from the woman who stood
watching her, a cigarette between her heavy, chapped lips,
her hair a cuckoo's nest, her face scarred and swollen from
many beatings, and her black eyes glittering like coal. Perhaps they both knew this, which was why, when, as rarely,
they addressed each other, they addressed each other as Sister.
As the singing filled the air the watching, listening faces un-
derwent a change, the eyes focusing on something within;
the music seemed to soothe a poison out of them; and time
seemed, nearly, to fall away from the sullen, belligerent, battered faces, as though they were fleeing back to their first
condition, while dreaming of their last. The barbecue cook
half shook his head and smiled, and dropped his cigarette and
disappeared into his joint. A man fumbled in his pockets for
change and stood holding it in his hand impatiently, as

though he had just remembered a pressing appointment further up the avenue. He looked furious. Then I saw Sonny, standing on the edge of the crowd. He was carrying a wide, flat notebook with a green cover, and it made him look, from where I was standing, almost like a schoolboy. The coppery sun brought out the copper in his skin, he was very faintly smiling, standing very still. Then the singing stopped, the tambourine turned into a collection plate again. The furious man dropped in his coins and vanished, so did a couple of the women, and Sonny dropped some change in the plate, looking directly at the woman with a little smile. He started across the avenue, toward the house. He has a slow, loping walk, something like the way Harlem hipsters walk, only he's imposed on this his own half-beat. I had never really noticed it before.

I stayed at the window, both relieved and apprehensive. As Sonny disappeared from my sight, they began singing again. And they were still singing when his key turned in the lock.

"Hey," he said.

"Hey, yourself. You want some beer?"

"No. Well, maybe." But he came up to the window and stood beside me, looking out. "What a warm voice," he said.

They were singing *If I could only hear my mother pray again!*

"Yes," I said, "and she can sure beat that tambourine."

"But what a terrible song," he said, and laughed. He dropped his notebook on the sofa and disappeared into the kitchen. "Where's Isabel and the kids?"

"I think they went to see their grandparents. You hungry?"

"No." He came back into the living room with his can of beer. "You want to come some place with me tonight?"

I sensed, I don't know how, that I couldn't possibly say no. "Sure. Where?"

He sat down on the sofa and picked up his notebook and

started leafing through it. "I'm going to sit in with some fellows in a joint in the Village."

"You mean, you're going to play, tonight?"

"That's right." He took a swallow of his beer and moved back to the window. He gave me a sidelong look. "If you can stand it."

"I'll try," I said.

He smiled to himself and we both watched as the meeting across the way broke up. The three sisters and the brother, heads bowed, were singing *God be with you till we meet again.* The faces around them were very quiet. Then the song ended. The small crowd dispersed. We watched the three women and the lone man walk slowly up the avenue.

"When she was singing before," said Sonny, abruptly, "her voice reminded me for a minute of what heroin feels like sometimes—when it's in your veins. It makes you feel sort of warm and cool at the same time. And distant. And—and sure." He sipped his beer, very deliberately not looking at me. I watched his face. "It makes you feel—in control. Sometimes you've got to have that feeling."

"Do you?" I sat down slowly in the easy chair.

"Sometimes." He went to the sofa and picked up his notebook again. "Some people do."

"In order," I asked, "to play?" And my voice was very ugly, full of contempt and anger.

"Well"—he looked at me with great, troubled eyes, as though, in fact, he hoped his eyes would tell me things he could never otherwise say—"they *think* so. And *if* they think so—!"

"And what do *you* think?" I asked.

He sat on the sofa and put his can of beer on the floor. "I don't know," he said, and I couldn't be sure if he were answering my question or pursuing his thoughts. His face didn't tell me. "It's not so much to *play.* It's to *stand* it, to be able to make it at all. On any level." He frowned and smiled: "In order to keep from shaking to pieces."

"But these friends of yours," I said, "they seem to shake themselves to pieces pretty goddamn fast."

"Maybe." He played with the notebook. And something told me that I should curb my tongue, that Sonny was doing his best to talk, that I should listen. "But of course you only know the ones that've gone to pieces. Some don't—or at least they haven't *yet* and that's just about all *any* of us can say." He paused. "And then there are some who just live, really, in hell, and they know it and they see what's happening and they go right on. I don't know." He sighed, dropped the notebook, folded his arms. "Some guys, you can tell from the way they play, they on something *all* the time. And you can see that, well, it makes something real for them. But of course," he picked up his beer from the floor and sipped it and put the can down again, "they *want* to, too, you've got to see that. Even some of them that say they don't—*some*, not all."

"And what about you?" I asked—I couldn't help it. "What about you? Do *you* want to?"

He stood up and walked to the window and remained silent for a long time. Then he sighed. "Me," he said. Then: "While I was downstairs before, on my way here, listening to that woman sing, it struck me all of a sudden how much suffering she must have had to go through—to sing like that. It's *repulsive* to think you have to suffer that much."

I said: "But there's no way not to suffer—is there, Sonny?"

"I believe not," he said and smiled, "but that's never stopped anyone from trying." He looked at me. "Has it?" I realized, with this mocking look, that there stood between us, forever, beyond the power of time or forgiveness, the fact that I had held silence—so long!—when he had needed human speech to help him. He turned back to the window. "No, there's no way not to suffer. But you try all kinds of ways to keep from drowning in it, to keep on top of it, and to make it seem—well, like *you*. Like you did something, all right, and now you're suffering for it. You know?" I said nothing. "Well you know," he said, impatiently, "why *do* people suffer? Maybe it's better to do something to give it a reason, *any* reason."

"But we just agreed," I said, "that there's no way not to suffer. Isn't it better, then, just to—take it?"

"But nobody just takes it," Sonny cried, "that's what I'm telling you! *Everybody* tries not to. You're just hung up on the *way* some people try—it's not *your* way!"

The hair on my face began to itch, my face felt wet. "That's not true," I said, "that's not true. I don't give a damn what other people do, I don't even care how they suffer. I just care how *you* suffer." And he looked at me. "Please believe me," I said, "I don't want to see you—die—trying not to suffer."

"I won't," he said, flatly, "die trying not to suffer. At least, not any faster than anybody else."

"But there's no need," I said, trying to laugh, "is there? in killing yourself."

I wanted to say more, but I couldn't. I wanted to talk about will power and how life could be—well, beautiful. I wanted to say that it was all within; but was it? or, rather, wasn't that exactly the trouble? And I wanted to promise that I would never fail him again. But it would all have sounded—empty words and lies.

So I made the promise to myself and prayed that I would keep it.

"It's terrible sometimes, inside," he said, "that's what's the trouble. You walk these streets, black and funky and cold, and there's not really a living ass to talk to, and there's nothing shaking, and there's no way of getting it out—that storm inside. You can't talk it and you can't make love with it, and when you finally try to get with it and play it, you realize *nobody's* listening. So *you've* got to listen. You got to find a way to listen."

And then he walked away from the window and sat on the sofa again, as though all the wind had suddenly been knocked out of him. "Sometimes you'll do *anything* to play, even cut your mother's throat." He laughed and looked at me. "Or your brother's." Then he sobered. "Or your own." Then: "Don't worry. I'm all right now and I think I'll *be* all right. But I can't forget—where I've been. I don't mean just the physical place I've been, I mean where I've *been*. And *what* I've been."

"What have you been, Sonny?" I asked.

He smiled—but sat sideways on the sofa, his elbow resting on the back, his fingers playing with his mouth and chin, not looking at me. "I've been something I didn't recognize, didn't know I could be. Didn't know anybody could be." He stopped, looking inward, looking helplessly young, looking old. "I'm not talking about it now because I feel *guilty* or anything like that—maybe it would be better if I did, I don't know. Anyway, I can't really talk about it. Not to you, not to anybody," and now he turned and faced me. "Sometimes, you know, and it was actually when I was most *out* of the world, I felt that I was in it, that I was *with* it, really, and I could play or I didn't really have to *play*, it just came out of me, it was there. And I don't know how I played, thinking about it now, but I know I did awful things, those times, sometimes, to people. Or it wasn't that I *did* anything to them—it was that they weren't real." He picked up the beer can; it was empty; he rolled it between his palms: "And other times—well, I needed a fix, I needed to find a place to lean, I needed to clear a space to *listen*—and I couldn't find it, and I—went crazy, I did terrible thing to *me,* I was terrible *for* me." He began pressing the beer can between his hands, I watched the metal begin to give. It glittered, as he played with it, like a knife, and I was afraid he would cut himself, but I said nothing. "Oh well. I can never tell you. I was all by myself at the bottom of something, stinking and sweating and crying and shaking, and I smelled it, you know? *my* stink, and I thought I'd die if I couldn't get away from it and yet, all the same, I knew that everything I was doing was just locking me in with it. And I didn't know," he paused, still flattening the beer can, "I didn't know, I still *don't* know, something kept telling me that maybe it was good to smell your own stink, but I didn't think that *that* was what I'd been trying to do—and—who can stand it?" and he abruptly dropped the ruined beer can, looking at me with a small, still smile, and then rose, walking to the window as though it were the lodestone rock. I watched his face, he watched the avenue. "I couldn't tell you when Mama died—but the reason I wanted to leave Harlem so bad was to get away from drugs. And then, when I ran away, that's what I was running from—really. When I came back, nothing had changed, *I* hadn't changed, I was just—older." And he stopped, drumming with his fingers on the windowpane. The sun had vanished, soon darkness would fall. I watched his face. "It can come again," he said, almost as though speaking to himself. Then he turned to me. "It can come again," he repeated. "I just want you to know that."

"All right," I said, at last. "So it can come again, All right."

He smiled, but the smile was sorrowful. "I had to try to tell you," he said.

"Yes," I said. "I understand that."

"You're my brother," he said, looking straight at me, and not smiling at all.

"Yes," I repeated, "yes. I understand that."

He turned back to the window, looking out. "All that hatred down there," he said, "all that hatred and misery and love. It's a wonder it doesn't blow the avenue apart."

We went to the only nightclub on a short, dark street, downtown. We squeezed through the narrow, chattering, jam-packed bar to the entrance of the big room, where the bandstand was. And we stood there for a moment, for the lights were very dim in this room and we couldn't see. Then, "Hello, boy," said a voice and an enormous black man, much older than Sonny or myself, erupted out of all that atmospheric lighting and put an arm around Sonny's shoulder. "I been sitting right here," he said, "waiting for you."

He had a big voice, too, and heads in the darkness turned toward us.

Sonny grinned and pulled a little away, and said, "Creole, this is my brother. I told you about him."

Creole shook my hand. "I'm glad to meet you, son," he said, and it was clear that he was glad to meet me *there*, for Sonny's sake. And he smiled, "You got a real musician in *your* family," and he took his arm from Sonny's shoulder and slapped him, lightly, affectionately, with the back of his hand.

"Well. Now I've heard it all," said a voice behind us. This was another musician, and a friend of Sonny's, a coal-black, cheerful-looking man, built close to the ground. He immediately began confiding to me, at the top of his lungs, the most terrible things about Sonny, his teeth gleaming like a lighthouse and his laugh coming up out of him like the beginning of an earthquake. And it turned out that everyone at the bar knew Sonny, or almost everyone; some were musicians, working there, or nearby, or not working, some were simply hangers-on, and some were there to hear Sonny play. I was introduced to all of them and they were all very polite to me. Yet, it was clear that, for them, I was only Sonny's brother. Here, I was in Sonny's world. Or, rather: his kingdom. Here, it was not even a question that his veins bore royal blood.

They were going to play soon and Creole installed me, by myself, at a table in a dark corner. Then I watched them, Creole, and the little black man, and Sonny, and the others, while they horsed around, standing just below the bandstand. The light from the bandstand spilled just a little short of them and, watching them laughing and gesturing and moving about, I had the feeling that they, nevertheless, were being most careful not to step into that circle of light too suddenly: that if they moved into the light too suddenly, without thinking, they would perish in flame. Then, while I watched, one of them, the small, black man, moved into the light and crossed the bandstand and started fooling around with his drums. Then—being funny and being, also, extremely ceremonious—Creole took Sonny by the arm and led him to the piano. A woman's voice called Sonny's name and a few hands started clapping. And Sonny, also being funny and being ceremonious, and so touched, I think, that he could have cried, but neither hiding it nor showing it, riding it like a man, grinned, and put both hands to his heart and bowed from the waist.

Creole then went to the bass fiddle and a lean, very bright-skinned brown man jumped up on the bandstand and picked up his horn. So there they were, and the atmosphere on the bandstand and in the room began to change and tighten. Someone stepped up to the microphone and announced them. Then there were all kinds of murmurs. Some people at the bar shushed others. The waitress ran around, frantically getting in the last orders, guys and chicks got closer to each other, and the lights on the bandstand, on the quartet, turned to a kind of indigo. Then they all looked different there. Creole looked about him for the last time, as though he were making certain that all his chickens were in the coop, and then he—jumped and struck the fiddle. And there they were.

All I know about music is that not many people ever really hear it. And even then, on the rare occasions when something opens within, and the music enters, what we mainly hear, or hear corroborated, are personal, private, vanishing evocations. But the man who creates the music is hearing something else, is dealing with the roar rising from the void and imposing order on it as it hits the air. What is evoked in him, then, is of another order, more terrible because it has no words, and triumphant, too, for that same reason. And his triumph, when he triumphs, is ours. I just watched Sonny's face. His face was troubled, he was working hard, but he wasn't with it. And I had the feeling that, in a way, everyone on the bandstand was waiting for him, both waiting for him and pushing him along. But as I began to watch Creole, I realized that it was Creole who held them all back. He had them on a short rein. Up there, keeping the beat with his whole body, wailing on the fiddle, with his eyes half closed, he was listening to everything, but he was listening to Sonny. He was having a dialogue with Sonny. He wanted Sonny to leave the shoreline and strike out for the deep water. He was Sonny's witness that deep water and drowning were not the same thing—he had been there, and he knew. And he wanted Sonny to know. He was waiting for Sonny to do the things on the keys which would let Creole know that Sonny was in the water.

And, while Creole listened, Sonny moved, deep within, ex- actly like someone in torment. I had never before thought of how awful the relationship must be between the musician and his instrument. He has to fill it, this instrument, with the breath of life, his own. He has to make it do what he wants it to do. And a piano is just a piano. It's made out of so much wood and wires and little hammers and big ones, and ivory. While there's only so much you can do with it, the only way to find this out is to try; to try and make it do everything.

And Sonny hadn't been near a piano for over a year. And he wasn't on much better terms with his life, not the life that stretched before him now. He and the piano stammered, started one way, got scared, stopped; started another way, panicked, marked time, started again; then seemed to have found a direction, panicked again, got stuck. And the face I saw on Sonny I'd never seen before. Everything had been burned out of it, and, at the same time, things usually hidden were being burned in, by the fire and fury of the battle which was occurring in him up there.

Yet, watching Creole's face as they neared the end of the

first set, I had the feeling that something had happened, something I hadn't heard. Then they finished, there was scattered applause, and then, without an instant's warning, Creole started into something else, it was almost sardonic, it was *Am I Blue*. And, as though he commanded, Sonny began to play. Something began to happen. And Creole let out the reins. The dry, low, black man said something awful on the drums, Creole answered, and the drums talked back. Then the horn insisted, sweet and high, slightly detached perhaps, and Creole listened, commenting now and then, dry, and driving, beautiful and calm and old. Then they all came together again, and Sonny was part of the family again. I could tell this from his face. He seemed to have found, right there beneath his fingers, a damn brand-new piano. It seemed that he couldn't get over it. Then, for awhile, just being happy with Sonny, they seemed to be agreeing with him that brand-new pianos certainly were a gas.

Then Creole stepped forward to remind them that what they were playing was the blues. He hit something in all of them, he hit something in me, myself, and the music tightened and deepened, apprehension began to beat the air. Creole began to tell us what the blues were all about. They were not about anything very new. He and his boys up there were keeping it new, at the risk of ruin, destruction, madness, and death, in order to find new ways to make us listen. For, while the tale of how we suffer, and how we are delighted, and how we may triumph is never new, it always must be heard. There isn't any other tale to tell, it's the only light we've got in all this darkness.

And this tale, according to that face, that body, those strong hands on those strings, has another aspect in every country, and a new depth in every generation. Listen, Creole seemed to be saying, listen. Now these are Sonny's blues. He made the little black man on the drums know it, and the bright, brown man on the horn. Creole wasn't trying any longer to get Sonny in the water. He was wishing him Godspeed. Then he stepped back, very slowly, filling the air with the immense suggestion that Sonny speak for himself.

Then they all gathered around Sonny and Sonny played. Every now and again one of them seemed to say, amen. Sonny's fingers filled the air with life, his life. But that life contained so many others. And Sonny went all the way back, he really began with the spare, flat statement of the opening phrase of the song. Then he began to make it his. It was very beautiful because it wasn't hurried and it was no longer a lament. I seemed to hear with what burning he had made it his, with what burning we had yet to make it ours, how we could cease lamenting. Freedom lurked around us and I understood, at last, that he could help us to be free if we would listen, that he would never be free until we did. Yet, there was no battle in his face now. I heard what he had gone through, and would continue to go through until he came to rest in earth. He had made it his: that long line, of which we knew only Mama and Daddy. And he was giving it back, as everything must be given back, so that, passing through death, it can live forever. I saw my mother's face again, and felt, for the first time, how the stones of the road she had walked on must have bruised her feet. I saw the moonlit road where my father's brother died. And it brought something else back to me, and carried me past it. I saw my little girl again and felt Isabel's tears again, and I felt my own tears begin to rise. And I was yet aware that this was only a moment, that the world waited outside, as hungry as a tiger, and that trouble stretched above us, longer than the sky.

Then it was over. Creole and Sonny let out their breath, both soaking wet, and grinning. There was a lot of applause and some of it was real. In the dark, the girl came by and I asked her to take drinks to the bandstand. There was a long pause, while they talked up there in the indigo light and after awhile I saw the girl put a Scotch and milk on top of the piano for Sonny. He didn't seem to notice it, but just before they started playing again, he sipped from it and looked toward me, and nodded. Then he put it back on top of the piano. For me, then, as they began to play again, it glowed and shook above my brother's head like the very cup of trembling.

JOHN ALLEN DAVIDSON, JR.

The Black Sons-of-Bitches

JOHN ALLEN DAVIDSON, JR., was born and raised in the
Smoky Mountains of North Carolina, but moved out for a few
months in 1968 at the age of twenty to spend the summer in
Sweden as an "ambassador" to Sweden from the University of
North Carolina, having been selected by the Experiment in In-
ternational Living, Putney, Vermont. He is a white senior at the
University of North Carolina. His father is employed by the North
Carolina Department of Veterans' Affairs and his mother is a high-
school teachers' aide.

The leaves of the rhododendrons and mountain laurels, dark
green and slick, were covered with a mist from a spring rain.
The puddles in the dirt road reflected the tall trees along the
river bank. I could feel the cool dampness on my bare feet
and the mud oozed up between my toes. The shower had come
up quickly in the deep river valley and had gone away. I
hoped the river wouldn't be muddy at the fishing hole.

I'd been up there many times in all kinds of weather, usually alone. When I was a kid, nine or ten years old, my grand-
father used to take me up there. But that was two or three
years ago, and now I could go alone.

I sat down on my rock and stuck my hand into the moss on the bottom of my lard can. The moss came alive as I touched it, the lizards crawling and twisting, jumping up the sides of the can, nipping at each other's tails, rolling around and around and over and under the moss, sliming and slicking and oozing reptile panic as I tried to get a grip on one of them. I caught a big fat black one and held him up. He looked at me with his bulging eyes and opened his soft, toothless mouth like a sock puppet. I looked at him and said, "Now listen, you ugly black bastard, I'm going to throw you in the water on a hook and you got to make those fish want to eat you. You hear, you black bitch?"

The lizard closed his mouth and wriggled as I hooked him through one eye and out the bottom of his jaw. I threw the line in and did the only thing a fisherman can do when he has thrown the line in. I sat down on the rock and watched the water.

I don't know how much help it is to cuss your bait, but Old Man Wailey used to cuss his, and he caught more fish and bigger ones with his cane pole than all the dudes with their million-dollar reels and hand-made Wiggle, Rebel Yell, and Spoonaroonie lures. Old Wailey used to hold up one of those five-dollar Dixie Diver lures with the streamers and spinners and beads and hooks hanging down and say, "Now, your fish ain't a smart critter, but sure to God, *nobody* would eat this!" Then he'd laugh and cuss his lizard, or his nightcrawler worm; "Listen here now, you dirt-eating son-of-a-bitch . . . ," he'd say, or maybe to a cricket, "Goddamned gangly chirping spit bug! Wiggle, you bastard!"

And I like to go fishing because I can sit out here and look at the water and cuss the lizards and maybe catch fish.

Sometimes you catch fish and sometimes you don't, and usually it doesn't matter. When I walk out here Mr. Lee at the grocery store sees me coming with my pole and can and stringer and he says, "You going fishing?" and I say no and he smiles like he thinks he's funny and says, "If you see anybody that's going fishing, put me in an order for a half-dozen big-mouth bass and a string of crappies," and then he laughs and I manage to grin at him a little and walk on.

The water was muddy on down the river, but where I sat it ran deep blue and clear. The land rises up just above the fishing hole and there are a hundred springs or more that run little trickles of cold water down to where I was sitting. The line was out, and it was moving around just a little, and some people would have thought it was a fish, but I just kept calm because it was the lizard swimming around down there, prob-ably trying to find a stump or something to hide under and get away from all those fish. I always assumed there were dozens of giant fish down there in the water, watching the lizard, and I guess he would be scared. A plastic Clorox bottle floated down past me and then a milk carton. Mysteries of life, I thought to myself. Nobody lives upriver from here, and there's not a road nearby that people can travel, and there are lots of other places away back in the mountains where no-body goes very much, but anywhere you go, there is always a plastic Clorox bottle nearby somewhere. I had just learned to accept them and not worry too much about why or where they came from.

I started to pull my line in, but it was hung up, and I strug-gled and turned and walked up and down the bank, trying to get it loose. I was glad my Dad wasn't there because he would kid me about catching a "Stump Muskie" or a "Wood Bass." Finally I had to break the line and tie on a new hook. I used to have to look very carefully and hard to tie the right kind of knot to hold a hook, but now I could do it without looking. I looked instead across the little river where the willow trees bent into the water on the other side. If it had all been blue it would have looked like the Chinese scenes on my aunt's dinner plates. The other side always looks better, I thought, but I won't try to get over there like I used to, because I did once and looked back and this side looked much better. I was older and wiser than in those days.

I finished tying on the hook and stuck my hand into the squirming black mass in my lard can. I caught a lizard and was lifting him up, but he oozed out of my hand and fell back into the can. I grabbed another lizard and hooked him and was about to throw him in, but I had forgotten to cuss him, so I pulled the line up again and caught the lizard behind his head, where his neck would have been if lizards had necks. I held him up in front of my face and stared at him, eye to eye. Maybe I hadn't been hard enough on the last one, and that's why he crawled under the stump. I looked into his eyes as sternly as I could and took a deep breath, because you have to be loud as well as strict. "You ugly, crawling, flat-nosed bastard!" I yelled. "You fork-tongued, beady-eyed, un-Christian, un-American, nasty Communist!" The lizard opened his mouth and hissed defiantly as I took a deep breath for the final cuss. "You big, black son-of-a-bitch!" I yelled as loud as I could.

"Who you calling a son-of-a-bitch?" a big voice boomed from the bushes behind me. I dropped the lizard and it went in the water, but I hardly noticed. I gasped and tried to speak but I just stood there with my mouth hanging open, looking at the biggest, blackest son-of-a-bitch I'd ever seen. He stood over six feet tall and looked at me with sharp black eyes, his arms bulging at the sleeves of his T-shirt. My mouth made noises but no words came out. I was staring at him and shaking all over. "Who you calling a son-of-a-bitch?" the big, deep voice of the Negro demanded.

I smiled weakly and tried to speak again. "I-I-I was just cussing the bait, mister . . . ," I said, my voice trembling.

"What's that?" the big man asked.

"Cussing the bait," I said louder. "I didn't mean you was a big black son-of-a-bitch. . . . I mean it wasn't about you."

"*Am* I a big, black son-of-a-bitch?" he asked with a little smile, walking toward me.

"No, sir, you sure ain't."

"I'm not?" he said jumping at me and looking me right in the eyes.

"Uh, yes sir, you sure are, sir, if you say so."

"Well I do say so. I am the biggest, blackest, and the meanest son-of-a-bitch in town! Do you hear me, boy!" He pointed a giant finger at my nose.

"Yes, sir," I said, looking cross-eyed at the finger.

"And don't you forget it. And if anybody wants to know it, you tell them you been jumped at by Felix, by God, Wheeler, the biggest, blackest, meanest son-of-a-bitch around!"

He grabbed me by the shoulders and shook me as the pole on the ground beside me started to slide in. "You getting a bite there, boy, grab that pole, you got a big one." He turned me around and I picked up the pole, and pulled hard on it, but the line was tight and moving around violently in the water.

"Horse him in! Horse him in!" the big black man cried, and I pulled as hard as I could, but I couldn't bring the line in. Felix grabbed the pole and gave it a big pull and the line went taut again and cracked like a whip and a giant silver-shiny fish snapped through the air and landed at my feet. Felix put his big foot on the head of the fish and said, "Goddam big one. Big-mouth bass. Get the stringer on him, boy! He's trying to chaw up my foot." I ran to get the stringer and hook him to it through his gills. He was a magnificent fish, with flat stupid fish eyes big as quarters.

Felix held him up by the stringer and for the first time, a big wide smile crossed Felix's face. "My, my, what a big one he is."

I smiled too. "He is a big one." I looked at Felix. "I couldn't have caught him if you hadn't been here to pull him in."

"Pulling them in ain't no big thing," Felix said. "You got to get them hooked first. That's the part of it that's fishing. What did you hook this one on? Lure?"

"Nope. Just an old spring lizard."

"I been fishing up there with lizards all morning without even a bite."

"Did you cuss the bait?" I asked him, intently.

Felix laughed, "Cuss the bait! Boy, what do you mean?"

"You got to cuss the bait. You just hold up the lizard or worm or everwhat you got and just give it blue hell right in its face. And that helps a lot. Makes you feel better even when you don't catch nothing," I said confidently, looking down at the big fish like it was just average size for me, nothing special.

Felix let out a big booming laugh like a thunderstorm coming up. "Man, you superstitious as hell. You like my old lady; she thinks she can witch and conjure and dee-vine and take off warts. *You* believe all that too." He laughed and slapped his knee and then the laughter began to trail off as he looked again at the big fish. He kept looking at the fish and then he shook his head and finally was not laughing any more.

The sun was going down on the hill above the river valley, so I started to get my stuff together. "I got to be going home now, Felix," I said. "You take this old fish on home with you and cook him up."

"But man, you caught him. You was the one hooked him up. You take him home."

"Naw," I said, trying to sound casual. "I can catch a lot more real easy."

"Cussing the bait?" he said, grinning.

"Yep. Got to cuss it."

"Man, you crazy," he chuckled, "but if you can catch another one of these I reckon I'll take him and make up a supper out of him."

I picked up all my stuff and put my pole across my shoulder and turned to go down the path away from the river.

"Good-bye, Felix. I'll see you around."

"Bye, boy," he said, reaching for his fishing pole at the water's edge.

I started down the path for home, but I stopped just a little way from the fishing hole and stood behind a bush to look back at Felix. He was holding up a big, fat lizard in his hand, looking at him eye to eye.

"You big, black bastard," he said slowly and softly. "You ugly son-of-a-bitch!"

IV

FROM "BIGGER" THOMAS TO PRINCETON

RICHARD WRIGHT

How "Bigger" Was Born

RICHARD WRIGHT, whose novel *Native Son* was the pioneer work of black fiction providing stimulus and influence to so many black writers in America who have since followed him, wrote a pamphlet on his character "Bigger" for his publishers, The Story Press—Harper & Brothers, the year the book was published, 1940. Wright, who died in Paris in November 1960 at the age of fifty-two, after a full life as a writer, ex-Communist, and racial spokesman, was born in a shack in Natchez, Mississippi, in 1908. After scanty formal schooling he began to work at fifteen at odd jobs in Memphis and later in Chicago. He was on the Federal Writers' Project in the Depression, wrote for radical magazines, and in 1938 won the STORY Magazine fiction prize for a group of short stories—really novellas, or long stories—published later that year under the title *Uncle Tom's Children*. *Black Boy* and other books followed, and with his white wife, Ellen Wright, he went to live in Paris, where their two daughters attended the Lycée where André Gide, in his day, had gone to school. His ashes are in the Columbarium Père Lachaise, Paris.

The basic symbols and images that went into the writing of *Native Son* were born of my living as a Negro in the United States. "How 'Bigger' Was Born" states how those symbols and images, over a long period of time, came to exercise a certain meaningful fascination over my mind and feelings. Here are fear, hate, guilt, murder, rape, brutality, deception, misguided kindness, and fumbling helpfulness. I don't think I ever enjoyed writing anything more than this preface and it was my first attempt to account publicly for the genesis of my attitude toward life.

If I were asked what is the one, over-all symbol or image gained from my living that most nearly represents what I feel to be the essence of American life, I'd say that it was that of a man struggling mightily to free his personality from the daily and hourly encroachments of American life. Bigger represents that to me.

• • •

I am not so pretentious as to imagine that it is possible for me to account completely for my own book, *Native Son*. But I am going to try to account for as much of it as I can, the sources of it, the material that went into it, and my own years' long changing attitude toward that material.

In a fundamental sense, an imaginative novel represents the merging of two extremes; it is an intensely intimate expression on the part of a consciousness couched in terms of the most objective and commonly known events. It is at once something private and public by its very nature and texture. Confounding the author who is trying to lay his cards on the table is the dogging knowledge that his imagination is a kind of community medium of exchange: what he has read, felt, thought, seen, and remembered is translated into extensions as impersonal as a worn dollar bill.

The more closely the author thinks of why he wrote, the more he comes to regard his imagination as a kind of self-generating cement which glued his facts together, and his emotions as a kind of dark and obscure designer of those facts.

Always there is something that is just beyond the tip of the
tongue that could explain it all. Usually, he ends up by discussing something far afield, an act which incites skepticism
and suspicion in those anxious for a straight-out explanation.

Yet the author is eager to explain. But the moment he
makes the attempt his words falter, for he is confronted and
defied by the inexplicable array of his own emotions. Emotions are subjective and he can communicate them only when
he clothes them in objective guise; and how can he ever be so
arrogant as to know when he is dressing up the right emotion in the right Sunday suit? He is always left with the uneasy notion that maybe *any* objective drapery is as good as
any other for any emotion.

And the moment he does dress up an emotion, his mind is
confronted with the riddle of that "dressed up" emotion, and
he is left peering with eager dismay back into the dim reaches
of his own incommunicable life. Reluctantly, he comes to the
conclusion that to account for his book is to account for his
life, and he knows that that is impossible. Yet, some curious,
wayward motive urges him to supply the answer, for there is
the feeling that his dignity as a living being is challenged by
something within him that is not understood.

So, at the outset, I say frankly that there are phases of *Native
Son* which I shall make no attempt to account for. There are
meanings in my book of which I was not aware until they
literally spilled out upon the paper. I shall sketch the outline
of how I *consciously* came into possession of the materials that
went into *Native Son,* but there will be many things I shall
omit, not because I want to, but simply because I don't know
them.

The birth of Bigger Thomas goes back to my childhood,
and there was not just one Bigger, but many of them, more
than I could count and more than you suspect. But let me
start with the first Bigger, whom I shall call Bigger No. 1.

When I was a bareheaded, barefoot kid in Jackson, Mississippi, there was a boy who terrorized me and all of the boys I played with. If we were playing games, he would saunter up and snatch from us our balls, bats, spinning tops, and marbles. We would stand around pouting, sniffling, trying to keep back our tears, begging for our playthings. But Bigger would refuse. We never demanded that he give them back; we were afraid, and Bigger was bad. We had seen him clout boys when he was angry and we did not want to run that risk. We never recovered our toys unless we flattered him and made him feel that he was superior to us. Then, perhaps, if he felt like it, he condescended, threw them at us and then gave each of us a swift kick in the bargain, just to make us feel his utter contempt.

That was the way Bigger No. 1 lived. His life was a continuous challenge to others. At all times he *took* his way, right or wrong, and those who contradicted him had him to fight. And never was he happier than when he had someone cornered and at his mercy; it seemed that the deepest meaning of his squalid life was in him at such times.

I don't know what the fate of Bigger No. 1 was. His swaggering personality is swallowed up somewhere in the amnesia of my childhood. But I suspect that his end was violent. Anyway, he left a marked impression upon me; maybe it was because I longed secretly to be like him and was afraid. I don't know.

If I had known only one Bigger I would not have written *Native Son*. Let me call the next one Bigger No. 2; he was about seventeen and tougher than the first Bigger. Since I, too, had grown older, I was a little less afraid of him. And the hardness of this Bigger No. 2 was not directed toward me or the other Negroes, but toward the whites who ruled the South. He bought clothes and food on credit and would not pay for them. He lived in the dingy shacks of the white landlords and refused to pay rent. Of course, he had no money, but neither did we. We did without the necessities of life and starved ourselves, but he never would. When we asked him why he acted as he did, he would tell us (as though we were little children in a kindergarten) that the white folks had everything and he had nothing. Further, he would tell us that we were fools not to get what we wanted while we were alive in this world. We would listen and silently agree. We longed to believe and act as he did, but we were afraid. We were Southern Negroes and we were hungry and we wanted to live, but we were more willing to tighten our belts than risk conflict. Bigger No. 2 wanted to live and he did; he was in prison the last time I heard from him.

There was Bigger No. 3, whom the white folks called a "bad nigger." He carried his life in his hands in a literal fashion. I once worked as a ticket-taker in a Negro movie house (all movie houses in Dixie are Jim Crow; there are movies for whites and movies for blacks), and many times Bigger No. 3 came to the door and gave my arm a hard pinch and walked into the theater. Resentfully and silently, I'd nurse my bruised arm. Presently, the proprietor would come over and ask how things were going. I'd point into the darkened theater and say: "Bigger's in there." "Did he pay?" the proprietor would ask. "No, sir," I'd answer. The proprietor would pull down the corners of his lips and speak through his teeth: "We'll kill that goddamn nigger one of these days." And the episode would end right there. But later on Bigger No. 3 was killed during the days of Prohibition: while delivering liquor to a customer he was shot through the back by a white cop.

And then there was Bigger No. 4, whose only law was death. The Jim Crow laws of the South were not for him. But as he laughed and cursed and broke them, he knew that some day he'd have to pay for his freedom. His rebellious spirit made him violate all the taboos and consequently he always oscillated between moods of intense elation and depression. He was never happier than when he had outwitted some foolish custom, and he was never more melancholy than when brooding over the impossibilty of his ever being free. He had no job, for he regarded digging ditches for fifty cents a day as slavery. "I can't live on that," he would say. Ofttimes I'd find him reading a book; he would stop and in a joking, wistful, and cynical manner ape the antics of the white folks. Generally, he'd end his mimicry in a depressed state and say: "The white folks won't let us do nothing." Bigger No. 4 was sent to the asylum for the insane.

Then there was Bigger No. 5, who always rode the Jim Crow streetcars without paying and sat wherever he pleased. I remember one morning his getting into a streetcar (all streetcars in Dixie are divided into two sections: one section is for whites and is labeled—FOR WHITES; the other section is for Negroes and is labeled—FOR COLORED) and sitting in the white section. The conductor went to him and said: "Come on, nigger. Move over where you belong. Can't you read?" Bigger answered: "Naw, I can't read." The conductor flared up: "Get out of that seat!" Bigger took out his knife, opened it, held it nonchalantly in his hand, and replied: "Make me." The conductor turned red, blinked, clenched his fists, and walked away, stammering: "The goddamn scum of the earth!" A small angry conference of white men took place in the front of the car and the Negroes sitting in the Jim Crow section overheard: "That's that Bigger Thomas nigger and you'd better leave 'im alone." The Negroes experienced an intense flash of pride and the streetcar moved on its journey without incident. I don't know what happened to Bigger No. 5. But I can guess.

The Bigger Thomases were the only Negroes I know of who consistently violated the Jim Crow laws of the South and got away with it, at least for a sweet brief spell. Eventually, the whites who restricted their lives made them pay a terrible price. They were shot, hanged, maimed, lynched, and generally hounded until they were either dead or their spirits broken.

There were many variations to this behavioristic pattern. Later on I encountered other Bigger Thomases who did not react to the locked-in Black Belts with this same extremity and violence. But before I use Bigger Thomas as a springboard for the examination of milder types, I'd better indicate more precisely the nature of the environment that produced these men, or the reader will be left with the impression that they were essentially and organically bad.

In Dixie there are two worlds, the white world and the black world, and they are physically separated. There are white schools and black schools, white churches and black churches, white businesses and black businesses, white graveyards and black graveyards, and, for all I know, a white God and a black God. . . .

This separation was accomplished after the Civil War by the terror of the Ku Klux Klan, which swept the newly freed Negro through arson, pillage, and death out of the United States Senate, the House of Representatives, the many state legislatures, and out of the public, social, and economic life of the South. The motive for this assault was simple and urgent. The imperialistic tug of history had torn the Negro from his African home and had placed him ironically upon the most fertile plantation areas of the South; and, when the Negro was freed, he outnumbered the whites in many of these fertile areas. Hence, a fierce and bitter struggle took place to keep the ballot from the Negro, for had he had a chance to vote, he would have automatically controlled the richest lands of the South and with them the social, political, and economic destiny of a third of the Republic. Though the South is politically a part of America, the problem that faced her was peculiar and the struggle between the whites and the blacks after the Civil War was in essence a struggle for power, ranging over thirteen states and involving the lives of tens of millions of people.

But keeping the ballot from the Negro was not enough to hold him in check; disfranchisement had to be supplemented by a whole panoply of rules, taboos, and penalties designed not only to insure peace (complete submission), but to guarantee that no real threat would ever arise. Had the Negro lived upon a common territory, separate from the bulk of the white population, this program of oppression might not have assumed such a brutal and violent form. But this war took place between people who were neighbors, whose homes adjoined, whose farms had common boundaries. Guns and disfranchisement, therefore, were not enough to make the black neighbor keep his distance. The white neighbor decided to limit the amount of education his black neighbor could receive; decided to keep him off the police force and out of the local national guards; to segregate him residentially; to Jim Crow him in public places; to restrict his participation in the professions and jobs; and to build up a vast, dense ideology of racial superiority that would justify any act of violence taken against him to defend white dominance; and further, to condition him to hope for little and to receive that little without rebelling.

But, because the blacks were so *close* to the very civilization which sought to keep them out, because they could not *help* but react in some way to its incentives and prizes, and because the very tissue of their consciousness received its tone and timbre from the strivings of that dominant civilization, oppression spawned among them a myriad variety of reactions, reaching from outright blind rebellion to a sweet, otherworldly submissiveness.

In the main, this delicately balanced state of affairs has not greatly altered since the Civil War, save in those parts of the South which have been industrialized or urbanized. So volatile and tense are these relations that if a Negro rebels against rule and taboo, he is lynched and the reason for the lynching is usually called "rape," that catchword which has garnered such vile connotations that it can raise a mob anywhere in the South pretty quickly, even today.

Now for the variations in the Bigger Thomas pattern. Some of the Negroes living under these conditions got religion, felt that Jesus would redeem the void of living, felt that the more bitter life was in the present the happier it would be in the hereafter. Others, clinging still to that brief glimpse of post-Civil War freedom, employed a thousand ruses and stratagems of struggle to win their rights. Still others projected their hurts and longings into more naïve and mundane forms —blues, jazz, swing—and, without intellectual guidance, tried to build up a compensatory nourishment for themselves. Many labored under hot suns and then killed the restless ache with alcohol. Then there were those who strove for an education, and when they got it, enjoyed the financial fruits of it in the style of their bourgeois oppressors. Usually they went hand in hand with the powerful whites and helped to keep their groaning brothers in line, for that was the safest course of action. Those who did this called themselves "leaders." To give you an idea of how completely these "leaders" worked with those who oppressed, I can tell you that I lived the first seventeen years of my life in the South without so much as hearing of or seeing one act of rebellion from *any* Negro, save the Bigger Thomases.

But why did Bigger revolt? No explanation based upon a hard and fast rule of conduct can be given. But there were always two factors psychologically dominant in his personality. First, through some quirk of circumstance, he had become estranged from the religion and the folk culture of his race. Second, he was trying to react to and answer the call of the dominant civilization whose glitter came to him through the newspapers, magazines, radios, movies, and the mere imposing sight and sound of daily American life. In many respects his emergence as a distinct type was inevitable.

As I grew older, I became familiar with the Bigger Thomas conditioning and its numerous shadings no matter where I saw it in Negro life. It was not, as I have already said, as blatant or extreme as in the originals; but it was there, nevertheless, like an undeveloped negative.

Sometimes, in areas far removed from Mississippi, I'd hear a Negro say: "I wish I didn't have to live this way. I feel like I want to burst." Then the anger would pass; he would go back to his job and try to eke out a few pennies to support his wife and children.

Sometimes I'd hear a Negro say: "God, I wish I had a flag and a country of my own." But that mood would soon vanish and he would go his way placidly enough.

Sometimes I'd hear a Negro ex-soldier say: "What in hell did I fight in the war for? They segregated me even when I was offering my life for my country." But he, too, like the others, would soon forget, would become caught up in the tense grind of struggling for bread.

I've even heard Negroes, in moments of anger and bitterness, praise what Japan is doing in China, not because they believed in oppression (being objects of oppression themselves), but because they would suddenly sense how empty their lives were when looking at the dark faces of Japanese generals in the rotogravure supplements of the Sunday newspapers. They would dream of what it would be like to live in a country where they could forget their color and play a responsible role in the vital processes of the nation's life.

I've even heard Negroes say that maybe Hitler and Mussolini are all right; that maybe Stalin is all right. They did not say this out of any intellectual comprehension of the forces at work in the world, but because they felt that these men "did things," a phrase which is charged with more meaning than the mere words imply. There was in the back of their minds, when they said this, a wild and intense longing (wild and intense because it was suppressed!) to belong, to be identified, to feel that they were alive as other people were, to be caught up forgetfully and exultingly in the swing of events, to feel the clean, deep, organic satisfaction of doing a job in common with others.

It was not until I went to live in Chicago that I first thought seriously of writing of Bigger Thomas. Two items of my experience combined to make me aware of Bigger as a meaningful and prophetic symbol. First, being free of the daily pressure of the Dixie environment, I was able to come into possession of my own feelings. Second, my contact with the labor movement and its ideology made me see Bigger clearly and feel what he meant.

I made the discovery that Bigger Thomas was not black all the time; he was white, too, and there were literally millions of him, everywhere. The extension of my sense of the personality of Bigger was the pivot of my life; it altered the complexion of my existence. I became conscious, at first dimly, and then later on with increasing clarity and conviction, of a vast, muddied pool of human life in America. It was as though I had put on a pair of spectacles whose power was that of an x-ray enabling me to see deeper into the lives of men. Whenever I picked up a newspaper, I'd no longer feel that I was reading of the doings of whites alone (Negroes are rarely mentioned in the press unless they've committed some crime!), but of a complex struggle for life going on in my country, a struggle in which I was involved. I sensed, too, that the Southern scheme of oppression was but an appendage of a far vaster and in many respects more ruthless and impersonal commodity-profit machine.

Trade-union struggles and issues began to grow meaningful to me. The flow of goods across the seas, buoying and depressing the wages of men, held a fascination. The pronouncements of foreign governments, their policies, plans, and acts were calculated and weighed in relation to the lives of people about me. I was literally overwhelmed when, in reading the works of Russian revolutionists, I came across descriptions of the "holiday energies of the masses," "the locomotives of history," "the conditions prerequisite for revolution," and so forth. I approached all of these new revelations in the light of Bigger Thomas, his hopes, fears, and despairs; and I began to feel far-flung kinships, and sense, with fright and abashment, the possibilities of *alliances* between the American Negro and other people possessing a kindred consciousness.

As my mind extended in this general and abstract manner, it was fed with even more vivid and concrete examples of the lives of Bigger Thomas. The urban environment of Chicago, affording a more stimulating life, made the Negro Bigger Thomases react more violently than even in the South. More than ever I began to see and understand the environmental factors which made for this extreme conduct. It was not that Chicago segregated Negroes more than the South, but that Chicago had more to offer, that Chicago's physical aspect—noisy, crowded, filled with the sense of power and fulfillment—did so much more to dazzle the mind with a taunting sense of possible achievement that the segregation it did impose brought forth from Bigger a reaction more obstreperous than in the South.

So the concrete picture and the abstract linkages of relationships fed each other, each making the other more meaningful and affording my emotions an opportunity to react to them with success and understanding. The process was like a swinging pendulum, each to and fro motion throwing up its tiny bit of meaning and significance, each stroke helping to develop the dim negative which had been implanted in my mind in the South.

During this period the shadings and nuances which were filling in Bigger's picture came, not so much from Negro life, as from the lives of whites I met and grew to know. I began to sense that they had their own kind of Bigger Thomas behavioristic pattern which grew out of a more subtle and broader frustration. The waves of recurring crime, the silly fads and crazes, the quicksilver changes in public taste, the hysteria and fears—all of these had long been mysteries to me. But now I looked back of them and felt the pinch and pressure of the environment that gave them their pitch and peculiar kind of being. I began to feel with my mind the inner tensions of the people I met. I don't mean to say that I think that environment *makes* consciousness (I suppose God makes that, if there is a God), but I do say that I felt and still feel that the environment supplies the instrumentalities through which the organism expresses itself, and if that environment is warped or tranquil, the mode and manner of behavior will be affected toward deadlocking tensions or orderly fulfillment and satisfaction. . . .

I don't know if *Native Son* is a good book or a bad book. And I don't know if the book I'm working on now will be a good book or a bad book. And I really don't care. The mere writing of it will be more fun and a deeper satisfaction than any praise or blame from anybody.

I feel that I'm lucky to be alive to write novels today, when the whole world is caught in the pangs of war and change. Early American writers, Henry James and Nathaniel Hawthorne, complained bitterly about the bleakness and flatness of the American scene. But I think that if they were alive, they'd feel at home in modern America. True, we have no great church in America; our national traditions are still of such a sort that we are not wont to brag of them; and we have no army that's above the level of mercenary fighters; we have no group acceptable to the whole of our country upholding certain humane values; we have no rich symbols, no colorful rituals. We have only a money-grubbing, industrial civilization. But we do have in the Negro the embodiment of a past

tragic enough to appease the spiritual hunger of even a James;
and we have in the oppression of the Negro a shadow athwart
our national life dense and heavy enough to satisfy even the
gloomy broodings of a Hawthorne. And if Poe were alive, he
would not have to invent horror; horror would invent him.

RALPH ELLISON

The Power Line Tapped

Prologue to Invisible Man

RALPH ELLISON, born March 1, 1914, in Oklahoma City, trained from 1933 to 1936 to be a musician. But after a meeting with Richard Wright in New York, he left Tuskegee Institute and turned to writing. His first book was *Invisible Man*, which won the National Book Award in 1952. From 1955 to 1957 he was a Fellow of the American Academy in Rome. He has taught at several universities and is a member of the American Institute of Arts and Letters and a Chevalier in the Order of Arts and Letters of France. He is married and lives in New York City and in Massachusetts. Thirteen years after *Invisible Man* was published, a poll of literary critics, authors, and editors considered the novel "the most distinguished single work published in America in the last twenty years." Appointed in 1971 to be Albert Schweitzer Professor in the Humanities at New York University, he outlined his plan for courses with the comment that "In the United States, European cultural styles, techniques and traditions have come into ceaseless contact with the imagination of Negro Americans who have been in the unique position of being inside the society and yet outside, thus allowing for a freedom of artistic improvisation which has been crucial in defining the American experience artistically."

I am an invisible man. No, I am not a spook like those who haunted Edgar Allan Poe; nor am I one of your Hollywood-movie ectoplasms. I am a man of substance, of flesh and bone, fiber and liquids—and I might even be said to possess a mind. I am invisible, understand, simply because people refuse to see me. Like the bodiless heads you see sometimes in circus sideshows, it is as though I have been surrounded by mirrors of hard, distorting glass. When they approach me they see only my surroundings, themselves, or figments of their imagination—indeed, everything and anything except me.

Nor is my invisibility exactly a matter of a bio-chemical accident to my epidermis. That invisibility to which I refer occurs because of a peculiar disposition of the eyes of those with whom I come in contact. A matter of the construction of their *inner* eyes, those eyes with which they look through their physical eyes upon reality. I am not complaining, nor am I protesting either. It is sometimes advantageous to be unseen, although it is most often rather wearing on the nerves. Then too, you're constantly being bumped against by those of poor vision. Or again, you often doubt if you really exist. You wonder whether you aren't simply a phantom in other people's minds. Say, a figure in a nightmare which the sleeper tries with all his strength to destroy. It's when you feel like this that, out of resentment, you begin to bump people back. And, let me confess, you feel that way most of the time. You ache with the need to convince yourself that you do exist in the real world, that you're a part of all the sound and anguish, and you strike out with your fists, you curse and you swear to make them recognize you. And, alas, it's seldom successful.

One night I accidentally bumped into a man, and perhaps because of the near darkness he saw me and called me an insulting name. I sprang at him, seized his coat lapels and demanded that he apologize. He was a tall blond man, and as my face came close to his he looked insolently out of his blue eyes and cursed me, his breath hot in my face as he struggled. I pulled his chin down sharp upon the crown of my head, butting him as I had seen the West Indians do, and I felt his flesh tear and the blood gush out, and I yelled, "Apologize! Apologize!" But he continued to curse and struggle, and I butted him again and again until he went down heavily, on his knees, profusely bleeding. I kicked him repeatedly, in a frenzy because he still uttered insults though his lips were frothy with blood. Oh yes, I kicked him! And in my outrage I got out my knife and prepared to slit his throat, right there beneath the lamplight in the deserted street, holding him by the collar with one hand, and opening the knife with my teeth—when it occurred to me that the man had not *seen* me, actually; that he, as far as he knew, was in the midst of a walking nightmare! And I stopped the blade, slicing the air as I pushed him away, letting him fall back to the street. I stared at him hard as the lights of a car stabbed through the darkness. He lay there, moaning on the asphalt; a man almost killed by a phantom. It unnerved me. I was both disgusted and ashamed. I was like a drunken man myself, wavering about on weakened legs. Then I was amused. Something in this man's thick head had sprung out and beaten him within an inch of his life. I began to laugh at this crazy discovery. Would he have awakened at the point of death? Would Death himself have freed him for wakeful living? But I didn't linger. I ran away into the dark, laughing so hard I feared I might rupture myself. The next day I saw his picture in the *Daily News,* beneath a caption stating that he had been "mugged." Poor fool, poor blind fool, I thought with sincere compassion, mugged by an invisible man!

Most of the time (although I do not choose as I once did to deny the violence of my days by ignoring it) I am not so overtly violent. I remember that I am invisible and walk softly so as not to awaken the sleeping ones. Sometimes it is best not to awaken them; there are few things in the world as dangerous as sleepwalkers. I learned in time though that it is possible to carry on a fight against them without their realizing it. For instance, I have been carrying on a fight with Monopolated Light & Power for some time now. I use their service and pay them nothing at all, and they don't know it. Oh, they suspect that power is being drained off, but they don't know where. All they know is that according to the master meter back there in their power station a hell of a lot of free current is disappearing somewhere into the jungle of Harlem. The joke, of course, is that I don't live in Harlem but in a border area. Several years ago (before I discovered the advantage of being invisible) I went through the routine process of buying service and paying their outrageous rates. But no more. I gave up all that, along with my apartment, and my old way of life: That way based upon the fallacious assumption that I, like other men, was visible. Now, aware of my invisibility, I live rent-free in a building rented strictly to whites, in a section of the basement that was shut off and forgotten during the nineteenth century, which I discovered when I was trying to escape in the night from Ras the Destroyer. But that's getting too far ahead of the story, almost to the end, although the end is in the beginning and lies far ahead.

The point now is that I found a home—or a hole in the ground, as you will. Now don't jump to the conclusion that because I call my home a "hole" it is damp and cold like a grave; there are cold holes and warm holes. Mine is a warm hole. And remember, a bear retires to his hole for the winter and lives until spring; then he comes strolling out like the Easter chick breaking from its shell. I say all this to assure you that it is incorrect to assume that, because I'm invisible and live in a hole, I am dead. I am neither dead nor in a state of suspended animation. Call me Jack-the-Bear, for I am in a state of hibernation.

My hole is warm and full of light. Yes, *full* of light. I doubt if there is a brighter spot in all New York than this hole of mine, and I do not exclude Broadway. Or the Empire State Building on a photographer's dream night. But that is taking advantage of you. Those two spots are among the darkest of our whole civilization—pardon me, our whole *culture* (an important distinction, I've heard)—which might sound like a hoax, or a contradiction, but that (by contradiction, I mean) is how the world moves: Not like an arrow, but a boomerang. (Beware of those who speak of the *spiral* of history; they are preparing a boomerang. Keep a steel helmet handy.) I know; I have been boomeranged across my head so much that I now can see the darkness of lightness. And I love light. Perhaps you'll think it strange that an invisible man should need light, desire light, love light. But maybe it is exactly because I *am* invisible. Light confirms my reality, gives birth to my form. A beautiful girl once told me of a recurring nightmare in which she lay in the center of a large dark room and felt her face expand until it filled the whole room, becoming a formless mass while her eyes ran in bilious jelly up the chimney. And so it is with me. Without light I am not only invisible, but formless as well; and to be unaware of one's form is to live a death. I myself, after existing some twenty years, did not become alive until I discovered my invisibility.

That is why I fight my battle with Monopolated Light & Power. The deeper reason, I mean: It allows me to feel my vital aliveness. I also fight them for taking so much of my money before I learned to protect myself. In my hole in the basement there are exactly 1,369 lights. I've wired the entire ceiling, every inch of it. And not with fluorescent bulbs, but with the older, more-expensive-to-operate kind, the filament type. An act of sabotage, you know. I've already begun to wire the wall. A junk man I know, a man of vision, has supplied me with wire and sockets. Nothing, storm or flood, must get in the way of our need for light and ever more and brighter light. The truth is the light and light is the truth. When I finish all four walls, then I'll start on the floor. Just how that will go, I don't know. Yet when you have lived invisible as long as I have you develop a certain ingenuity. I'll solve the problem. And maybe I'll invent a gadget to place my coffee-pot on the fire while I lie in bed, and even invent a gadget to warm my bed—like the fellow I saw in one of the picture magazines who made himself a gadget to warm his shoes! Though invisible, I am in the great American tradition of tinkers. That makes me kin to Ford, Edison and Franklin. Call me, since I have a theory and a concept, a "thinker-tinker." Yes, I'll warm my shoes; they need it, they're usually full of holes. I'll do that and more.

Now I have one radio-phonograph; I plan to have five. There is a certain acoustical deadness in my hole, and when I have music I want to *feel* its vibration, not only with my ear but with my whole body. I'd like to hear five recordings of Louis Armstrong playing and singing "What Did I Do to Be so Black and Blue"—all at the same time. Sometimes now I listen to Louis while I have my favorite dessert of vanilla ice cream and sloe gin. I pour the red liquid over the white mound, watching it glisten and the vapor rising as Louis bends that military instrument into a beam of lyrical sound. Perhaps I like Louis Armstrong because he's made poetry out of being invisible. I think it must be because he's unaware that he *is* invisible. And my own grasp of invisibility aids me to understand his music. Once when I asked for a cigarette, some jokers gave me a reefer, which I lighted when I got home and sat listening to my phonograph. It was a strange evening. Invisibility, let me explain, gives one a slightly differ-ent sense of time, you're never quite on the beat. Sometimes you're ahead and sometimes behind. Instead of the swift and imperceptible flowing of time, you are aware of its nodes, those points where time stands still or from which it leaps ahead. And you slip into the breaks and look around. That's what you hear vaguely in Louis' music.

Once I saw a prizefighter boxing a yokel. The fighter was swift and amazingly scientific. His body was one violent flow of rapid rhythmic action. He hit the yokel a hundred times while the yokel held up his arms in stunned surprise. But suddenly the yokel, rolling about in the gale of boxing gloves, struck one blow and knocked science, speed and footwork as cold as a well-digger's posterior. The smart money hit the canvas. The long shot got the nod. The yokel had simply stepped inside of his opponent's sense of time. So under the spell of the reefer I discovered a new analytical way of listening to music. The unheard sounds came through, and each melodic line existed of itself, stood out clearly from all the rest, said its piece, and waited patiently for the other voices to speak. That night I found myself hearing not only in time, but in space as well. I not only entered the music but descended, like Dante, into its depths. And *heneath the swiftness of the hot tempo there was a slower tempo and a cave and I entered it and looked around and heard an old woman singing a spiritual as full of Weltschmerz as flamenco, and beneath that lay a still lower level on which I saw a beautiful girl the color of ivory pleading in a voice like my mother's as she stood before a group of slave owners who bid for her naked body, and below that I found a lower level and a more rapid tempo and I heard someone shout:*

"Brothers and sisters, my text this morning is the 'Blackness of Blackness.' "

And a congregation of voices answered: "That blackness is most black, brother, most black . . ."

"In the beginning . . ."

"At the very start," they cried.

". . . there was blackness . . ."

"Preach it . . ."

". . . and the sun . . ."
"The sun, Lawd . . ."
". . . was bloody red . . ."
"Red . . ."
"Now black is . . ." the preacher shouted.
"Bloody . . ."
"I said black is . . ."
"Preach it, brother . . ."
". . . an' black ain't . . ."
"Red, Lawd, red: He said it's red!"
"Amen, brother . . ."
"Black will git you . . ."
"Yes, it will . . ."
". . . an' black won't . . ."
"Naw, it won't!"
"It do . . ."
"It do, Lawd . . ."
". . . an' it don't."
"Halleluiah . . ."
". . . It'll put you, glory, glory, Oh my Lawd, in the WHALE'S
BELLY.*"*
"Preach it, dear brother . . ."
". . . an' make you tempt . . ."
"Good God a-mighty!"
"Old Aunt Nelly!"
"Black will make you . . ."
"Black . . ."
". . . or black will un-make you."
"Ain't it the truth, Lawd?"

And at that point a voice of trombone timbre screamed at me, "Git out of here, you fool! Is you ready to commit treason?"

And I tore myself away, hearing the old singer of spirituals moaning, "Go curse your God, boy, and die."

I stopped and questioned her, asked her what was wrong.

"I dearly loved my master, son," she said.

"You should have hated him," I said.

"He gave me several sons," she said, "and because I loved my sons I learned to love their father though I hated him too."

"I too have become acquainted with ambivalence," I said. "That's why I'm here."

"What's that?"

"Nothing, a word that doesn't explain it. Why do you moan?"

"I moan this way 'cause he's dead," she said.

"Then tell me, who is that laughing upstairs?"

"Them's my sons. They glad."

"Yes, I can understand that too," I said.

"I laughs too, but I moans too. He promised to set us free but he never could bring hisself to do it. Still I loved him . . ."

"Loved him? You mean . . ."

"Oh yes, but I loved something else even more."

"What more?"

"Freedom."

"Freedom," I said. "Maybe freedom lies in hating."

"Naw, son, it's in loving. I loved him and give him the poison and he withered away like a frost-bit apple. Them boys woulda tore him to pieces with they homemake knives."

"A mistake was made somewhere," I said, "I'm confused." And I wished to say other things, but the laughter upstairs became too loud and moan-like for me and I tried to break out of it, but I couldn't. Just as I was leaving I felt an urgent desire to ask her what freedom was and went back. She sat with her head in her hands, moaning softly; her leather-brown face was filled with sadness.

"Old woman, what is this freedom you love so well?" I asked around a corner of my mind.

She looked surprised, then thoughtful, then baffled. "I done forgot, son. It's all mixed up. First I think it's one thing, then I think it's another. It gits my head to spinning. I guess now it ain't nothing but knowing how to say what I got up in my head. But it's a hard job, son. Too much is done happen to me in too short a time. Hit's like I have a fever. Ever' time I starts to walk my head gits to swirling and I falls down. Or if it ain't that, it's the boys; they gits to laughing and wants to kill up the white folks. They's bitter, that's what they is . . ."

"But what about freedom?"

"Leave me 'lone, boy; my head aches!"

I left her, feeling dizzy myself. I didn't get far.

Suddenly one of the sons, a big fellow six feet tall, appeared out of nowhere and struck me with his fist.

"What's the matter, man?" I cried.

"You made Ma cry!"

"But how?" I said, dodging a blow.

"Askin' her them questions, that's how. Git outa here and stay, and next time you got questions like that, ask yourself!"

He held me in a grip like cold stone, his fingers fastening upon my windpipe until I thought I would suffocate before he finally allowed me to go. I stumbled about dazed, the music beating hysterically in my ears. It was dark. My head cleared and I wandered down a dark narrow passage, thinking I heard his footsteps hurrying behind me. I was sore, and into my being had come a profound craving for tranquility, for peace and quiet, a state I felt I could never achieve. For one thing, the trumpet was blaring and the rhythm was too hectic. A tom-tom beating like heart-thuds began drowning out the trumpet, filling my ears. I longed for water and I heard it rushing through the cold mains my fingers touched as I felt my way, but I couldn't stop to search because of the footsteps behind me.

"Hey, Ras," I called. "Is it you, Destroyer? Rinehart?"

No answer, only the rhythmic foosteps behind me. Once I tried crossing the road, but a speeding machine struck me, scraping the skin from my leg as it roared past.

Then somehow I came out of it, ascending hastily from this underworld of sound to hear Louis Armstrong innocently asking,

> *What did I do*
> *To be so black*
> *And blue?*

At first I was afraid; this familiar music had demanded action, the kind of which I was incapable, and yet had I lingered there beneath the surface I might have attempted to act. Nevertheless, I know now that few really listen to this music. I sat on the chair's edge in a soaking sweat, as though each of my 1,369 bulbs had every one become a klieg light in an individual setting for a third degree with Ras and Rinehart in charge. It was exhausting—as though I had held my breath continuously for an hour under the terrifying serenity that comes from days of intense hunger. And yet, it was a strangely satisfying experience for an invisible man to hear the silence of sound. I had discovered unrecognized compulsions of my being—even though I could not answer "yes" to their promptings. I haven't smoked a reefer since, however; not because they're illegal, but because to *see* around corners is enough (that is not unusual when you are invisible). But to hear around them is too much; it inhibits action. And despite Brother Jack and all that sad, lost period of the Brotherhood, I believe in nothing if not in action.

Please, a definition: A hibernation is a covert preparation for a more overt action.

Besides, the drug destroys one's sense of time completely. If that happened, I might forget to dodge some bright morning and some cluck would run me down with an orange and yellow street car, or a bilious bus! Or I might forget to leave my hole when the moment for action presents itself.

Meanwhile I enjoy my life with the compliments of Monopolated Light & Power. Since you never recognize me even when in closest contact with me, and since, no doubt, you'll hardly believe that I exist, it won't matter if you know that I tapped a power line leading into the building and ran it into my hole in the ground. Before that I lived in the darkness into which I was chased, but now I see. I've illuminated the blackness of my invisibility—and vice versa. And so I play the invisible music of my isolation. The last statement doesn't seem just right, does it? But it is; you hear this music simply because music is heard and seldom seen, except by musicians. Could this compulsion to put invisibility down in black and white be thus an urge to make music of invisibility? But I am an orator, a rabble rouser—Am? I *was*, and perhaps shall be again. Who knows? All sickness is not unto death, neither is invisibility.

I can hear you say, "What a horrible, irresponsible bastard!" And you're right. I leap to agree with you. I am one of the most irresponsible beings that ever lived. Irresponsibility is part of my invisibility; any way you face it, it is a denial. But to whom can I be responsible, and why should I be, when you refuse to see me? And wait until I reveal how truly irresponsible I am. Responsibility rests upon recognition, and recognition is a form of agreement. Take the man whom I almost killed: Who was responsible for that near murder—I? I don't think so, and I refuse it. I won't buy it. You can't give it to me. *He* bumped *me, he* insulted *me*. Shouldn't he, for his own personal safety, have recognized my hysteria, my "danger potential"? He, let us say, was lost in a dream world. But didn't *he* control that dream world—which, alas, is only too real!—and didn't *he* rule me out of it? And if he had yelled for a policeman, wouldn't *I* have been taken for the offending one? Yes, yes, yes! Let me agree with you, I was the irresponsible one; for I should have used my knife to protect the higher interests of society. Some day that kind of foolishness will cause us tragic trouble. All dreamers and sleepwalkers must pay the price, and even the invisible victim is responsible for the fate of all. But I shirked that responsibility; I became too snarled in the incompatible notions that buzzed within my brain. I was a coward . . .

But what did *I* do to be so blue? Bear with me.

EDWARD RIVERA

In Black Turf

EDWARD RIVERA is a Puerto Rican-born writer who, since the age of seven, has lived in New York City's Spanish Harlem. He attended a parochial grammar school for seven years, then public school, later working at odd jobs and attending the Art Students League and Pratt Institute at night. After five months with the U.S. Army in Heidelberg, Germany, he returned to New York, was graduated from City College in 1967, and began private-school teaching. He received a Master of Fine Arts degree from Columbia University in 1969, after studying with the writer Jean Stafford, and others, and since then has been teaching English in the SEEK program at the College of the City of New York. He is married and lives on the upper West Side of Manahattan. A story of his won him a first prize in the STORY College Creative Awards Contest among contestants from all over the United States and Canada. "In Black Turf" is here published for the first time.

———————

The day before, I had made up my mind to cut Sunday mass for the fourth straight week. In parochial school, the Christian Brothers gave you no choice about religious matters. But I was out of their clutches now, and there was no punishment to worry about if I got to mass late, or if I didn't get there at all. Giving up the Holy Ghost and the rest of the religious business was a serious decision, the most serious I'd made to date. I was beginning to feel like a real grown-up. But because it was a critical decision, I couldn't bring myself to make it all at once; growing up, I knew, was a slow process, and I was in no hurry to become a full-grown man before my time. I decided to spend Sunday morning strolling with my buddy Panna in the wilds of Central Park.

At 9:45, fifteen minutes before the young people's mass began, I came down and found Panna sitting on the steps of my stoop. His real name was Teodoro, but to his friends he was "Panna," because he called everyone he liked "Partner." He'd picked up the word from cowboy movies. He was small, undernourished, and about as black a Puerto Rican as I'd ever known. I don't think he had a drop of white blood in him. Half his ancestors must have been shipped to the Caribbean from Africa, and the other half, the Indian side of his family tree, must have been waiting for them on the island long before Ponce de Leon got there. He had an immense head topped with an abundance of thick, unwashed kinky hair, and tiny rotting teeth. People sometimes took him for an American black, but he was as Puerto Rican as I was. Maybe more so, because at least he didn't try to deny his origins by getting rid of his East Harlem accent.

My own accent was closer, though not really close, to the speech of American disc jockeys and TV-radio detergent pushers. This was a result of having spent eight submissive years under the influence of the hard-driving Christian Brothers, who subscribed as faithfully to the myth of the American melting pot as they did to their vows of poverty, chastity, and obedience. Nobody had ever taken me for someone whose veins might contain Negro or Arab or Caribbean Indian blood. I was too light-skinned for that. On various occasions I had been mistaken for a Jew, an Italian, a Greek, even a Hungarian; and each time I had come away feeling secretly proud

of myself for having disguised my Spick accent, and with it
my lineage. I could almost feel myself melting smoothly and
evenly into the great American pot.

The north end of Central Park was right across from our
block. Our goal was to scout around for girls who might be
willing to join us in the bushes. This was a favorite fantasy
of ours. It gave our excursions in the Park a specific purpose,
and it satisfied one part of a favorite daydream of mine: saving a nice-looking girl from rape. She could be a Puerto Rican
dusky, or an American blonde, it didn't matter, as long as she
was equipped with big, plump boobs and a nice round rump.

The time would be early evening, just as the sun was about
to drop between the tall tenements of Central Park West; the
place, a clump of bushes near the baseball diamonds. I would
arrive on the scene just as the pervert, a big, muscular black
man with a shaved head, was tearing off her pink polka-dot
panties with one hand and unzipping his fly with the other.
With a baseball bat or a sawed-off broomstick I just happened
to be carrying, I would splinter the lecher's skull. By risking
my life for the poor girl's chastity, I'd be putting her in my
debt. To remind her of this would be crude; but she'd know
it, and she would want to repay me in kind. At this juncture
I would stoop to pick up her panties, and when I offered them
to her, she would take my hand and lead me into the bush for
a satisfactory settlement. Afterward, holding hands, we would
walk off toward Loui's Luncheonette on the corner of 108th
and Fifth. After a thick malted (two straws, one glass), she'd
leave me her name, address, and phone number, and an open
invitation to come and see her whenever I had time.

What usually happened, whenever a girl saw Panna and me
approaching her with a look of undisguised lust in our eyes,
was that she would clutch her purse to her chest, turn
abruptly, and scamper off for the nearest exit. Copping a girl's
drawers in that park was even more difficult than stealing a
squirrel's hoard of nuts, but we liked to pretend it was easy.

The only people in the Park at ten in the morning were mounted cops on their big, brown, huge-assed horses, perverts like ourselves, and members of the Puerto Rican Baseball League. At the baseball diamonds we watched one inning that lasted over a half hour (the beer-bellied pitchers couldn't get the ball over the plate, which wouldn't have mattered much since catcher and batters were too sleepy to see the ball; and the fielders, undernourished and weighted down with heavy, loose-fitting uniforms, couldn't catch up with fly balls and ground balls), and when we decided that Puerto Rican baseball had no future as a national pastime, we headed north toward the black people's section of Central Park.

Acros the bicycle path, on a grassy area where Puerto Rican families picnicked on sunny weekends, we looked for empty beer and soda bottles. If we found enough empties, we could get them "changed" at Miguel's *bodega* on Madison and head for the movies or Loui's Luncheonette. All we found was a bag of dried chicken bones crawling with ants, and a used condom. Panna picked up the condom with a crooked stick and came at me swishing it like a secondhand sword inches from my face. I tore off down the sloped picnic grounds and stumbled to a halt in front of a marshy stream that divided "our" section of the Park from the black people's section.

Like a scrawny, scraggly blackbird, Panna stumbled after me and jabbed playfully at my chest with his stick and condom.

I stooped and picked up a wet, scummy stone. "Don't touch me with that thing, Mother-fo!" I warned him, taking a full windup.

Thrown off guard by my unexpected counterattack, he halted. He was a few inches smaller than me and about half as strong. His head, with its thick tangle of kinky hair, was attached to his thin neck like a bowling ball to a skinny long finger; it swayed uneasily from side to side on its precarious stem. His round, coarse face, dotted here and there with pimples, made him look about five year older than his actual age. He was fourteen, my age, but already half his teeth were hopelessly rotting. No amount of dental work could save them. One had been knocked out in a fight with his older brother. I don't think he'd ever seen a dentist. Maybe that was why girls took off when they saw us coming.

"All right," he said, thrusting his head forward and closing in on me with quick little hops, like a hungry starling advancing on a worm. "Drop the rock or I'll plug you with my fuckin' scumbag."

Stabbed helpless with laughter, I lurched backward. He opened his mouth wide and grinned at me, the evil guy stalking his helpless victim. The sight of his putrid teeth, with the black, blank gap in the middle, disarmed me completely. I slipped on the slimy grass, dropped the rock and tried to fall forward. But I splashed into the stream, flat on my ass.

Panna hurled himself to the ground in convulsions.

"See what you did?" I screamed, already worrying about what my mother would say when she saw what I'd done to my best pair of pants. Panna was too busy laughing to hear me.

"You black fuck!" I snapped. "You think it's funny, huh?"

Cut short by my sharp slur, he suddenly became silent. He hurled the stick in the stream while I got to my feet. I was completely soaked from the waist down. Green slime dripped from my Sunday pants and clung to my recently polished shoes.

"Don't call me that shit, Mannie."

I stood up and slapped at my pants. "Well, you asked for it. Look what the hell you did."

"Just don't call me that," he said, biting his big lower lip. "I don't like nobody calling me a black fuck, understand?"

"Just watch it next time," I said, half-sorry I had insulted him.

He bent his head a little and stared at my throat, as if

readying himself for a savage fight. "You better say you're sorry, Mannie."

I was sure I could take him, if he wanted a fight, but the thought of fighting him was as repulsive to me as the condom he had just threatened to stick in my face. He was my "panna."

"All right, forget it, okay?" I had to raise my voice so he wouldn't think I was backing down.

He raised his dark eyes to my face. "So say you're sorry."

"All right, shit. I'm sorry. You satisfied?"

He jerked his shoulders and started to walk off alongside the shallow stream, kicking at the grass with his sneakers.

I followed him.

"Hey, man," I said, "You heard me say I'm sorry, right?"

"Yeah, I heard you." He was staring at the ground.

I walked in front of him and faced him. He stopped abruptly, tilted his large head and scanned me with a scowl. His hands were clenched tight at his sides.

"I don't wanna fight witchu, Panna," I told him in a soft, nervous voice.

"So whatchu want then?"

"Say you're sorry."

"For *what?*"

I slapped my sopping pants. "You made me fall in the water."

He stepped to the side and shrugged his shoulders. If we got into a fight, the only thing I'd have to guard against was his head. He could crack my jaw with one butt of that solid bowling ball.

"Look man," he said, lifting his voice for emphasis, "I didn't touch you."

"You stuck that dirty scumbag in my face, Panna. It was *your* fault."

He shook his head and produced a slow-motion smirk. "Look, Mannie, I don't wanna argue witchu."

"So say it."

He hesitated, squinting at the stream. Like me, he wasn't used to apologizing. It was a sign of weakness, a retreat. "Okay," he said finally, in a weak voice, "I'm sorry you got wet. All right?"

"Forget it," I said, satisfied. "It was my fault, too."

We continued walking, quietly, keeping the distance between us a little wider than usual. I was afraid he'd hold a lifetime grudge against me for the insult. What I couldn't understand was that he and his older brother, who was a little lighter than he was, were always calling each other names like "nigger" and "spook" whenever they got into an argument, and never thought anything about it. With them it was a game.

What the hell was he being so sensitive about all of a sudden? We spoke the same language, lived in the same block, and shared the same friends. Maybe he'd had another fight with his brother earlier that morning and was taking it out on me. I should have kicked his ass when he poked the condom in my face.

The stream dipped and disappeared under a rise of large, jagged rocks which formed a natural bridge to the "black" part of the Park. People got killed there, I'd heard, women raped. It was a hilly area where the vegetation grew thicker than anywhere else in the Park, and for that reason, darker. People from our side of the Park, from our neighborhood, stayed away from that section. It was strictly for blacks. I seldom ventured there, never on my own.

When we got to within a few feet of the stone bridge, Panna broke into a quick run and leaped onto a rock.

"Where you going?" I asked.

"Thataway, partnuh." He pointed to the other side of the stream.

I was pleased at his rapid change of mood. "Whatchu going there for?"

"Whatchu mean what I'm going there for? Ain't you coming?"

I stared at a dragonfly hovering over the little stream below the rocks. "What for, man?"

He dropped his hands and shrugged. "I don't know. Maybe we can find some empties."

I grinned. "Or some broads."

He grinned back. "Or some scumbags."

The dragonfly was swooping and circling less than an inch over the water, searching for insects.

"Whatsa matter, Mannie, you scared?"

"Whatchu mean scared?" I leaped up on the rock next to him.

"So let's go."

I let him lead the way.

On the other side of the stream, we had to climb a steep hill on all fours; the ground was damp and loose, even though it hadn't rained in over a week. Every time I grabbed a small plant for support, it came up by the roots and I would slide back a foot or more. I was wearing my Sunday shoes, leather soled and tight fitting. Panna was wearing sneakers and had less trouble climbing. As long as he didn't tilt his huge head backward, he was all right.

When I got to the top, minutes after he did, he was staring at an old fortress a short way off to our left.

"Hey, you know," he said, shielding his eyes with one hand and pointing with the other, "George Washington fought in there." He spoke like a grammar-school teacher hammering home a startling fact to his students.

"Bullshit," I panted.

"No shit, Mannie. He whipped them redcoats right there in that fuckin' fort. How you like that?"

"Who told you that?"

He clucked his tongue at my ignorance. "Whatchu mean who told me that? I been here before lots of times."

"No you ain't."

He picked up a small stone and pitched it at the fortress. "Man, don't tell me what I know. *Every*body knows it. Where you been at?"

"You're jiving me."

"I'll betchu."

"You ain't got no money."

"That's all right," he said, "I can pay you back tomorrow when I get some bread."

"Forget it," I said, uninterested. "I don't wanna take your bread."

He was always broke. His spending money came mostly from empties or from tips he got delivering groceries on Saturdays. But he always managed to spend it all on candy and the movies before the day was out, because if he didn't, he said, his big brother would go through his pockets at night and steal it.

He turned his head toward the fortress. "You *know* I'm right."

"You got a way to prove it?"

"Damn right," he said. "Come on, I'll show you." He trotted off toward the old fort.

I hesitated. "I ain't going in there, Panna."

"What the hell you scared of, partnuh?"

I followed him down some rocks and onto a narrow dirt path thick with weeds. Below I could hear the traffic going in both directions along 110th Street.

We squeezed through a small opening that had been knocked into the stone wall like the holes in playground fences, only this one must have been smashed with a sledge hammer. Inside there was nothing but tall grass, weeds, a few bushes, and a strong smell of human shit. Not far from where I stood, close to the wall, someone had dropped a sizable load; flies, hundreds of them, buzzed around it like maggots. In the center of the fortress, rising from a jungle of grass, a shredded, faded American flag flapped on a thin white pole like wash on the line.

"C'mon," Panna called. He was several feet ahead of me, up to his neck in grass.

"Fuck you," I said. "I'm staying right here. There ain't nothing in there but shit."

"There's an old, whatchamacallit, plaque, around here someplace, Mannie."

I could just about make out his head now, a huge, black, kinky-haired ball rolling slowly along the grass, like an immense sunflower minus the petals.

"That's where it says George Washington whipped the redcoats right here in this spot."

"All you're gonna find in there is a big lump of shit," I called. "There ain't no plaque. You'll fall in a hole and break your leg. Come on, let's go back."

I was getting hungry. The mass I'd missed should have been over long ago, and I was anxious to change into dry clothes.

I leaned against the stone wall and waited for him to emerge. "Panna," I yelled, "let's go, man. Forget the fuckin' plaque. George Washington never came near this place, you jerk."

A pebble bounced off my head. I looked up and saw one, two, then four black faces. They were standing and sitting on the ledge of the wall, staring down at me. The sun was almost directly overhead now, and I had to squint and shield my eyes to see them clearly.

"Whatchu doin' in there, white boy?" the tallest of the four said. He was about six feet, and he was tapping the wall with the heels of his sneakers and cracking his knuckles. I moved back a few steps for a better look. They were all very black, blacker than Panna even; the noon sun gave their faces a smooth, rubbery look.

"I'm waiting for my friend," I said. My legs began to sag

slightly below the knees. I couldn't have run more than a few yards before they caught up with me. But even a speed-runner didn't stand a chance in that trap.

"Where your friend at?" another one asked. He wasn't much taller than me, but he had the arm muscles of a professional athlete or a truck loader in the garment district. His pants were the color of orange soda; he was holding a stickball bat out in front of him like a fishing pole.

I pointed toward the tall grass. "He's in there." I realized my mistake immediately. Panna had probably spotted them before I did; that was why he hadn't answered when I called him.

When I squinted up again, only one of them was sitting on the wall. He was the smallest, an inch or two smaller than Panna. A blue beret, spattered with dust, was tilted dramatically to one side of his head.

"Don't move, motherfucker," he said.

I pressed my back to the wall and looked for a possible way out; the hole I'd come in through was impassable: they would be coming in any second. There was nothing but grass, the long, white flagpole, and the pile of human shit with its frantic flies. If there was an exit, it would have to be across the field, on the other side. If Panna had found it, he must have escaped. That bastard, I thought. It was all his fault, and now he had copped out on me.

The three came in through the hole in the wall one at a time and surrounded me. I stared at the ground, waiting stiffly for the first blow and regretting that I didn't have a gun on me and that I had never taken judo lessons.

The six-foot one stepped up to me and looked down for a few seconds. I listened to the roar of a crosstown bus far away.

"Where's your buddy, stud?"

"I told you," I said, "he's in there somewhere."

"What he doin' there?"

"He's looking for a plaque."

The one with orange-colored pants stroked the grass with his stickball bat. "A what?"

"A plaque," I said. "My friend says there's this plaque in here that says George Washington fought the redcoats here during the Ci-Ci-Civil War."

They looked at each other, shook their heads, smiled and broke into laughter. One of them slapped the side of his head and came down on his knees, almost touching the ground. He had on a sleeveless white sweat shirt with "Clinton High School" lettered across the chest.

"Man, you must be outta your fuckin' skull," he said to me when he had straightened out. "Old Georgie Washington never came near this fuckin' place."

"He puttin' us on," the tall one said.

"I ain't puttin' you on," I insisted, failing to see what was so funny. "That's what my friend said."

The one in orange pants snapped his fingers. "Maybe he mean *Booker T.* Washington." He stepped up to me and tapped me on the shoulder with his stick. "You tell your friend to come on out here 'fore I go in there and get him out myself."

I hesitated.

"You better do like he say, son," the one from Clinton said. "He ain't playing witchu."

I cleared my throat. The strong sun was beginning to give me a headache. "Hey, Panna," I called. "C'mere, man."

No answer.

They looked at me with skeptical frowns. I could see they thought I had lied to them about Panna and the plaque.

I called again. "Hey, Panna, man, come on out!"

Nothing. I was sure he was back in the block, or in his house stuffing himself with peanut-butter sandwiches and very likely enjoying the thought that I was getting just what I deserved for having called him a black fuck.

The one with the stick stared off in the direction of the flagpole. "Man," he said, "if I don't find your friend in there, I'm gonna crack your hea-ud with this stick, dig?" In a few seconds he had disappeared. I could hear his stick stroking the grass.

"I didn't do nothing," I said to the tall one.

"Nobody say you did, Jack."

"How much brea-ud you got, son?" the one with the sleeveless sweat shirt asked me. He was flexing the muscle of his right arm and staring at it as if it were some abnormal growth that had suddenly emerged into full view. It resembled a large sweet potato. I knew I didn't stand a chance.

" 'Scuse me?"

"I said how much brea-ud you got? You know, *mmoneh, honeh.*"

Before I left the house that morning, my mother had given me a quarter for the church collection. I had planned on treating Panna to a soda at Loui's Luncheonette, but now he could go screw himself.

"I ain't got nothin' on me," I said.

"Put your hands behind your head," the tall one commanded.

I inched away from him. "What for?"

He grabbed my shirt collar and pushed me hard against the stone wall. A small shock of pain shot through my spine. My legs felt like two heavy pieces of lumber.

"Put your hands behind your hea-ud," the Clinton student said. He was standing so close to me now that I could smell his bad breath.

I lifted my arms and clasped my hands behind my head, the way I'd seen it done on the block whenever the cops were frisking a suspected criminal.

The big one stuck his hand in one of my pockets, then in the other, and came up with the quarter.

His mouth spread in a thick-lipped smile. "Dig," he told

his friends. He pinched the shiny quarter between two long fingers and held it up for the others to see. The solemn, silver face of George Washington flashed in the sun.

"Maybe he got a wallet on him," the one sitting on the wall called down.

The tall one slipped the quarter in his pocket and patted my head. "Turn around, man."

I turned quickly and raised both arms high over my head, the palms flat against the warm wall, while he slapped my back pockets. Where was Panna? I refused to believe he had run off. Not that it made any difference. He was too small to defend himself against one of them, let alone all four. Only the gang from the block could pull me out of this mess, and they were all far away, ignorant of the trap I had walked into. This was strange turf for me; I was only used to dealing with Spicks like myself. In the block my name stood for something among my friends; here it was less than shit. It was useless to tell these black guys that I had many friends who would decend on them in an all out war if they didn't release me unharmed. That kind of threat might only get me a busted head.

"Sheeet, he ain't got nothin' on him," the tall one told his friends after he had gone through my pockets. "Turn around."

I dropped my hands and turned slowly.

The Clinton student grabbed my right arm and jerked it upwards. A pain shot down my shoulder. "Nobody say to drop your hands."

I raised them again, stretching them to their limits, to show that I hadn't meant any harm.

"And keep them up, mother," the lookout man on the wall yelled down.

Suddenly the six-foot one stuck his long leg between my legs and rammed the heel of his hand against my shoulder. I stumbled, scraped my back on the wall, and collapsed with a squeal on something soft. A swarm of flies, thousands it seemed, exploded around me, and in seconds I was immersed in the odor of human shit. I sat there, too overcome with disgust and rage to move. And the flies swarmed and buzzed around me, in a frenzy of delicious delight.

Not because I had been pushed around and robbed of a quarter, which had not been mine to begin with, nor even because I had been smeared in shit, which could be washed off, but because I had been humiliated without any possibility of fighting back, of standing up for myself—for that reason I began to cry. I didn't cry loudly or hysterically; only girls and women had the right to that kind of display. I cried softly, missing my breath once in a while and sucking back in the thin, fibrous liquid that spilled from my nostrils. A slow accumulation of pain, brought on by the strong noon sun, began to tighten around my forehead. I dropped my head and waited for them to kick my face in.

But they just stood there, silently staring down at me.

From the grassy area where Panna and his pursuer had disappeared, I could hear voices and a stick slashing grass. I waited, resigned to the stink of the shit I was sitting on and the sting and buzz of the flies. The voices had the sound of calm conversation rather than conflict.

In a few moments, Panna and his captor emerged. I watched them through half-closed eyes. They were still talking. Panna was smiling.

When he saw me he stopped, clapped a hand to his mouth, and whispered: "Holy shit! Oh, lordie."

I rubbed two fists in my eyes.

"Who you got there?" the tall one asked the one who had found Panna.

"This here's Ramirez, my friend," he said, slapping Panna on the back. "We went to junior high school together. He's all right. Foo! Whatchu-all been doin' to white boy here?"

"He pushed me in," I said.

The one with the Clinton sweat shirt kicked some dirt in front of me. "I make you eat that, too, if you don't shut your big mouth."

"He's my friend," Panna told him.

The tall one sucked his teeth and looked him up and down. "So whatchu be hangin' out with him for? He ain't none o' your kind."

"We live in the same block," Panna explained.

His school friend held out the stickball bat to me. "Here, man, grab on to this."

I shook my head, suspecting a trick.

"Go on, Mannie," Panna said. "Get up, man."

I grabbed the stick cautiously and pulled myself up quickly, in case he might decide to release his hold on it.

The scat of my pants felt wet. Repulsed by the stink, the others backed up a few steps.

"Man, you full of shit," the kid on the wall said. He was holding his nose.

The tall one stuck his hand in his pocket and brought out my quarter. "Here," he told me, "take your fuckin' George Washington back. I don't want your quarter."

I put out my hand suspiciously and let him slap the shiny quarter in the palm.

"Let me tell you somethin', white boy," he began. "This here's our turf, understand?"

I nodded, unconsciously biting my lip.

"And it don't make no difference to me who your friend is, even if he black as an asshole. You stick to your side of the Park."

I kept nodding my head.

"Otherwise I make you eat that shit. Just keep that in mind."

Then he turned to Panna. "And you, shorty with the big hea-ud, don't think cause you black all over and ugly as sin you can bring who you want around here."

Panna nodded. "Okay."

A long silence followed. I stared intently at the flagpole and longed to be back on my small block, where there were no territorial divisions.

"You better get on home, Ramirez," the school friend said to Panna.

I let Panna go on ahead and tried to remain calm during the few seconds it took to squeeze through the hole in the wall of the fort. But just as I was about to emerge on the other side, I heard a voice behind me: "Man, you full of sheeet," followed by a fit of laughter.

We walked slowly side by side until we reached the top of the hill, from where we could see part of the baseball diamonds, and beyond them the mansions of Fifth Avenue. I started down in a half-run, then broke into an awkward, stumbling rush down the steep hill until I was on the safe side of the little stream.

From somewhere behind me I could hear Panna calling. "Hey, Mannie, man. Slow down. Whatchu scared of?"

I ignored him and picked up speed. Near the baseball diamonds, I heard the reassuring sounds of Spanish and slowed down. "Nothin'," I said to myself. "I ain't scared of nothing." I stopped and looked back for Panna. He was nowhere in sight. I continued walking at a steady, brisk pace, leaving a strong stench behind me.

JOHN HOWARD GRIFFIN

Black Again, White Again

In October of 1959, JOHN HOWARD GRIFFIN, a white man from Mansfield, Texas, decided that he wanted to see what it felt like to be a Negro in the South, and shortly afterward he set out by foot and bus, his skin dyed black, on a unique search for a place to eat, rest, work, or sleep. It was a notable journey. He is of old Georgia stock, but much of his formal education was had in France, as a musicologist. He is an authority on Gregorian chant. In World War II, as a bombardier in the American Air Force, he served in the Pacific and was blinded by an exploding shell. He regained his sight only after ten years, when he saw his wife and two oldest children for the first time. He is the author of two novels, *The Devil Rides Outside* and *Nuni,* and a number of short stories. His experiences in *Black Like Me* are by now known to hundreds of thousands of readers in many languages.

November 25

. . . The morning was bright and cool. Before long a car with two young white boys picked me up. I quickly saw that they were, like many of their generation, kinder than the older ones. They drove me to a small-town bus station where I could catch a bus.

I bought a ticket to Montgomery and went to sit outside on the curb where other Negro passengers gathered. Many Negroes walked through the streets. Their glances were kind and communicative, as though all of us shared some common secret.

As I sat in the sunlight, a great heaviness came over me. I went inside to the Negro rest room, splashed cold water on my face and brushed my teeth. Then I brought out my hand mirror and inspected myself. I had been a Negro more than three weeks and it no longer shocked me to see the stranger in the mirror. My hair had grown to a heavy fuzz, my face skin, with the continued medication, exposure to sunlight and ground-in stain, was what Negroes call a "pure brown"— a smooth dark color that made me look like millions of others.

I noted, too, that my face had lost animation. In repose, it had taken on the strained, disconsolate expression that is written on the countenance of so many Southern Negroes. My mind had become the same way, dozing empty for long periods. It thought of food and water, but so many hours were spent just waiting, cushioning self against dread, that it no longer thought of much else. Like the others in my condition, I was finding life too burdensome.

I felt a great hunger for something merely pleasurable, for something people call "fun." The need was so great that deep within, through the squalor and the humiliations of this life, I took some joy in the mere fact that I could be alone for a while inside the rest-room cubicle with its clean plumbing and unfinished wood walls. Here I had a water faucet to drink from and I could experience the luxury of splashing cold water on my face as much as I wanted. Here, with a latch on the door, I was isolated from the hate stares, the contempt.

The smell of Ivory livened the atmosphere. Some of the stain came off and I wondered how long it would be before I could pass as white again. I decided to take no more pills for a while. I removed my shirt and undershirt. My body, so long unexposed to the sun or the sun lamp, had paled to a *café-au-lait* color. I told myself I would have to be careful not to undress unless I had privacy henceforth. My face and hands were far darker than my body. Since I often slept in my clothes, the problem would not be great.

I wet my sponge, poured dye on it and touched up the corners of my mouth and my lips, which were always the difficult spots.

We boarded the bus in late afternoon and rode without incident to Selma, where I had a long layover before taking another bus into the state capital.

In deep dusk I strolled through the streets of the beautiful town. A group of nicely dressed Negro women solicited contributions for missionary activities. I placed some change in their cup and accepted a tract explaining the missionary program. Then, curious to see how they would fare with the whites, I walked along with them.

We approached the stationkeeper. His face soured and he growled his refusal. We walked on. In not a single instance did a white hear them out.

Two well-dressed men stood talking in front of the Hotel Albert.

"Pardon us, sir," one of the women said, holding a tract in her hand. "We're soliciting contributions for our missionary—"

"G'wan," the older one snapped, "I got too many of them damned tracts already."

The younger man hesitated, dug in his pocket and tossed a handful of change into the cup. He refused the tract, saying, "I'm sure the money'll be put to good use."

After we had gone two blocks, we heard footsteps behind us. We stopped at a street corner, not looking back. The younger man's voice came to us. "I don't suppose it does any

good," he said quietly, "but I apologize for the bad manners
of my people."

"Thank you," we said, not turning our heads.

As we passed the bus station, I dropped out of the little
group and sat on a public bench near an outside phone booth.
I waited until I saw a Negro use the phone, and then I hurried to it, closed the door and asked the long-distance operator
to call my home collect.

When my wife answered, the strangeness of my situation
again swept over me. I talked with her and the children as
their husband and father, while reflected in the glass windows
of the booth I saw another man they would not know. At this
time, when I wanted most to lose the illusion, I was more than
ever aware of it, aware that it was not the man she knew, but
a stranger who spoke with the same voice and had the same
memory.

Happy at least to have heard their voices, I stepped from
the booth to the night's cooler air. The night was always a
comfort. Most of the whites were in their homes. The threat
was less. A Negro blended inconspicuously into the darkness.

> *Night coming tenderly*
> *Black like me.*

At such a time, the Negro can look at the starlit skies and
find that he has, after all, a place in the universal order of
things. The stars, the black skies affirm his humanity, his
validity as a human being. He knows that his belly, his lungs,
his tired legs, his appetites, his prayers and his mind are
cherished in some profound involvement with nature and
God. The night is his consolation. It does not despise him.

The roar of wheels turning into the station, the stench of
exhaust fumes, the sudden bustle of people unloading told
me it was time to go. Men, better and wiser than the night,
put me back into my place with their hate stares.

I walked to the back of the bus, past the drowsers, and

found an empty seat. The Negroes gave me their sleepy smiles and then we were off. I leaned back and dozed along with the others.

November 25

In Montgomery, the capital of Alabama, I encountered a new atmosphere. The Negro's feeling of utter hopelessness is here replaced by a determined spirit of passive resistance. The Reverend Martin Luther King, Jr.'s influence, like an echo of Gandhi's, prevails. Nonviolent and prayerful resistance to discrimination is the keynote. Here, the Negro has committed himself to a definite stand. He will go to jail, suffer any humiliation, but he will not back down. He will take the insults and abuses stoically so that his children will not have to take them in the future.

The white racist is bewildered and angered by such an attitude, because the dignity of the Negro's course of action emphasizes the indignity of his own. It is a challenge to him to needle the Negro into acts of a baser nature, into open physical conflict. He will walk up and blow cigarette smoke in the Negro's face, hoping the Negro will strike out at him. Then he could repress the Negro violently and claim it was only self-defense.

Where the Negro has lacked unity of purpose elsewhere, he has in Montgomery rallied to the leadership of King. Where he has been degraded elsewhere by unjust men of both races, here he is resisting degradation.

I could not make out the white viewpoint in Montgomery. It was too fluid, too changeable. A superficial calm hung over the city. At night police were everywhere. I felt that the two races stood like blocks of concrete, immovable, and that the basic issues of right and wrong, of justice and injustice, were lost from view by the whites. The issues had degenerated to who would win. Fear and dread tensed both sides.

The Negroes with whom I associated feared two things. They feared that one of their own might commit an act of violence that would jeopardize their position by allowing the whites to say they were too dangerous to have their rights. They dreaded the awful tauntings of irresponsible white men, the jailing, the frames.

The white man's fears have been widely broadcast. To the Negro these fears of "intermingling" make no sense. All he can see is that the white man wants to hold him down—to make him live up to his responsibilities as a taxpayer and soldier, while denying him the privileges of a citizen. At base, though the white brings forth many arguments to justify his viewpoint, one feels the reality is simply that he cannot bear to "lose" to the traditionally servant class.

The hate stare was everywhere practiced, especially by women of the older generation. On Sunday, I made the experiment of dressing well and walking past some of the white churches just as services were over. In each instance, as the women came through the church doors and saw me, the "spiritual bouquets" changed to hostility. The transformation was grotesque. In all of Montgomery only one woman refrained. She did not smile. She merely looked at me and did not change her expression. My gratitude to her was so great it astonished me.

November 27

I remained in my room more and more each day. The situation in Montgomery was so strange I decided to try passing back into white society. I went out only at night for food. My heart sickened at the thought of any more hate. Too, I wanted no more sunlight until I had the medication sufficiently out of my system to allow me to lighten.

November 28

I decided to try to pass back into white society. I scrubbed myself almost raw until my brown skin had a pink rather than black undertone. Yes, looking into the mirror, I felt I could pass. I put on a white shirt, but by contrast it made my face and hands appear too dark. I changed to a brown sports shirt which made my skin appear lighter.

This shift was nerve-racking. As a white man I could not be seen leaving a Negro home at midnight. If I checked into a white hotel and then got too much sun, it would, in combination with the medication still in my system, turn me too dark and I would not be able to return to the hotel.

I waited until the streets were quiet outside and I was sure everyone in the house slept. Then, taking my bags, I walked to the door and out into the night.

It was important to get out of the neighborhood and into the white sector as quickly and inconspicuously as possible. I watched for police cars. Only one appeared in the distance and I dodged down a side street.

At the next intersection a Negro teen-ager strode by. I stepped out and walked behind him. He glanced at me and then kept his eyes to the front. Obviously thinking I might harass him, he pulled something from his jacket and I heard a click. Though I could not see what he held in his hand, I have no doubt it was a switch-blade knife. To him I was nothing more than a white stranger, a potential source of harm against whom he must protect himself.

He stopped at the corner of a wide street and waited to cross. I came up beside him.

"It's geting cold, isn't it?" I said, seeking to reassure him that I had no unfriendly intentions.

He stood like a statue, unresponsive.

We crossed the street into a brighter downtown section. A

policeman strolled toward us and the boy quickly dropped his weapon into his jacket pocket.

The policeman nodded affably to me and I knew then that I had successfully passed back into the white society, that I was once more a first-class citizen, that all doors into cafés, rest rooms, libraries, movies, concerts, schools and churches were suddenly open to me. After so long I could not adjust to it. A sense of exultant liberation flooded through me. I crossed over to a restaurant and entered. I took a seat beside white men at the counter and the waitress smiled at me. It was a miracle. I ordered food and was served, and it was a miracle. I went to the rest room and was not molested. No one paid me the slightest attention. No one said, "What're you doing in here, nigger?"

Out there in the night I knew that men who were exactly as I had been these past weeks roamed the streets and not one of them could go into a place and buy a cup of coffee at this time of the night. Instead of opening the door into rest rooms, they looked for alleys.

To them as to me, these simple privileges would be a miracle. But though I felt it all, I felt no joy in it. I saw smiles, benign faces, courtesies—a side of the white man I had not seen in weeks, but I remembered too well the other side. The miracle was sour.

I ate the white meal, drank the white water, received the white smiles and wondered how it could all be. What sense could a man make of it?

I left the café and walked to the elegant Whitney Hotel. A Negro rushed to take my knapsacks. He gave me the smiles, the "yes, sir—yes, sir."

I felt like saying, "You're not fooling me," but now I was back on the other side of the wall. There was no longer communication between us, no longer the glance that said everything.

The white clerks registered me, surrounded me with smiles,

sent me to my comfortable room accompanied by a Negro who carried my bags. I gave him his tip, received his bow and realized that already he was far from me, distant as the Negro is distant from the white. I locked the door, sat on the bed and smoked a cigarette. I was the same man who could not possibly have bought his way into this room a week ago. My inclination was to marvel at the feel of the carpet beneath my feet, to catalogue the banal miracle of every stick of furniture, every lamp, the telephone, to go and wash myself in the tile shower—or again to go out into the street simply to experience what it was like to walk into all the doors, all the joints and movies and restaurants, to talk to white men in the lobby without servility, to look at women and see them smile courteously.

November 29

Montgomery looked different that morning. The face of humanity smiled—good smiles, full of warmth; irresistible smiles that confirmed my impression that these people were simply unaware of the situation with the Negroes who passed them on the street—that there was not even the communication of intelligent awareness between them. I talked with some—casual conversations here and there. They said they knew the Negroes, they had had long talks with the Negroes. They did not know that the Negro long ago learned he must tell them what they want to hear, not what is. I heard the old things: the Negro is this or that or the other. You have to go slow. You can't expect the South to sit back and let the damned Communist North dictate to it, especially when no outsider can really "understand." I listened and kept my tongue from giving answer. This was the time to listen, not to talk, but it was difficult. I looked into their eyes and saw sincerity and wanted to say: "Don't you know you are prattling the racist poison?"

Montgomery, the city I had detested, was beautiful that day; at least it was until I walked into a Negro section where I had not been before. I was a lone white man in a Negro neighborhood. I, the white man, got from the Negro the same shriveling treatment I, the Negro, had got from the white man. I thought, "Why me? I have been one of you." Then I realized it was the same stupidity I had encountered at the New Orleans bus station. It was nothing I had done, it was not me, but the color of my skin. Their looks said: "You white bastard, you ofay sonofabitch, what are you doing walking these streets?" just as the whites' looks had said a few days before: "You black bastard, you nigger sonofabitch, what are you doing walking these streets?"

Was it worth going on? Was it worth trying to show the one race what went on behind the mask of the other?

December 1

I developed a technique of zigzagging back and forth. In my bag I kept a damp sponge, dyes, cleansing cream and Kleenex. It was hazardous, but it was the only way to traverse an area both as Negro and white. As I traveled, I would find an isolated spot, perhaps an alley at night or the brush beside a highway, and quickly apply the dye to face, hands and legs, then rub off and reapply until it was firmly anchored in my pores. I would go through the area as a Negro and then, usually at night, remove the dyes with cleansing cream and tissues and pass through the same area as a white man.

I was the same man, whether white or black. Yet when I was white, I received the brotherly-love smiles and the privileges from whites and the hate stares or obsequiousness from the Negroes. And when I was a Negro, the whites judged me fit for the junk heap, while the Negroes treated me with great warmth.

*　*　*

As the Negro Griffin, I walked up the steep hill to the bus station in Montgomery to get the schedule for buses to Tuskegee. I received the information from a polite clerk and turned away from the counter.

"Boy!" I heard a woman's voice, harsh and loud.

I glanced toward the door to see a large, matriarchical woman, elderly and impatient. Her pinched face grimaced and she waved me to her.

"Boy, come here. Hurry!"

Astonished, I obeyed.

"Get those bags out of the cab," she ordered testily, seeming outraged with my lack of speed.

Without thinking, I allowed my face to spread to a grin as though overjoyed to serve her. I carried her bags to the bus and received three haughty dimes. I thanked her profusely. Her eyebrows knitted with irritation and she finally waved me away.

I took the early afternoon bus for Tuskegee, walked through a Southern town of great beauty and tranquility. The famed Tuskegee Institute was, I learned, out of the city limits. In fact the major portion of the Negro residential area is out of the city limits—put there when the city fathers decided it was the simplest way to invalidate the Negro vote in local elections.

The spirit of George Washington Carver hangs strongly over the campus—a quiet, almost hauntingly quiet area of trees and grass. It radiates an atmosphere of respect for the work of one's hands and mind, of human dignity. In interviews here, my previous findings were confirmed: with the exception of those trained in professions where they can set up independent practice, they can find jobs commensurate with their education only outside the South. I found an atmosphere of great courtesy, with students more dignified and more soberly dressed than one finds on most white campuses. Education for them is a serious business. They are so

close to the days when their ancestors were kept totally illiterate, when their ancestors learned to read and write at the
risk of severe punishment, that learning is an almost sacred
privilege now. They see it also as the only possible way out
of the morass in which the Negro finds himself.

Later that afternoon, after wandering around the town,
I turned back toward the Institute to talk with the dean. A
white man stood in front of a Negro recreation parlor near
the college entrance gates and waved to me. I hesitated at first,
fearing he would be just another bully. But his eyes pleaded
with me to trust him.

I crossed slowly over to him.

"Did you want me?" I asked.

"Yes—could you tell me where is Tuskegee Institute?"

"Right there," I said, pointing to the gates a block away.

"Aw, I know it," he grinned. I smelled whisky in the fresh
evening air. "I was just looking for an excuse to talk to you,"
he admitted. "Do you teach here?"

"No, I'm just traveling through," I said.

"I'm a Ph.D.," he said uncomfortably. "I'm from New York
—down here as an observer."

"For some government agency?"

"No, strictly on my own," he said. I studied him closely,
since other Negroes were beginning to watch us. He appeared
to be in his early fifties and was well enough dressed.

"How about you and me having a drink?" he said.

"No, thanks," I said and turned away.

"Wait a minute, dammit. You people are my brothers. It's
people like me that are your only hope. How do you expect
me to observe if you won't talk to me?"

"Very well," I said. "I'll be glad to talk with you."

"Hell, I've observed all I can stomach," he said. "Let's us
go get just roaring blinko drunk and forget all this damned
prejudice stuff."

"A white man and a Negro," I laughed. "We'd both hear from the merciful Klan."

"Damned right—a white man and a Negro. Hell, I don't consider myself any better than you—not even as good, maybe. I'm just trying to show some brotherhood."

Though I knew he had been drinking, I wondered that an educated man and an observer could be so obtuse—could create such an embarrassing situation for a Negro.

"I appreciate it," I said stiffly. "But it would never work."

"They needn't know," he whispered, leaning close to me, an almost frantic look in his eyes as though he were begging not to be rejected. "I'm going to get soused anyway. Hell, I've had all this I can stand. It's just between you and me. We could go into the woods somewhere. Come on—for brotherhood's sake."

I felt great pity for him. He was obviously lonely and fearful of rejection by the very people he sought to help. But I wondered if he could know how offensive this overweaning "brotherhood" demonstration was. Others stood by and watched with frowns of disapproval.

At the moment a Negro drove up in an old car and stopped. Ignoring the white man, he spoke to me. "Would you like to buy some nice fat turkeys?" he asked.

"I don't have any family here," I said.

"Wait a minute there," the white man said. "Hell, I'll buy all your turkeys . . . just to help you out. I'll show you fellows that not all white men are bastards. How many've you got in there?" We looked into the car and saw several live turkeys in the back seat.

"How much for all of them?" the white man asked, pulling a ten-dollar bill from his wallet.

The vendor looked at me, puzzled, as though he did not wish to unload such a baggage on the generous white man.

"What can you do with them when you get them out of the car?" I asked.

"What're you trying to do," the white man asked belliger-
ently, "kill this man's sale?"

The vendor quickly put in: "No . . . no, mister, he's not
trying to do that. I'm glad to sell you all the turkeys you want.
But where you want me to unload them? You live around
here?"

"No, I'm just an observer. Hell, take the ten dollars. I'll
give the damned turkeys away."

When the vendor hesitated, the white man asked: "What's
the matter—did you steal them or something?"

"Oh, no sir . . ."

"You afraid I'm a cop or something?"

The unpardonable had been said. The white man, despite
his protestations of brotherhood, had made the first dirty suggestion that came to his mind. He was probably unaware of
it but it escaped none of us. By the very tone of his question
he revealed his contempt for us. His voice had taken on a
hard edge, putting us in our place, as they say. He had become
just like the whites he decried.

"I didn't steal them," the turkey man said coldly. "You can
come out to my farm. I've got more there."

The white man, sensing the change, the resentment, glared
at me. "Hell, no wonder nobody has any use for you. You
don't give a man a chance to be nice to you. And damn it, I'm
going to put that in my report." He turned away grumbling.
"There's something 'funny' about all of you." Then he raised
his head toward the evening sky and announced furiously:
"But before I do anything else, I'm going to get drunk, stinking drunk."

He stamped off down the road toward open country. Negroes around me shook their heads slowly, with regret. We
had witnessed a pitiful one-man attempt to make up for some
of the abuses the man had seen practiced against the Negro.
It had failed miserably. If I had dared, I would have gone

after him and tried to bridge the terrible gap that had come between him and us.

Instead, I walked to the street lamp and wrote in my notebook.

"We must return to them their lawful rights, assure equality of justice—and then everybody leave everybody else to hell alone. Paternalistic—we show our prejudice in our paternalism—we downgrade their dignity."

It was too late to visit the dean of Tuskegee, so I went to the bus station and boarded a bus for Atlanta, via Auburn, Alabama.

The trip was without incident until we changed buses at Auburn. As always, we Negroes sat at the rear. Four of us occupied the back bench. A large, middle-aged Negro woman sat in front of us to the left, a young Negro man occupied the seat in front of us to the right.

At one of the stops, two white women boarded and could find not place to sit. No gallant Southern white man (or youth) rose to offer them a place in the "white section."

The bus driver called back and asked the young Negro man and the middle-aged Negro woman to sit together so the white women could have one of the seats. Both ignored the request. We felt the tensions mount as whites craned to stare back at us.

A readheaded white man in a sports shirt stood up, faced the rear and called out to the Negro. "Didn't you hear the driver? Move out, man."

"They're welcome to sit here," the Negro said quietly, indicating the empty seat beside him and the one beside the woman across the aisle.

The driver looked dumfounded and then dismayed. He walked halfway to the rear and, struggling to keep his voice under control, said: "They don't want to sit with you people, don't you know that? They don't want to—is that plain enough?"

We felt an incident boiling, but none of us wanted the young Negro, who had paid for his ticket, to be forced to vacate his seat. If the women did not want to sit with us, then let one of the white men offer his seat and he could come and sit with us. The young Negro said no more. He gazed out the window.

The readhead bristled. "Do you want me to slap these two jigaboos out of their seats?" he asked the driver in a loud voice.

We winced and turned into mummies, staring vacantly, insulating ourselves against further insults.

"No—for God's sake—please—no rough stuff," the driver pleaded.

One of the white women looked toward us apologetically, as though she were sorry to be the cause of such a scene. "It's all right," she said. "Please . . ." asking the driver and the young man to end their attempts to get her a seat.

The readhead flexed his chest muscles and slowly took his seat, glaring back at us. A young teen-ager, sitting halfway to the front, sniggered: "Man, he was going to slap that nigger, all right." The white bully was his hero, but other whites maintained a disapproving silence.

At the Atlanta station we waited for the whites to get off. One of them, a large middle-aged man, hesitated, turned and stepped back toward us. We hardened ourselves for another insult. He bent over to speak to the young Negro. "I just wanted to tell you that before he slapped you, he'd have had to slap me down first," he said.

None of us smiled. We wondered why he had not spoken up while whites were still on the bus. We nodded our appreciation and the young Negro said gently: "It happens to us all the time."

"Well, I just wanted you to know—I was on your side, boy." He winked, never realizing how he had revealed himself to us by calling our companion by the hated name of "boy." We nodded wearily in response to his parting nod.

I was the last to leave the bus. An elderly white man, bald and square of build, dressed in worn blue work clothes, peered intently at me. Then he crimped his face as though I were odious and snorted, "Phew!" His small blue eyes shone with repugnance, a look of such unreasoning contempt for my skin that it filled me with despair.

It was a little thing, but piled on all the other little things it broke something in me. Suddenly I had had enough. Suddenly I could stomach no more of this degradation—not of myself but of all men who were black like me. Abruptly I turned and walked away. The large bus station was crowded with humanity. In the men's room, I entered one of the cubicles and locked the door. For a time I was safe, isolated; for a time I owned the space around me, though it was scarcely more than that of a coffin. In medieval times, men sought scantuary in churches. Nowadays, for a nickel, I could find sanctuary in a colored rest room. Then, sanctuary had the smell of incense permeated walls. Now it had the odor of disinfectant.

The irony of it hit me. I was back in the land of my forefathers, Georgia. The town of Griffin was named for one of them. Too I, a Negro, carried the name hated by all Negroes, for former Governor Griffin (no kin that I would care to discover) devoted himself heroically to the task of keeping Negroes "in their place." Thanks in part to his efforts, this John Griffin celebrated a triumphant return to the land from which his people had sprung by seeking sanctuary in a toilet cubicle at the bus station.

I took out my cleansing cream and rubbed it on my hands and face to remove the stain. I then removed my shirt and undershirt, rubbed my skin almost raw with the undershirt, and looked into my hand mirror. I could pass for white again.

I repacked my duffel, put my shirt and coat back on and wondered how I could best leave the colored rest room without attracting attention. I guessed it was near midnight, but the traffic in and out remained heavy.

Oddly, there was little of the easy conversation one generally hears in public rest rooms, none of the laughter and "woofing." I waited, listening to footsteps come and go, to the water-sounds of hand-washing and flushing.

Much later, when I heard no more footsteps, I stepped from my cubicle and walked toward the door that led into the main waiting room. I hurried into the crowd unnoticed.

The shift back to white status was always confusing. I had to guard against the easy, semiobscene language that Negroes use among themselves, for coming from a white man it is insulting. It was midnight. I asked a doorman where to find a room for the night. He indicated a neon sign that stood out against the night sky—YMCA, only a block or so away. I realized that though I was well dressed for a Negro, my appearance looked shabby for a white man. He judged me by that and indicated a place where lodging was inexpensive.

Interviewed and televised, in New York and elswhere, and hanged in effigy where he had lived in Mansfield, Texas, Mr. Griffin wrote his experiences in Black Like Me, *parts of which appeared in* Sepia *magazine, became a hard cover (Houghton Mifflin) book, and a paperback which long since went into its forty-first edition (Signet). His experiences altered the author's life and he concluded his book with the following two entries:*

EPILOGUE

August 14

It was late in the afternoon of a cloudy, humid day. My parents, unable to bear the hostility, had sold their home and all their furniture and left Mansfield for Mexico where they hoped to find a new life. We, too, were going, since we had decided that it was too great an injustice to our children to remain.

But I felt I must remain a while longer, until the bullies had a chance to carry out their threats against me. I could not allow them to say they had "chased" me out. They had promised to fix me on July 15th, and now they said they would do it August 15th.

Across the pastures, the incredible vulgarity of highly amplified hillbilly music drifted from the café on the highway. I sat in the barren studio where I had worked so many years, emptied now of all except the table and the typewriter and the bed, stripped of its sheets, with only the mattress ticking staring up at the ceiling. Empty bookshelves surrounded me. A few yards away, my parents' house stood equally empty. I wandered back and forth from my barn to the house.

August 17

I stayed on, and the lane leading to my barn office remained empty. They did not come for me.

I hired a Negro youth to come and help me clean up my parents' house so it would be spotless for the new owners. The youth knew me and had no reticence in talking since he was sure I was "one of them" so to speak. Both Negroes and whites have gained this certainty from the experiment—because I was a Negro for six weeks, I remained partly Negro or perhaps essentially Negro.

While we swept and burned old newspapers, we talked.

"Why do the whites hate us—we don't hate them?" he asked.

We had a long conversation during which he brought out the obvious fact that whites teach their children to call them "niggers." He said this happened to him all the time and that he would not even go into white neighborhoods because it sickened him to be called that. He said revealing things:

"Your children don't hate us, do they?"

"God, no," I said. "Children have to be taught that kind of filth. We'd never permit ours to learn it."

"Dr. Cook's like that. His little girl called me nigger and he told her if he ever heard her say that again he'd spank her till she couldn't sit down."

The Negro does not understand the white any more than the white understands the Negro. I was dismayed to see the extent to which this youth exaggerated—how could he do otherwise?—the feelings of the whites toward Negroes. He thought they all hated him.

The most distressing repercussion of this lack of communication has been the rise in racism among Negroes, justified to some extent, but a grave symptom nevertheless. It only widens the gap that men of good will are trying desperately to bridge with understanding and compassion. It only strengthens the white racist's cause. The Negro who turns now, in the moment of near-realization of his liberties, and bares his fangs at a man's whiteness, makes the same tragic error the white racist has made.

And it is happening on a wider scale. Too many of the more militant leaders are preaching Negro superiority. I pray that the Negro will not miss his chance to rise to greatness, to build from the strength gained through his past suffering and, above all, to rise beyond vengeance.

If some spark does set the keg afire, it will be a senseless tragedy of ignorant against ignorant, injustice answering injustice—a holocaust that will drag down the innocent and right-thinking masses of human beings.

Then we will all pay for not having cried for justice long ago.

ROBERT K. DURKEE

The Negro at Princeton

ROBERT K. DURKEE, as a white student at Princeton, began research on this study in the spring of 1967, "talking with incoming black freshmen during their first days in the fall, and after further research, wrote the piece in two nights in October." It was published in the *Daily Princetonian,* which the author later was to serve as editor-in-chief. The article won first prize in journalism in the STORY College Creative Awards Contest and appeared in STORY: *The Yearbook of Discovery.* The author graduated frim Princeton in 1969 and is teaching fifth grade in the Trenton, New Jersey, public schools. He served as Director of Public Relations for the campus-based Movement for a New Congress and contributed to the Movement's book, *Vote Power.* He was born in Brooklyn in 1942. He has added an updating footnote at the end of his article.

Maybe you are a student at Princeton. Maybe you are black. Maybe you are one of the fifty-six men in the world who are both. Maybe then you know what it is like to be a Negro at Princeton.

But the chances are highly unlikely.

There have been fewer than one hundred Negro undergraduates at Princeton in its 221-year history. More than half of those are on campus today. Still, the Negro today accounts for the less than two per cent of the undergraduate body at an educational institution which many rank among the nation's best.

The Princeton image is not colored. The pictures of Old Nassau are still taken with only white students strolling along the shaded paths. The university's colors are orange and black. But the black refers to Tiger stripes—and not to people.

The Negro at Princeton is black. That means something. It means he is somehow different. It means he is uniquely visible. It means he is subject to certain pressures and certain problems which his fellow undergraduates don't face, aren't aware of, and, all too often, can't understand.

Obviously, the Negro at Princeton is primarily a person. He is concerned with the same things that concern other students. But there is more to it. As one Negro sophomore put it: "How do you feel when you have to go back for your Commons card if you forget it while others who forget theirs can use their U-Store cards as identification?

"How do you feel if the same security patrolman asks you three times within one week whether or not you go to Princeton?

"How would you feel if you walked by a room on campus and saw a big confederate flag stretched across the wall?

"How would you feel if you heard 'Dixie' played with such exuberance at basketball games?

"How would you feel when your date, who this time happens to be white, is called a tramp, simply because there are 3,100 other guys for her to date?

"How would you feel if other fellows appeared to gape and cringe because you were walking with two of your friends who share a common shade of black?

"How would you feel if old grads remarked, 'In my days, we fortunately didn't have any of them'?

"How would you feel? You'd feel like a Negro at Princeton."

Things have changed considerably since that day in the 1840s when Theodore Wright enrolled at Princeton. Theodore Wright was a seminary student in Princeton's graduating class of 1848. He was Princeton's first Negro. For almost 100 years, he was Princeton's only Negro.

No one is quite sure how Wright became an undergraduate at Old Nassau. Legend tells of Negroes who accompanied their masters when they came to Princeton in return for their freedom at his graduation. Some speculate that Wright had been part of a student's slave retinue before he became an undergraduate. Another version is that Wright was a slave brought North by a clergyman who recognized his natural intellectual abilities.

At any rate, the story of the Negro at Princeton begins with Theodore Wright. Until World War II, the story of the Negro at Princeton also ended with Theodore Wright. During and after the War, Princeton sporadically admitted a token Negro or two. But the prospects for a Negro at Princeton in the middle of this century were not much better than his prospects a century before.

Even in 1967, 120 years after Theodore Wright received his diploma, Princeton graduated only three Negroes. But a change was beginning to take place. Princeton was becoming concerned with Negroes and its role in their education. One hundred years after the Emancipation Proclamation, Princeton decided that color was not a valid academic criterion.

In 1963, President Goheen announced a new university policy to accept as many qualified Negro students as could be found. He said the Office of Admission would actively seek applications from such Negroes.

In a speech at the Princeton Playhouse, the president noted that "The university's policies are open and nondiscrimina-

tory." He pointed out that the administration for a decade
had been primarily concerned with procuring students from
underdeveloped countries. "It took a shock (the civil rights
movement) to make us realize our problems at home."

Mr. Goheen called upon Director of Admission E. Alden
Dunham '53—who had been appointed in 1962—to actively
recruit Negro applicants. In the fall of 1962, Princeton admitted its first *group* of Negro students—six of them. In 1963,
six more were admitted, and eleven were among the freshman
class the following year.

A year after the president's Playhouse speech, Princeton
made another significant move. Carl A. Fields was appointed
to a position in the Bureau of Student Aid—thereby making
him a member of the administration. He is a Negro.

Carl Fields had been one of the Negroes who shattered the
color barrier at St. John's University in Brooklyn. He was
the first Negro to attend St. John's on full scholarship. He
had been the first black student to captain a major college
team at St. John's. He is still the only Negro ever named to
that university's honor society. At Princeton he was hired to
advise the administration, to prevent mistakes that could be
avoided. For the administration, he was "instrumental in
shaping policies, plans, and processes to make the Negro more
completely a Princeton student." For the Negro students, Mr.
Fields became an unofficial adviser, consultant, and innovator.

When he came to Princeton, the administration, in some
areas, had not planned sufficiently for Negro students. In
other areas, the administration had not planned at all.

"The Negro student used to enter Princeton hoping that,
like other students, his main problem would simply be dealing with the new academic experience," says Mr. Fields.
"Then he experienced what could have been prepared for,
but wasn't."

Much at Princeton is done according to tradition. "Negroes

had it tough because they didn't know the traditions to which other students conformed," Mr. Fields says.

The Negro went to mixers just like any other freshman only to find no Negro girls present. He hoped to benefit from free and easy camaraderie with his classmates, but he found many white students obviously unprepared to share their community with black students. The university placed him in a single room in a new dormitory, thinking it was doing him a favor by allotting him a "prime" room. He felt the university had isolated him. The Negro began to feel uncomfortable in an environment that didn't seem ready for him. He began to feel lonely. And he began to wonder why the university had accepted him in the first place.

To fill the gaps in university planning, Mr. Fields began a series of programs such as a foster parent program, giving every Negro freshman a family sponsor in the Princeton community while simultaneously involving Princeton's Negro community with the affairs of campus. The family offers the Negro advice as where to go for haircuts, where to meet girls, and where to put up dates. The family increases his network of contacts in the university area and gives him someone to talk with.

Mr. Fields has also been instrumental as adviser to the Princeton chapter of the Association of Black Collegians (ABC)—founded by Paul Williams '68 and A. Dean Buchanan '68 last year. The ABC fellowship enables Negroes to express "a consciousness of responsibility" for black brothers in the ghettos, allows them to participate in the university's quest for black applicants, and offers them a forum for their opinions and experiences.

The Negro search for an identity in the Princeton environment is furthered by the efforts of Mr. Fields and the initiative of the black students themselves. Some progress has been slow; some downright discouraging.

During Mr. Fields' first three years at Princeton, Negroes

entering increased with each class. Eleven Negroes entered with the Class of 1968. For the Class of 1969 the number was 16. The Class of 1970 had 18. Negroes thought the progression too slow, but at least it was in the right direction. Then last year only 24 Negroes were admitted to the Class of 1971. Only 16 accepted. The Negroes on campus want to know what happened. And they want to make sure that it doesn't happen again.

Director of Admission John T. Osander '57 admits that last year's decline was disappointing, but he says that "our search for Negro applicants is still a high-priority item. We don't intend to let up on our efforts." Mr. Osander points out that his office "takes more than an average number of risks academically with Negroes and students from disadvantaged backgrounds generally."

Princeton University is a landmark of white middle-class and white aristocratic America. The Negro, on the other hand, is black and his roots are in the ghettos and cotton fields of second-class citizenry.

It may be true that every student at Princeton has his own problems and personal conflicts. But beyond these elements common to humanity, the Negro at Princeton encounters obstacles and difficulties directly resulting from his color and heritage.

There are special social problems; questions of attitudes; decisions about future participation in society; psychological pressures and reformulations of personal philosophy. There are matters of values, identities, and goals. For most Negroes at Princeton, however, the essential problem is strictly one of numbers. They feel that there are just too few black students on campus. There are also far too few Negroes in faculty and administration posts, they say.

The paucity of Negro undergraduates involves a two-fold problem. First, concerning the Office of Admission, there is debate about the attitudes and efforts of the university in seeking Negro applicants. There is also discussion about what criteria should be utilized in evaluating potential Negro undergraduates. Second, there is the question of why Negro applications have decreased and why admitted Negroes don't accept.

Theoretically, Princeton handles Negro applicants just like any others. It has not lowered its standards to take applicants below normal standards for the college. But Mr. Fields and many undergraduate blacks point out that many intelligent Negroes capable of performing at a Princeton level are disadvantaged by background and lack of motivation. They feel that the university should be willing "to go out on a limb" to bring more Negroes to Princeton and should establish programs to train and motivate promising Negro students in stifling environments.

Nathaniel E. Mackey '69 likens the situation to a 100-yard dash where one contestant is given a 50-yard head start. The Negro is on the starting line and the white is halfway to the finish line. It is meaningless to say that each contestant will then proceed at an even pace.

"The man who starts out 50 yards behind needs a boost," Mackey contends. "The university has to make a sacrifice; it has to create qualified students." The university, he says, also has to actively recruit. Representatives from Harvard and Yale talk with top-ranking Negroes before Princeton shows up, if Princeton shows up at all, he says.

Once a Negro has been accepted, there is no guarantee that he will enroll. If he has been admitted to Harvard or Yale, he will consider the fact that both of those schools have a longer history of concern with Negroes and have greater numbers of Negroes on their campuses.

There is also the reality that the Princeton "Southern gentleman" stereotype is still accepted by many. According to Mackey, this image was not helped by the fact that President

Goheen openly denounced the black power ideas of Stokely Carmichael last year while not denouncing the policies of George Wallace.

(In addition, there is sometimes the feeling that an Ivy League institution simply cannot offer anything of meaning to black students. As one Negro wrote recently in the Columbia University *Spectator:* "Subsequent classes of black students will reject the mediocre goals this institution says they ought to aspire to; they will resolutely refuse the man's benevolent offer of a '32nd vice-niggership' at General Motors.

". . . Columbia College has nothing of significance to offer black students and never will until it ceases to regard us as essentially white students with black skins.")

There have been some efforts by the administration and Negro undergraduates to improve the state of admissions. The university is involved in such programs as the Princeton-Trenton Institute for Teachers which seeks to orient students from the ghetto toward universities. The ABC is informing the Office of Admission about potential applicants from their home towns and trying to dispel stereotypes among black students.

Some Negroes do enroll at Princeton. Few have any idea what to expect.

"It wasn't until after I arrived and found out that the administration was concerned about the problem of being a Negro on the Princeton campus that I began to wonder about my next four years here as a black student," said one Negro, now a junior.

Another remarked, "Apparently, my naïveté was not in thinking that Princeton University had no history of poor race relations, but in holding the belief that prejudices that had been instilled in my white associates both from the North and South since the days they learned from primers that black dogs were bad and white dogs were good could be eradicated by my very presence."

Negroes come to Princeton for many different reasons. Some want to prove they can handle the challenge. Some see an opportunity to help their black brothers. Some are swayed solely by academic or financial considerations. And some come to try to reason with the white student, to expose whites who have been isolated to Negroes. One senior said: "My course is Negro 204, held every day from 8 A.M. to 2 A.M."

But in many ways, it isn't as bad as it used to be in the days when the Negro at Princeton was known as "window dressing," if he was known at all. Back then, relations were particularly strained between Negroes on campus and the town's black community. According to Mackey, black students in those days thought of themselves as "Princeton students first, Americans second, and Negroes last."

Also, in those days, Negroes would avoid talking with or even being near each other because they were afraid of being accused of "congregating."

Today's Negro undergraduates matriculate in a racial context transformed by the civil rights movement. There are more Negroes. And Mr. Fields has told the black students not to be afraid to be seen with each other.

But still there is a white reaction when more than two Negroes gather at any one place. Negroes are accused of segregating themselves, of "racism in reverse," when they room together, party together, or walk along McCosh Walk together. "You can almost tell how scared some of the white students feel, or how much reservation they have about seeing a group of Negroes together in the library or students' center. We're not supposed to gather together because that presupposes some conspiracy or evil toward whites."

Negroes do tend to gravitate toward each other. Why? Mr. Fields claims "because the black students have common interests, common dialect, similar backgrounds and attitudes, and tastes. These are different from those of whites.

"The Negroes' problem is that they're visible. If several

religion majors walk together you have no way of identifying them visually. But you can't escape noticing . . . Negroes . . . together."

The Negroes explain that there are differences of manner, music, and conversation that whites just can't understand. They explain that the music and the frolicking which are part of white parties don't jive with their tastes in "soul" and dancing. They explain that they feel more comfortable with each other at times. Most of the black students have white roommates and white friends. "It's just that sometimes we like to get away from the white culture in which we don't always feel at home," said one.

Another explained, "Honestly, when a white boy comes up to you and tries to make you feel 'wanted' by telling you how much he digs 'soul music,' you soon begin to feel repulsed. If, in fact, we are 'set apart,' it is our response to the overzealous actions of the white students."

Negroes have been forced to join together in some instances because of deficiencies in the university structure. One junior said: "The black students here at Princeton are in the process of building structures that can serve for the growth of the brothers who come here in the future."

There are no Negro girls at mixers, so the black students joined together in suite parties with Negro contingents from the seven sister schools whose white girls traditionally populate Princeton mixers.

As much as anyone else, the Negro would like to see Princeton coeducational. He would like to see the dorm rule modified because "most Negro college students are accustomed to keeping late hours during a party."

The Negro can add to, or modify, the institution within which he functions. Over time, the university itself can adapt to the needs of its black undergraduates. But the attitudes of the members of the university community and the prejudices of the campus society, some feel, are difficult to deal with and are slow to change.

"There aren't too many displays of open bitterness at Princeton," a black student explains. "Things are done in a very subtle fashion, such as a faint smile or a refusal to acknowledge a Negro—especially if he is with a number of his brothers."

The Negro finds that most whites expect him to be at Princeton because he is an athlete. He finds that "white people try to force you to be one of those 'responsible' Negroes, one of the black leaders—but they want to dictate the terms of that responsibility and that leadership."

Some Negroes find that the only things whites feel comfortable talking about with them are sports and civil rights. The Negro finds that whites want their opinions justified by these "elite" of the black race. When the conversation does turn to civil rights, the Negro finds the white afraid to disagree. He tends to "overzealously confirm and back up every word we say" or simply "nod his head, seemingly afraid to differ."

The Negro finds whites suggesting that Negroes at Princeton are not real representatives of blacks—that they are "not Negroes in a certain sense." One Negro tells how a white girl thought she was complimenting him when she told him that he was such a fine person that he "deserved to be white."

For most of the black students, the Princeton campus provides the background for perplexing psychological pressures and profound philosophical probings.

"The main psychological pressure on me at Princeton," says one, "is to maintain my identity as a Negro and not to feel that I can crawl up in this academic hole and forget about the unjust treatment of the black people in the nation." Most Negroes at Princeton are concerned about losing touch with black society, alienation from their race.

Not all Negroes at Princeton perceive a black consciousness and a need for educated blacks to return to their people. Some Negroes try to pass for white. Some feel they should integrate with white society and avoid their "black brothers," others that they can best help the Negro cause by attaining individual success according to white values and serving as an example to both races.

But Mackey asserts the majority of Negroes at Princeton supports some variation of black power and expresses some sense of commitment to the Negro community. A junior said: "All too often, I've heard black students in predominantly white colleges say 'I want to be considered as an individual, not as a Negro.' Frankly, I would have no respect for myself as an individual if I ended up ignoring the needs of my people."

Mackey says that most Negroes at Princeton think in terms of leadership of the black people in one way or another. But he stresses that the method of leadership they choose will have to seem relevant to those expected to follow.

A Negro in the Ivy League is likely to be termed a running boy or puppet for the white establishment. "The black middle class," he contends, "is the only thing now being criticized more than the white middle class."

Mackey says that Negroes are advised when they leave their home communities not to forget where their roots are. "Don't let them mess up your mind too much; don't get too optimistic about making it in white society."

For that half of the black students which comes from white neighborhoods, Princeton usually means a transformation to greater militancy, according to Mackey. Often it results in summers spent close to the ghettos or at least close to the Negro representatives of the masses.

For Mackey, Princeton tends to imbed racial consciousness and responsibility through the reaction of its white students to the Negro. "Racial barbs at Princeton sting more than most because you realize that for all you've done, people still

won't change their opinion of you until you change the color
of your skin," he says. "Your concern is primarily with in-
tangibles. You realize that you must change society. For society as it exists now, you know that nothing you can do can
make them respect you or recognize your dignity. You cannot
help but develop a racial pride."

To cope with his challenges, the Negro finds it easiest to
maneuver primarily within his own subculture. "It's not that
we are antiwhite," claims one Negro. "It's just that there are
so many problems which the black man must solve for himself, that we don't have time to worry about the white man."

The problems facing the black students go far beyond the
boundaries of the Princeton campus. Through the ABC and
Princeton undergraduates who are town residents, Negro
students have become involved with the black man's problems
throughout the nation and, particularly, in the town of
Princeton.

The ABC is only one of several national associations of
black collegians. Last spring, the organization sponsored a
regional conference. Representatives from 46 Eastern schools
met at Princeton. Committees for regional communication,
fellowship, black culture, and community relations were
formed, including an organization of students and town
youths to improve relations between the two societies. The
group's name is "Pseukay," Greek for "soul."

Undergraduate concern with Negroes elsewhere is mir-
rored in the university's involvement with Lincoln University, a Negro institution 50 miles southwest of Philadelphia.
Princeton participates in a cooperative program with the
school, known as "the Negro Princeton." The program is designed to bring about student exchanges between the two universities.

The Negro at Princeton is an unfinished story. The lines of
communication, commitment, and concern have been established. Some questions have been asked; some problems have

been solved. The situation of the Negro at Princeton parallels the situation of the Negro in American society at large. On the other hand, some of the experiences encountered at Princeton are unique.

Essentially, the Negro comes to Princeton for an education. He finds that "there are things that black people don't understand and things that white people don't understand." Princeton institutions, attitudes, traditions, and stereotypes can be alien to him, and prove difficult. His presence on campus signals difficulties for white students. An interplay—somewhat uncertain and somewhat unnatural—hesitantly takes place.

This interplay and confrontation, this mutual re-evaluation, this contact of two societies "must become part of the experience of every white and every black in this pluralistic society," asserts Mr. Fields. "We are going to have to find ways by which each can naturally come to know and live and become involved with the other and be comfortable in this."

It is still too early to tell what percentage of Negroes at Princeton is going to become the norm. It is still too early to tell what effect Paul Mattox—a Negro employed in the admissions office since September—will have. It is still too early to tell what the eventual dialogue between whites and Negroes at Princeton will sound like or what the Princeton of another decade will look like.

It is still too early to tell when Negro professors will become commonplace. It is still too early to tell what will happen to the Negroes who graduate from Princeton. It is still too early to tell exactly what role Princeton is destined to play for the changing American Negro.

It is still too early to tell. But it is not too early to ask.

Maybe someday, the pictures of Princeton will show black faces among the shadows of Nassau Hall. Perhaps someday, the story of the Negro at Princeton will be no more unique than the story of the history major at Princeton or the Californian at Princeton or the atheist at Princeton. Maybe someday, Princeton will become in practice what she aspires to in theory.

Maybe. Just maybe.

Note to "The Negro at Princeton"

I wrote my story on the Negro at Princeton as a new era was beginning and just before students and scholars began earnestly to research and write about the topic. Since 1967, the life of the Negro at Princeton has changed a great deal, and his story has been more fully and accurately told.

In 1970, more than 120 blacks came to Princeton in its freshman class (and they are blacks, not Negroes). This meant that almost 15 per cent of the incoming class was black and it meant that there were almost 250 black undergraduates on campus. In 1969, a twenty-one-year-old black was elected to Princeton's Board of Trustees, and in 1970 a black junior was elected president of Princeton's student body. Princeton has an Afro-American Studies program now and there are more black graduate students and faculty members. Black administrators have become almost commonplace and, in fact, the whole question of black at Princeton, while not fully resolved, has been overshadowed by other much more pressing issues.

Black students now are expressing very little concern with the university as such. Their concern is with their people, and their attention is directed off the campus. There is less concern with identity and symbols of blackness on campus because blacks have defined themselves in terms of this country's black communities and they are living their blackness. They have resolved for themselves the questions of why they are at Princeton and what they are living for. Efforts to create an all-black dormitory collapsed last year when the blacks who would live there realized, first, that they were away from

campus so regularly they would not be at the dorm very
much, and second, that they did not feel they *had* to be "with
their own kind" in order to enjoy black music or use the
black idiom or congregate with their "brothers."

Because of increased numbers and because of a clearer
sense of direction, blacks at Princeton have changed. But, just
as importantly, so have whites. Today's youth, white and
black, is alienated together. Whites at Princeton don't share
a race pride (and may even suffer a race guilt), but they much
better understand blacks, are much more sensitive to their
humanity, and have much more in common with blacks than
Princetonians of only a few years back.

Research into the history of blacks at Princeton has un-
covered a few more blacks scattered throughout the university's past than were known about when I prepared my article.
There may even have been a black or two at Princeton before
1840. But the essentials of history presented in my article are
still quite accurate: the saga of the Princeton Negro did not
begin until the 1960's and the first real story of blacks at
Princeton is being written only now.

BOB TEAGUE

Fallout: A Letter to a Black Boy

BOB TEAGUE, nightly television news broadcaster for NBC, began his *Letters to a Black Boy* when Adam, his infant son, was less than a year old. The collection of heart-to-heart missives may, as someone has said, "help white readers to understand what it means to be black in a racist society." A popular football player at the University of Wisconsin, Mr. Teague later became a newspaperman with the *Milwaukee Journal* and then *The New York Times.* He lives in New York City. His wife, Matt Turney, performs with the Martha Graham Dance Company, and their "black boy," Adam Fitz-James Teague, is now in the neighborhood of three.

Dear Adam,

The fallout from the poisonous cloud of racism that hovers over this country can infect every square inch of a black man's life. And not just in his dealings with white men.

A few weeks ago, your daddy promised the black director of a ghetto youth center to come up and give my talk to his boys. Let's call the director Harry Day. We had never met face to face, but Harry was well known to every newsman in town after a stormy career as a full-time civil rights picket.

Now—Harry explained on the phone—he had given up on demonstrations. He was instead trying to guide black boys out of the crippling despair that was settling over their lives—he called it "the ghetto mentality."

"I hate to admit it," he told me, "but I'm caught up in the same thing myself. I've given up on freedom in my time. I must've walked thirty thousand miles with a picket sign in the last three years, and look at where we are today. Like nowhere. Hell, you can't shake Whitey up unless you use a Molotov cocktail or a gun. I just can't see myself doing that. So all I got left to hope on is the kids. But they won't make it neither unless we get inside their heads and move them to where they start believing they got some kind of a chance."

When I arrived this afternoon in Harry's neighborhood, I found it dreary, dirty and depressing. Like ghettos around the world. His youth center was a dingy brick building, four stories tall, in the middle of a long block lined on both sides by almost identical buildings barely resisting the urge to crumble. There were rusty cans overflowing with garbage along the curbs. Trash piles littered the sidewalks—mostly broken discarded furniture. Dozens of yammering black youngsters with old faces played in the trash piles or between them on the sidewalks. The stench from the garbage was unbearable. I was reminded of a story about Adolf Hitler walking through a concentration camp on an inspection tour. Hitler turned up his nose and said. "Jews stink." What he sniffed, of course, was Nazism.

Inside Harry's youth center, I was surprised. Everything was neat, clean and freshly painted in white trimmed with green—tables, chairs, bookshelves, everything. I could hear the uproar of manly teen-age voices coming from the upper floors. I found Harry sitting at an ancient roll-top desk in a cramped cubicle on the ground floor.

"Hey, man," he greeted me with a grin, extending his right hand. "Like welcome. Glad you got here so early."

We shook hands. Harry waved me into his chair—there was no room for another—and perched on the edge of the desk. He looked much younger than he had seemed on television. Perhaps thirty. Tall, dark and likable.

"I told the boys they could meet us in the rec room on the top floor at three-thirty," Harry said. "That means we got about fifteen minutes. Now I've read a lot about you, and I know you got a thing about talking to kids in the ghettos. Like I got my bag, and this is yours. But I want you to do something a little different today. A special favor."

"Like, man, you name it," I said. It was catching.

He rewarded me with a grin. "Well, let me explain something first. You have to understand that the kids living in this hell-hole ain't like a lot of other kids you've seen. This is Endsville, man, Endsville. They been left out of everything, and they know it. Only reason they listen to me at all when I tell 'em to stay out of trouble is they know I'm one of them. Just older. Like I was a high school dropout. You dig? I've done time. I ain't been able to make it.

"Now we come to you. These kids, they look at a guy like you—it's like you're somebody from outer space. You dig?"

"Not quite," I said, wondering what Harry was driving at.

"Well, here's the thing. You and me, we amount to about half the joker what could get through to these kids all the way. Wouldn't do no good for me to talk to 'em about staying in school and doing good deeds and all. Like they'd bust out laughing in my face. Okay. So we fudge a little. When you talk to 'em, you mess up your background a little. Don't make it sound so easy like it sounds in the stuff I read about you. Just say like you dropped out of school for a while. You got in trouble with the cops. Maybe you did a little time in reform school. Then you wised up; you straightened out, and you made it. You see what I mean? You made it with a second chance."

I saw.

"You mean you want me to lie for a good cause."

Harry shook his head, disgusted.

"Man, that ain't the way to look at it. Like we're talking about kids, man. Kids. We do it for the kids."

I didn't say anything for several seconds. I was a little stunned. The words I had planned to say to those kids were in my mind—accept responsibility, respect other people, keep your word. I would have choked on the words Harry wanted me to say.

When I tried, inadequately, to explain to Harry, he lost his temper.

"Don't hand me that Sunday school crap," he said fiercely. "Like this is the *real* world. You sound just like Whitey. Maybe you learned to be too much like Whitey to give us any help here."

I said I was sorry. Then I picked up my hat and left.

Driving home, I found it difficult to blame Harry Day. It was that damned, lousy fallout again. What he had asked me to do made me feel guilty and embarrassed. Guilty because I had spent my life grabbing first chances. Afraid, like Harry's boys, that there wouldn't be any second. Embarrassed because what he had said made mad sense in a society that conspired to keep black boys in that ghetto. I could not look into those young-old black faces and tell them more lies.

V

THE ELEVENTH HOUR

MICHAEL THELWELL

The Organizer

MICHAEL THELWELL was born in Jamaica, West Indies, in 1938 and came to the United States in 1959. His first published story won a college short-story contest in 1962 when he was a student at Howard University, Washington, D.C. Two others won subsequent honors in following years, and "The Organizer" won the STORY College Creative Awards first prize in 1968-69. Mr. Thelwell has been active in the civil-rights movement in the South. He now lives in Amherst, Massachusetts, where he is a member of the faculty of Amherst College and chairman of the W. E. B. Dubois Department of Afro-American Studies.

The river of that name cuts in half the town of Bogue Chitto, Mississippi. All of importance is east of the river—the jail, the drugstore and Western Union, the hotel, the Greyhound station and the Confederate memorial in the tree-shaded park. West of the river one comes to a paper mill, a cemetery, a junk yard, which merges with a garbage dump, and the Negro community.

Perched on a rise overlooking the dump and cemetery on one side and the Negro shacks on the other is the Freedom House. A low, unpainted concrete structure with a huge store-

front window, it had been built for us as a roadhouse in expectation of a road that had turned out to be campaign
oratory. When the road failed to materialize, the owner left
the state feeling, with some justification, that he had been
misled, and the building remained unused until the present
tenants moved in.

It is reported that when Sheriff John Sydney Hollowell
was told of the new arrivals he said, "Wal, they sho' chose a
mighty good place—ain't nothin' but trash nohow, an' mighty
subjeck to needin' buryin'."

This sally was savored, chuckled over and repeated, rapidly
making its rounds out of the jail house, to the bench sitters in
the park, the loungers in the general store, to be taken home
and repeated over the supper table. Thus by ten o'clock that
same night it had filtered up by way of the kitchens to the
tenants of the Freedom House.

"That peckerwood is a comical son-of-bitch, ain't he?"
Travis Peacock asked, and the thought came to him that perhaps the first thing to be done was to board up the big store-
front window. Either he forgot or changed his mind, for when
the other members of his project arrived they painted
"BOGUE CHITTO COMMUNITY CENTER, FREE-
DOM NOW" on the glass in huge black letters. Two weeks
later, while everyone was at a mass meeting in the Baptist
Church, someone demolished the window with three loads of
buckshot. Peacock boarded it up.

Time passed.

Peacock lay on his back in the darkness listening to the
clock on the town hall strike eleven. He turned on his side,
then sat up and unsnapped the straps of his overalls. "Too
damn tight, no wonder I can't sleep," he muttered, reached
under the cot for the pint bottle that Mama Jean had slipped
to him at the café that afternoon, laughing and cautioning
him, "Now doan go gittin' yore head all tore up, honey."

He had no intention of getting his head "tore up," but the fiery stump likker was a comfort. He jerked to a sitting position, listening. It was just the creaking, rusty Dr. Pepper sign moaning as the wind came up. He made a note to fix the sign tomorrow: "Damn thing run me crazy soon."

He lit a cigarette and sat in the darkness listening to the squeaking sign and shaking. He had never before spent a night alone in the Freedom House. Maybe I do need that rest up North, he thought. At the last staff meeting when Truman had hinted at it he had gotten mad. "Look, if you don't like the way I'm running the project come out and say so, man." And Truman had muttered something about "owing it to the movement to take care of our health." Maybe he did need that rest.

He thought of going down to Mama Jean's or the Hightowers' and spending the night there. He pulled on his boots to go, then changed his mind. The first rule for an organizer, and maybe the hardest, was never to let the community know that you were afraid. He couldn't go, even though the people had all tried to get him to stay in the community that night. That afternoon when he was in the café Mama Jean had suggested that he stay in her son's room.

"Shoot, now, honey," she beamed, "yo' doan want to be catchin' yo' death o' cold up theah on thet cold concrete by yo'se'f."

Raf Jones had chimed in, "Yeah man, we gon' drink us some stump juice, tell some lies, and play some Georgia Skin tonight." But he had declined. And Old Mrs. Ruffin had met him and repeated her urging to come stay a few nights at her place. But that was above the call of duty. A standing joke on the project was that the two places in Bogue Chitto to avoid were, "Buddy Hollowell's jail, and Ol' Miz Ruffin's kitchen. She a nice ol' lady, but she the worse cook in Mississippi. Man, that ol' lady burn Kool-aid."

As the afternoon progressed and he received two more invitations, he realized that the community was worried. They knew that the other three staff members were in Atlanta for a meeting and they didn't want him spending a night alone in the office.

By his watch it was nearly midnight. He took a drink and lit another cigarette. Maybe they'd skip tonight. He was tempted to take the phone off the hook. "Hell no," he muttered. "I ain't going give them that satisfaction." But what did it mean if the phone didn't ring? At least when they on the phone you know they ain't sneaking around outside with a can of kerosene.

He got off the cot and went into the front room, the "office." It was the big public part of the building with a couple of desks, a table, chairs, mimeo machine and a few old typewriters, and in one section a blackboard where small meetings and literacy classes were held. He sat at a desk with the phone, staring at the boarded-up window.

"Ring, you son-ovva-bitch, ring. You kept me up, now ring." He calmed himself down by reading the posters. A black fist holding a broken chain. "Freedom." Goddamn you, ring. Another poster, "Pearl River County Voters' League: One Man One Vote." Would it be a man or a woman this time? It was five after midnight. They were late. That was unusual.

Maybe they wouldn't call tonight. They always seemed to know what was happening. Maybe they thought that everyone was gone to Atlanta. Suppose they thought that and came to wreck the office? Peacock was still, listening. He was certain that he heard the sounds of movement outside. He went into the storeroom, tripped over a box of old clothes and swore. He came back with the shotgun just as the phone rang, piercingly loud. He dropped the gun and jumped for the phone.

"Pearl River County Voters' League, can we help you?" His voice is steady and that gives him some satisfaction.

There is a low laugh coming over the receiver. "Heh, heh, heh."

"Hello, you are late tonight," Travis says.

"Nigger," the voice asks, "you alone up theah, ain'tchu?"

It's a man's voice. Good. The women are hysterical and foul-mouthed.

"You alone up theah?" The voice persists. Travis' nervousness has become anger. He starts to say, "No Charlie, I ain't alone, yo' Momma's here with me." But restrains himself.

"I'm not alone, there are three of us here." He says and laughs, yeah me, Jesus and mah shotgun.

"Ah know you alone. Thet pointy-head nigger an' the Jewboy gone to Atlanta. Heh, heh."

"If you think so, come up and find out." Peacock invited in an even voice. "Why don't you do that?" There was a pause.

"We comin' direckly, boy, an' you can sell the shithouse, cause hit's going to be yore ass." Peacock doesn't answer. He stands holding the phone listening to the hoarse breathing from the other end. "Heh, heh. Nigger, yo' subjeck to bein' blowed up." Click. The phone goes dead and Peacock, shaking violently, stands listening to his own breathing.

Somehow that final click is the most terrifying part. As long as you can feel that there is a human being on the other end, despite the obscenity and the threats, you have some contact. Peacock broke the shotgun and loaded it. The phone rings. Briefly he debates not answering it but he knows he has to. With Ray and Mac on the road, he has to; they could be in trouble. He picks up the phone.

"Hello." That demented chuckling.

"Knowed yo' wasn't sleepin', Nigger. Ain't nevah goin' sleep no mo'."

"If I don't, neither will you, brother."

"Boy, yo' subjeck to bein' blowed up." Click.

Well, hope that's over for the night. But it isn't. They're

going to take turns calling. He went to get what was left of the bottle wishing he could remove the phone from the hook. They must rotate the telephone duty, everyone volunteering to give up a night's sleep on a regular basis. Damn.

Peacock began to regret his decision not to go to the meeting. It would have been nice to see everyone again and find how things were on other projects. In Alabama, things looked pretty mean. But so were things here. That was one of the reasons he had stayed. As project director he thought that he should stay with the community in case some crisis broke. Where did his responsibility end?

Sitting there waiting for the phone to ring, he began to leaf idly through the progress report that he had sent to the meeting. He had done a damn good organizing job. The community was together, and had really strong local leadership, whose skill and competence were increasing rapidly.

Morale was high. They had formed a voters' organization and elected Jesse Lee Hightower chairman. He was a good man with real leadership potential for the entire state. And every act of intimidation seemed to increase his determination and that of the community. After the deacon board of the New Hope Baptist Church had been informed that the insurance of the church would not be renewed, they had met and voted to continue to hold meetings there. A week later the church was a total loss. The Sheriff attributed its destruction to a mysterious and very active arsonist called Faulty Wiring who had been wreaking havoc with other Negro churches in the state.

Then Mama Jean's café came under fire. She had been publicly displaying posters and announcements. The merchants in town cut off her credit, and refused to sell her supplies for cash. She had been selling beer and wine for fifteen years with the approval of three sheriffs, although the county was allegedly dry. Now she was charged with the illegal sale of alcohol and a hearing scheduled for the purpose of cancelling her license.

When the news reached Peacock he had been worried. The huge, loud, tough-talking woman was a leader and a symbol in the community—it was Mama Jean and Jesse who had been the first to go across the river to try to register to vote—Mama Jean wearing her floppy, terrible flowered hat, gloves and long black coat in the summer heat. They had been met by the Sheriff and three deputies.

"This office is closed till four o'clock."

"We come to register, Sheriff Hollowell."

"This office is closed."

"Why, thass all right, honey." Mama Jean's gold teeth were flashing. "Usses done waited a hunnerd yeahs, be plumb easy to wait till fo' o'clock." And she swept into the hall, marched to the only chair available and composed herself to wait. Hollowell and his deputies, obviously not prepared for that, had remained muttering veiled threats and caressing their guns. All knew the office would not open that afternoon.

Without her and the Hightowers, Peacock could never have gotten started in the community. If she broke, the community would crumble overnight. So he had been very worried when he ran to her café that afternoon. He was somewhat surprised to find her behind the bar laughing and joking.

"Mama Jean, what are you going to do?"

"Whut ah'm gon' do? Do 'bout whut, honey?" she was looking at him as though surprised at the question.

"Didn't they cut your credit? I heard . . ."

"Oh shush now, take mo'n thet li'l bitty ol' sto'keeper to stop Mama Jean. Jes' doan yo' fret yo'se'f none, heah. Ah be keepin' on keepin' on like ah always done." And she had. No more was heard about the illegal sale of liquor, and twice a week she got into Jesse Lee's pickup truck and drove into Louisiana to buy supplies. She claimed it was much cheaper.

Then the town council tripled the tax assessment on her café. Peacock got her a lawyer, and she was challenging the assessment, even threatening to file a damage suit.

"Damn," Peacock muttered, "if that lady was thirty years younger I swear I'd ask her to marry me." Thinking of Mama Jean cheered him. Some of the people in that poverty-stricken, hard-pressed community were so great, like the Hightowers and the Joneses, he felt warm with pride and love; it was as if he had returned to a home he had never known, but always missed.

He had lived with the Hightowers at first, while he met the people and learned the community. He felt closer to them than to his natural family who now seemed to him shadowy figures leading barren and futile lives in their Northern suburb.

He thought of Miss Vickie. Jesse's wife, a small fragile appearing woman always hovering around her burly husband, expressing her support by small, thoughtful acts. And the two kids, Richie and Fannie Lou who was extremely bright and curious beneath her shyness. Peacock loaned her books and had long talks with her, constantly being surprised at the range and breadth of her curiosity. The Negro school only went to the ninth grade, and she had long surpassed her teachers. She had finally quit, and was now a full-time volunteer, doing the typing and running the office.

His favorite was eight-year-old Richie, like his father a leader and a born organizer. He had created an organization to blanket the community with leaflets. Then he had badgered and begged until Miss Vickie bought him a denim jacket and overalls "like Travis'." A hell of an organizer he will be when he grows up, Peacock reflected.

Peacock noticed that his bottle was almost empty. He could feel the effects of the liquor, particularly potent after his recent tension.

"Hell, no wonder, you sittin' here getting so sentimental.

A sixteen-year-old girl has a crush on you, her kid brother thinks you are Jesus, and your leader complex runs away again." But he felt easier now and tired. He went into the back room and stretched out on the cot, feeling his limbs relax as he gave in to exhaustion. But his mind wouldn't turn off.

He was in that half-way zone between sleep and wakefulness in which thoughts disguise themselves as dreams, when he heard the sound. That is, he sensed it, a kind of silent, dull reverberation, that reached his mind before the sound came to him—the heavy, somehow ponderous boom of dynamite. Silence, then a yapping, howling chorus as every dog in town began to bark.

Peacock froze on the cot. *Oh God. Oh God. Let it be a church, not anyone's house.*

He wanted to pull on his boots but was paralyzed. His stomach felt empty and weak. He retched and puked up all the hot acid liquor. His fear returned and he began to shake violently. *Somebody's dead. They killed someone. Mama Jean. I don't want to know. I can't go.* He sat there smelling his vomit, until he heard the pounding on the door. "Travis, ho, Travis!"

He stumbled into the front room, going for the door. Then he returned for the shotgun. His voice came as a hoarse whisper and it took two efforts to make himself audible. "Who is it?"

"Us, Raf Jones and Sweezy. We alone."

Peacock knew the men. They had both been fired from the paper mill after attempting to register. When there was money in the project he gave them subsistence, other times they helped Mama Jean in the café in return for meals. He opened the door. Jones and Sweezy were carrying rifles. They didn't know what had happened, either, having been outside the Freedom House when they heard the noise.

In a few moments they were running down the hill, past

the edge of the cemetery toward the town and the café. Peacock was sure that the nightriders had tried for the café, but when, panting and gasping, they reached there, they found it intact. So was the little church that was now being used for meetings. Where was the explosion? A car turned into the road, going fast and raising a cloud of dust. The headlights picked them out, and they dived into the ditch. The car roared past.

"Hit's the Sher'f," Raf said. "Trouble taken place fo' sho'." They set out running in the car's dust. It passed two side roads, then turned. Peacock had no doubt where it was headed now.

"Good God Almighty." He half moaned, half shouted and stopped. The two men ran on without him, then stopped and turned.

"Yo' awright?"

Peacock nodded and waved them on. His eyes and nose were filled with dust. His chest heaved. He coughed. Whatever had happened wouldn't change before he got there. He even had a momentary urge to turn back, to run somewhere and hide, certain that something terrible and irrevocable had happened. He stood bent double in the road, clutching his sides, coughing, eyes streaming water, no longer gut-scared but filled with dread. He couldn't go on.

Wait, maybe no one had been hurt. A house can be rebuilt. He personally would go North to raise the money. He would gouge it out cent by cent from his family and their affluent and secure neighbors. If it was only the house! Then he was running again. He could smell burnt powder now. It seemed like the entire town was crowded in the road before him. He recognized faces, people, everyone was talking.

"Wha' happen? Wha' happen?"

"Whole family daid?"

"Two white fellers in a car."

Pushing his way through the crowd, Peacock realized that

he was still carrying the shotgun. He didn't know what to do
with it. The people would be looking to him, and if he had a
gun. . . . Besides it'd be in every lousy newspaper in the country that the local representative of the organization had arrived on the scene carrying a weapon.

He pushed his way to the front of the crowd, no one called
his name. Was it his imagination or were they stepping away
from him? Oh God, were they blaming him?

The Sheriff's car was right in front of the house, its search-
light beaming into the living room. The front of the house
was a shambles, porch completely gone, the front wall torn
away. A pair of deputies stood facing the crowd carrying tear-
gas guns, cumbersome, futuristic looking weapons that
seemed to belong in a Flash Gordon kit. "Y'awl keep on back
now. Sheriff's orduhs."

Clutching the shotgun, Peacock darted out of the crowd
toward the house. One deputy turned to face him.

"Wheah yew going?"

"I'm kin," Peacock said without stopping. The deputy
turned back to the crowd which had surged forward.

Peacock ran around the house and came up to the back
door. The smell of burnt powder lingered strong. At the
kitchen door he stopped, looking in; the kitchen was filled
with people. Mama Jean turned to the door and saw him.

"Oh Travis, Travis, honey. They done hit. They done kilt
Jesse." The people gave a low moan of assent. It seemed to
Travis that they were looking at him accusingly, the stranger
who had brought death among them. Then Mama Jean was
holding him. He clung to her without shame, comforting
himself in her large, warm strength. He was sure now that
there was hostility in the room. The people gathered there
had kept aloof from the Voters' League, explaining that they
had to avoid commitment so that they could keep their position flexible and talk with the white community. He recognized the school principal, the minister from the big Baptist

church, and the undertaker. No one spoke. Then Mama Jean
was leading him into the bedroom. "The fam'ly bin askin'
fo' yo', Travis."

Their heads all turned to Peacock as they entered. Fanny
Lou was holding Richie, their eyes big, black solemn pools in
their young faces. Miss Vickie huddled on the bed, leaning
forward, her back sharply curved, hunch-shouldered, clutching her clasped hands between her knees. Her face seemed set,
polished from smooth black stone. When she turned her head
to the door her eyes showed nothing.

"See, he come. He all right, nothing happen to him."
Mama Jean's tone was soothing, meant to reassure them. But
for one second Peacock heard only a reproach for his own
safety and survival. *You must say something. You have to tell
these folks something.*

From the next room he heard a low wailing hum. They
were half humming, half singing one of those slow, dirge-like
songs that was their response in times when no other response
was possible. *"Shiine on Mee, Oh, shiiine on Meee . . ."*

Peacock crossed to Miss Vickie. His limbs felt heavy, as
though he were moving through some heavy liquid medium,
but his footsteps sounded loud. He bent and took her hands.
They were limp at first, then they imprisoned his in a quick
fierce grip. He was looking into her eyes for some sign of
warmth, life, recognition, but most of all for some sign of ab-
solution, forgiveness.

Jumbled phrases crowded through his mind. Trite, traditional words, phrases that were supposed to bear comfort, to
move, to stir, to strengthen, and ultimately to justify and
make right. But the will of which God? Whose God, that this
man, this husband . . . *I am not to blame. I didn't do it.*
Silently Peacock looked at her. She returned his look blankly.
Then she pitched forward and her head rested on his arms.

"We will do everything . . . we must keep on . . . brave and good man . . . do what he would want us to do . . . death not in vain."

Which voice was that spewing out tired political phrases we hear too often. It couldn't have been me, please it was someone else. What hard hands she has. "Miss Vickie, I'm sorry," Peacock said, "I'm sorry."

"Hush chile. T'aint yore fault." Mama Jean's deep voice cracked. "T'aint none of us heah fault, cept we shoulda moved long time ago. Hit's a long time they been killin' us, little by little . . ."

"Ahmen," Miss Vickie said. Richie started to cry. Peacock picked him up, surprised at how light he was. The boy threw his skinny arms around Peacock's neck and buried his wet cheeks in his neck. Hugging him tightly, Travis felt his own tears starting for the first time.

"Who is comforting who?" he asked himself.

There was a soft knock on the door, and the elderly unctuous minister clad in his black suit glided in from the kitchen.

"Miz Hightower, hit's the Sher'f come to talk to you." Miss Vickie sat up, a mixture of emotions crossing her face.

"Thet 'Buddy' Hollowell have no shame. Effen he did . . ." Mama Jean began as Sheriff Hollowell strode into the room, accompanied by a man in a business suit. "Seems like some folks doan even knock fo' they come bustin' into folks' houses," Mama Jean snorted.

The Sheriff stood in the center of the room. He ran his glance over the group, fingering his jowl. He was a big, solid man, heavy-boned, thick-waisted and with enormous red hands. He was wearing his khaki uniform and a planter's Stetson. He stared at the floor just in front of Miss Vickie, and his jaw moved slowly and steadily.

"Ah just come to git a statement from the widow." His voice must have sounded subdued and apologetic in his own ears for he paused briefly and continued in a louder voice. "So theah ain't no need fer anyone else to be saying nothin'."

Mama Jean snorted. Then there was dead silence in the room. Rev. Battel who had been standing in the doorway made a sidling self-effacing motion and was frozen by a glare from Mama Jean.

"Well, which a yew is the widow?" the Sheriff asked.

"Ah'm Mrs. Hightower," Miss Vickie said and pulled herself up erect. She looked at the official with an expression of quiet, intense contempt that seemed to be almost physical, coming from a depth of outrage and grief beyond her will. Peacock would swear that Miss Vickie had no knowledge of what was in her eyes. His own spirit shrank within him.

"Sheriff Hollowell," he said softly, "there's been a death in this house."

The second man flushed and removed his hat. The Sheriff gave no sign of having seen or heard anything. "Yew have another room where ah can git yore statement?" He could have been addressing anyone in the room.

"We used to." Miss Vickie said. "Anythang need to be said kin be said right here. These my husband's family and friends."

Hollowell produced a notebook and flipped his Stetson back on his head. The second man was also holding a pad. "Wal, whut happened?" Again there was a pause.

" 'What happened? What happened,' Jesus God Almighty." The words flashed through Peacock's mind, and he only realized that he had spoken when Hollowell said "Ah'm not gon' tell yew to shut up again, boy."

Miss Vickie's voice was calm and low, without inflection or emphasis. "Ah wuz sleepin' an' then ah woke up. Heard like a car drive up in the road going slow like. Hit drive past three times like they was lookin' fo' something. Ah see that Jesse Lee wun't in the bed. Ah listen fo' a spell an' didn' heah nothin' so I call out an' he answer from the front.

" 'Hit's allright, go to sleep.' But ah knew hit wuz somethin' wrong and ah started to get up . . . Then, then like the room light up an' ah feel this hot win' an' the noise an' hit was nothin' but smoke an ah heah mah daughter scream . . ." Her voice broke off and she began to sob softly. The two children began to sob too. Mama Jean turned and stared at the wall.

"Is this necessary, Sheriff?" Peacock asked.

"Boy, yew not from round heah are yew?"

"You know who I am," Peacock said. Miss Vickie began to speak.

"An' thass all. Evrah thang wuz like yo' see hit now, only the children wuz cryin' and Jesse Lee was lyin' on the floor in the front room. Ah nevah seen no car."

"Jes' one thang more, Miz Hightower." Hollowell's voice was almost gentle. "Yew know any reason fo' anyone to dew a thang lak' this?"

Peacock stared at the Sheriff incredulously.

"Same reason he got arrest three time for drunk drivin' when evrah-body know he nevah did drink," Mama Jean said.

"Ah doan know why some folks do whut they do," Miss Vickie said.

"Wal, ah'l sho let yew know soon as ah find out anything." Hollowell snapped his book. "Mighty sorry myself. Only one thang more, this gentleman heah, be wanting to ask yew a few questions." His companion seemed uncomfortable, his Adam's apple bobbing jerkily in his thin neck. His cheek twitched and he passed a hand quickly over his thinning hair. "I think I've got all I need," he began. Hollowell looked at him. "Well maybe just one thing. I'm from the Associated Press in New Orleans, happened to be passing through." He darted a quick look at the Sheriff, and spoke more rapidly. "I want you to know how sorry I am. This is a terrible, terrible thing. I want you to know that you have the sympathy of every decent person in the state, Mrs. Hightower. I hope . . . I'm sure that whoever did this will be found and punished. I was wondering if there is anything that you would like to say, any kind of personal statement . . ."

"Why can't you leave the family in peace?" Peacock was on his feet. "What more statement do you want, isn't what happened statement enough? For God's sake, what more do you want?" But Peacock's anger was not at the timid little man, but at what he knew was to come for the family—an ordeal that would be as painful as the night before them and in its own way more obscene than the brute fact of death. He was lashing out at that future and the role that he could neither escape nor resolve.

"Now ah've warned yew." The Sheriff was advancing toward him.

"Mist'r Hollowell, come quick before something happen." A deputy was standing in the door. "Hit's the niggers, yew bettah come." The deputy disappeared, followed by Hollowell and the reporter.

"Preacher," the Sheriff called over his shoulder, "maybe yew better come on." The old man followed silently, and then Peacock heard the crowd. Waves of boos and shouts came in spurts, and in between shouted angry words:

"Thet sho' doan sound good. Them folks is mad. Them peoples is afixin' to turn this town out an' ah swears thet in mah heart ah doan blame 'em."

"Ain't that the truth," Peacock said, "but I'd blame myself. You know the Safety Patrol is coming, and maybe even the Army. Them peckerwoods will shoot us down like dogs. And we gotta do something. The only people can stop them is right here in this room." He looked at Miss Vickie. She rocked back and forth and wouldn't look at him. He thought for a while that she hadn't heard. Then she spoke very softly.

"Travis, ah jes' doan know no mo'. Seems like either they gits kilt tonight or one by one nex' week. Maybe this is what hit had to come to. Ah jes' ain't straight in mah own min'."

Peacock sat down silently on the bed, his head bowed. He

understood how she felt. He too longed for the swift liberating relief of wild, mindless, purging violence, ending maybe in death. But survival, what of that? Suppose he was one of the survivors. It was a nightmare that had hovered in the back of his consciousness ever since he had joined the movement—yet he saw himself limping away from the burning town, away from the dead and maimed, people to whom he had come to singing songs of freedom and rewarded with death and ashes. The organizer is always responsible. That was the second rule.

"Miss Vickie. You know how much I loved Jesse, more than my natural father. I ain't got to tell you how I feel, but you know Jesse would feel this way too. If you won't come with me to speak to the folks, lemme give them a word from you." Miss Vickie did not answer immediately. There was a new frenzy of shouting outside, louder, more hysterical than before. Peacock couldn't wait for an answer, and Mama Jean followed him as he ran out into the shouting. . . .

"Look at them peckerwoods. Look at them. See who them guns pointing at. We din' kill nobody. We din' bomb no house. Hit wuzn't us, but who the guns pointing at? Why ain't they go find the killers? Why? 'Cause they knows who they is, they brothahs an' they cousins, thass who!"

Peacock recognized Raf Jones. Himself and Sweezy and some of the younger men were grouped in front of the police car. They were armed. "Look at thet Raf, fixin' to get hisse'f kilt too." Mama Jean muttered. "Yo' right Travis, now whut is we gon' do?" They walked over to the car. Hollowell began to talk through a bull horn, his flat, nasal voice magnified and echoing through the night.

"Awright, awright. This is Sher'f Hollowell. That's enough, ah want yew to cleah these streets." Angry shouts from the crowd. "Yew good collud folks of this town know me."

"Yo' damn right we does." Raf shouted back.

"Yew know me, and ah know most of yew. Ah know yew're

good, decent folk that don't want no trouble. An' this town din' have no trouble till them agitators pull in heah to disrup' and destroy whut we had. Now a man was kilt heah tonight. Ah wanna ask yew, yew all sensible folks, ah wanna ask yew. Was theah any trouble fore these trouble-makers started hangin' round heah?"

"Allus bin trouble," Raf screamed. "Allus bin killin's." The crowd roared agreement.

"An' ah want to tell yew, ah have mah own feelin's bout who done this terrible thang heah tonight. Ah tell yew, yew got evrah right to be mad. Why, hit could'a jes' as easy bin a white man got blowed up. Yew're decent folk, ah know thet. Ah know hit wasn't none o' yew did this thang. We got a good town heah. But ah want to ask yew this. Dew yew *know* anythang 'bout these outsiders yew bin harboring? What dew yew know bout them? Tell me, dew yew thank thet these race mixahs an' agitators mean this town any good? Wheah dew they come from? Right now ah only see one ov 'em. Where's the othah two raht now? Ah want yew to go hom an' thank 'about thet. Yew will git the true answers, you cain't plant corn an' hit come up cotton. Y'awl go on home now an' thank 'bout whut ah said."

The crowd was silent, shuffling sullenly. No one left. "Ah want yew to go now. Ah'm ordering yew to break this up. Stay and yew break the law. Ah've called the Safety Patrol barracks an' troopers is on the way. In ten minutes they be heah. Anyone still heah goes to jail. Yew heah me?" Silence.

"Awright, awright. Ah got someone heah yew all know. He is one of yew, a fine collud gentleman. He got somethin' to say, thcn he goin' lead yew in prayer, an' that'll be awl. Step up heah, Preacher Battel." Before the old man could move Mama Jean stepped in front of him, one hand on her hip, the other wagging in his face. Peacock heard her saying, ". . . Swear 'fo' Gawd, effen yo' git up now an' start in to Tommin' fo' thet cracker, ah'm gon' run ye outta town myse'f.

Yo' heah me, Charlie Battel, ah'm sick an' tard of bein' sick
an' tard of yo' selling the folks out." Battel backed away before her fury. Hollowell came over fingering his gun.

"An' as fo' yo' Bo Hollowell, the onliest true thang yo' say
wuz thet we knows yo'. An' ah knows yo' pappy befo' yo'. Yo'
wuz none o' yo' any good. No mo' good than a rattlesnake.
Whoa now, Bo Hollowell, yo' lay a han' to me an' hit's yo' las'
living ack. Me 'n' Travis gon' git the folks to go home, but
hit's gon' be our way. We gon' do hit cause we doan want no
mo' peoples kilt, an' thass whut you fixing to do. But if hit's
mo' dying tonight, t'aint only black folks gon' die."

She turned her back on him and marched over to the car,
walking past an immobilized Hollowell as though he were not
present. The passionate power of the fat, middle-aged woman
was awesome even to Peacock, against whom it was not
directed. He followed her automatically.

"Gi'mme a han' up," she demanded. She balanced herself
on the fender of the car, holding Travis' shoulder for support.
Silently she surveyed the crowd, her broad chest heaving, hair
unkempt and standing out on her head. "Lookaheah. Hit's
me, Mama Jean, an' ah ain't got much to say. But yo' all hear
that rattlesnake talking 'bout outside agitators. Yo' all
knowed he wuz talking 'bout Travis. Wal, maybe he is a
agitator. But yo' seen the agitator in yo' white folks' washing
machine. Yo' know what hit do, hit git the dirt out. Thass
right, an' thass what Travis gon' do now. Listen to him, he
got a message from Miss Vickie. An' he gon' git out all the
dirt thet Hollowell bin asayin'." She jumped down. "Go on,
son, talk some sense to the folks. Ah'm jes' too mean mad
mese'f, but yo' kin tell them lak hit is."

Hollowell stepped up. "Don't look like ah got much choice."
He drew his pistol from its holster. "So yew say yore piece,
but remember ah'l be raht heah behind yew. Yew git them
to go home now. Say one wrong word . . ." He waved his pistol
suggestively.

Travis climbed onto the bonnet of the car and waved his arms for silence. The skin of his back crawled, sensitive to the slightest pressure of his shirt and waiting for the first probing touch of Hollowell's bullet. He closed his eyes and waited for the crowd's attention.

"Friends. Friends, you got to be quiet now, cause I ain't got no bull horn like Hollowell, an' I want you to hear every word." That's right, keep your voice low so they have to calm down to hear. "You all can see that house right there, least what the crackers left of it. There's a lady inside there, a black lady. And her husband's dead. They killed her husband an' she grievin'. You know she grievin'. Seem like thass all we black folk know to do, is grieve. We always grievin', it seem like." Peacock shook his head and bowed his head as though in grief or deep thought. A woman gave a low scream, "Jesus, Jesus," and began to sob, deep, animal, racking sounds that carried into the crowd. Peacock waited, head bowed, until he heard a few more muffled sobs from the crowd.

"Yes, some o' us cryin'. Thass all right, let the good sister cry, she got reason. Will ease huh troubled heart. Lady inside thet bombed-out, burned-out house cryin' too. She cryin' right now but while her soul cry for the dead, her min' is on the livin'. She thinking 'bout you. That's the kind of lady she is. She say to tell you the time for weeping is almost over. Soon be over. She say she cryin' for her man tonight, an' she don't want to cry for her brothers and sisters tomorrow. She say they already kill one, don't give them a chance to kill no more. She say to go home peacefully."

"Why?" Raf shouted, "so they kin git the rest o' us when we lyin' up in the bed? Ah say, GIT ON WIT THE KILLIN'!" There was a roar from the people, but Peacock judged that it came mainly from Raf's little group. Raf, shut up, please. Every time you say something like that, I can just feel that cracker's finger jerking. He had to find something to divert the people. "Miss Vickie, say to go home, it's what

Jesse Lee would want." A deep murmur of rejection came back.

"Jesse Lee was a fighter!" Raf yelled. This was greeted with cheers.

"Lookaheah," Travis said, raising his voice and adopting the accent of the folk. "Lookaheah, y'awl heard the Sheriff." *I sure hope Hollowell doesn't loose his cool. I got to do this now.* A small muscle in his back kept twitching. "Yeah, ah'm talkin' 'bout Bo Hollowell, that ugly ol' lard-ass, big belly, Bo Hollowell." Peacock held his breath. No sound came from behind him. There was scattered laughter in the crowd.

"Yeah," Peacock continued, "look at him. Ain't he the sorriest, pitifullest thang yo' evah saw? Ain't he now? Looka him. See him standing there holdin' thet gun. He scared. Yo' heard him say he called fo' the troopers. Wal, he did. Yo' know he did, cause he scared as hell. Hit's too many angry black folk heah fo' him. He scared. Look at him." Peacock turned and pointed. Hollowell was standing in front of his deputies. His Stetson was pulled down to hide his eyes, but Peacock could see the spreading black stain under his arms, and his heavy jaw grinding as he shook with barely controlled fury. But there were cheers and laughter in the crowd now.

"He scared lak a girl," Peacock shouted and forced himself to laugh. "Why ol' bad-assed Bo Hollowell standin' theah shaking jes' lak a dawg tryin' to shit a peach stone." That cracked the people up, real laughter, vindictive and punitive to the lawman, but full, deep and therapeutic to the crowd.

"Yessuh, lak a dawg tryin' to shit a peachstone," Peacock repeated, and the people hooted. *Jesse, I know you understand,* Peacock apologized. *I got to do this.* He waved for silence and got it. His voice was soft now.

"But looka heah, very close now. Sho' he scared. But he scared jes' lak them peckerwoods whut blowed up this house. An' yo' knows whoevah done it ain't even folks. They scared, they sick. Thass right. Whenevah peckerwoods git scared, niggers git kilt. Ahuh, thass lak hit is, whenevah white folks git scared, black folks git kilt. Yo watch 'at ol' big belly Bo. He scared right enough to kill me right heah." Peacock was sweating in the night breeze. I have to do it just right, one word too much and he's goin' break, he warned himself.

"See," he said, "an' when them othah crackers git heah, they goin' be scared too. They gon' start whuppin' heads an shootin' folks lak we wuz rabbits."

"Thass right.'

"He right."

"Tell the truth."

"See. An' they's a lot of women an' chillun, beautiful black chillun out heah. What's gon' happen to them? Now yo' men got yo' guns. An' thass good. If Jesse Lee hada had his'n he might be alive this minute. So we gotta be ready. But whoevah stay heah now, bettah be ready to die. Thass right, *be ready to die.*"

"We dyin' right now," Raf shouted.

"That wuz true. An' hit still is. But not no mo'. Hit's a new day comin'. Hit's gotta come. A new day. Thass whut scared them peckerwoods, why they kill Jesse Lee. 'Cause Jesse was a free man. He didn't take no mess. Y'awl know that? An' he was tryin' to git y'awl to come with him. That's what scare them folks. He was a free man. His min' was free. He was not afraid."

"Tell it."

"Right. Thass right."

"Yes, brothahs an' sistuhs, thass whut scare 'em. Black folks wuz fixin' to be free. Ahuh. See, an' ol' Bo knew thet. Them peckerwoods is mighty tricky. Yo' gotta study 'em, they *awful* tricky."

"Yes Jesus, they sho' is."

"So now, lookaheah very careful now. Inside that house is this black lady, an' she mournin' fo' her husband. An' she say, Go home. She say, Go home, cause she love yo', an' she cain't

stan' no mo' grievin'. Then out heah, yo' got Bo Hollowell
an' his gun. He say, Go home, too. Now why would he say
that? 'Cause he scared? Thass part of hit. But mostly, yo' know
why he say thet, 'cause he know we sick an' tard. He know
we sick an' tard o' bein' whupped." Peacock was now chant-
ing in the sing-song cadence of the ecstatic sermon with the
full participation of the people.
   "Sick an tard o' being starved."
   "Oh yes, oh yes."
   "Sick an' tard o' being worked to death."
   "Oh yes, yes Jesus."
   "Sick an' tard o' bein' cheated."
   "Jesus Gawd, yes."
   "Sick an' tard o' bein' kilt."
   "Yeah, mah brothahs an' sistuhs, that cracker know we sick
an' tard, thet we sick an' tard o' *bein' sick an' tard.*"
   "Tell it, tell it."
   "Yeah, that cracker sure do know thet so long as we live,
we gon' be free. He know that if he say go home, yo' gon'
stay. An' yo' know somethin', even though he scared, he mad
too. An' cause he scared he want yo' to go home. An' cause
he mad, he kinda hope yo' gon' stay. An' yo' know why? Yo'
know why that cracker, yeah look at him, yo' know why he
want yo' to stay? SO HE CAN KILL SOME MO' BLACK
FOLKS. Thass right. Evra one heah know he bin sayin' he
gon' come down heah an' clean the niggers out. Yo' know he
say thet evrah time he git drunk."
   "Thass right."
   "The gospel truth."
   "Yo' right, man."
Peacock waved his hands for silence. He spoke softly and
clearly now as though he were revealing a great secret. He
tried to inject into his voice certitude and calm authority. Yet
he was tired and the slowness of his speech was not entirely
for effect. His dripping body was lethargic, relaxed, and a

peacefulness crept over him. For the first time he did not care about Hollowell's gun at his back.

"So whut we gon' do, mah brothers? We are going to go home like Miss Vickie say do. We going to trick ol' Bo Hollowell this time. No more black folk going to die tonight. We men with the guns going to get the women and kids home. We going to get them there safe. And then we going to stay there. When those troopers come, there ain't going to be no folks standing around for them to beat on, all right? And we are going to stay home so that if any more bomb-toting crackers come we can defend our children an' our homes, all right?"

The crowd shouted assent.

"But that's only tonight. We aren't going to let Jesse Lee Hightower jes' die like that, are we? No. Uhuh. Tomorrow night we going come back to a meeting. Tomorrow night at eight o'clock, we all going to come to a meeting an' plan and decide just what we going to do."

"Yes, we is!" the crowd roared.

"An' we going to do it all together. Us folks gotta stick together. And you know where the meeting is going to be tomorrow night? In Rev. Battel's church, that's where. Rev'ren' say he done seen the light, an' out of respect fo' Jesse Lee, he gon' let us have the church."

Peacock listened to the cries of surprise and approval from the people. They all knew that Battel had kept himself and his church apart from the activities of the movement. Glancing behind he could see Mama Jean rocking with mirth at a thoroughly unhappy looking Preacher Battel.

"All right, so we going home now. Raf an' Sweezy, will you get everything all straight so that folks get home safe? But before we do that, one more thing. Rev'ren' Battel will give us a prayer. An' we not going to pray for no forgiveness, we going to pray for justice, an' for the soul of our brother."

Battel stepped forward. "Let us bow our haids an' ask the Almighty . . ." he intoned.

"Wait," Peacock shouted. Battel stopped. Bowed heads were raised. Peacock pointed to Hollowell and his deputies. "Folks, I didn't mean to interrupt the prayer. But remember what happened here tonight. A man is dead, murdered. And I know that Sheriff Hollowell and his men don't mean no disrespect. But I believe we should ask them to remove their hats. Even if *they* don't believe in prayer."

The crowd stood stock still for a moment, a low murmur growing and thickening. The officers made no move. Peacock could not see Hollowell's face which was shaded by the brim of the Stetson.

"Jesse Lee Hightower is one black man they had to respeck in life," Mama Jean boomed, "an they bettah respeck him in death too."

Slowly the crowd was closing the distance between itself and the lawmen. It had become very quiet, the only sound that Peacock heard was the soft hum of feet on the dusty road. The people were no longer a diffuse crowd, but had become a single unit.

The click of Hollowell's pistol cocking was sharp and clear. Peacock cursed himself; it had been such a close thing and now he had torn it.

"Take them off, take off the damned hats!" He thought that he had screamed, but apparently there had been no sound. The deputy on the left took a half pace backward. Hollowell's lips moved stiffly. "Hope the bastard's praying," Peacock murmured, but he was sure that Hollowell was only threatening the deputy. But the man's nerve had broken. Peacock saw his hand moving, stealthily, unbearably slowly in the direction of his head. It sneaked up, tremulously, then, faster than a striking rattler, streaking up to snatch the hat from the head. . . . The other deputy looked at Hollowell, then at the crowd. He made his choice. Hollowell was the last.

MICHAEL THELWELL [326

Peacock did not see it happen. But the Sheriff's hat was suddenly cradled against his leg. The crowd let out a great moaning sigh, and Battel resumed the prayer in a quavering voice. Peacock felt an arm on his shoulder. He slumped onto Mama Jean's shoulder putting his arm around her neck and they stood watching the people disperse.

"Yo' done jes' great. Travis, hit was beautiful. But yo' know them crackers jes' ain't gon' take the way yo' done them tonight. Careful how yo' walk. Like ef that Hollowell should stop yo' on the road by yo'se'f . . . . Her voice trailed off.

"I know, Mama Jean." Peacock squeezed her shoulder. "An' I'm gonna be watching him. But ain't nothing he can do for the next few weeks." And that's the truth, Peacock reflected. Come tomorrow this town is going to be so full of newsmen and TV cameras that everyone is going to be careful as hell.

"Yeah, but yo' know he ain't nevah gon' forget. He *cain't*."

"Surprised to hear you talking like that, Mama Jean. Way you light into him an' Battel, jes' like a duck on a June bug. Don't you know you gettin' a little old to be doing folks like that?"

"Who ol'?" she growled. "Long as ah keeps mah strength ah ain't nevah gon' be too ol'. Ef they want to stop me, they gon' have to kill me. An' ah ain't sho' but whut the ones thet gits kilt ain't the lucky ones. Whut 'bout those thet lef'?" She looked toward the broken house.

Yes, Peacock thought, what about them? Us? He watched the police car drive slowly down the road behind the last group. What about them? He wondered if the family in the house had heard him. Jesse wasn't four hours dead, and already he had cheapened and manipulated that fact. He had abstracted their grief and his own, used it, waved it in front of the crowd like a matador's cape and this was only the beginning.

* * *

Inside the house, Mama Jean took charge, bustling around collecting whatever she felt the family would need next morning. She was taking them to spend the night at her place. They still sat in the bedroom, as though they had not changed position during the time Peacock had been away. Looking at his watch, Peacock discovered that the incident outside had taken less than forty minutes. He looked up to meet Fannie Lou's eyes, big and dark with grief, staring at him. What was she thinking? Of her father? Or of him, the stranger who had come to live with them like the big brother she never had? How did they feel now? Miss Vickie used to call him her son, to introduce him to visitors that way. And he had felt closer to this family than to the family he never saw and rarely thought about. But there was nothing he could say. Everything that came to him sounded weak and inadequate, incapable of expressing the burden of his feeling. Unless he could find new words that would come fresh and living from his heart, that had never been said before, he could not say anything.

When Raf and the men came back they left for the café, Peacock walking between the mother and daughter and holding a sleepy Richie. He felt Fannie Lou's light touch on his arm.

"Travis, yo' gon' stay?" Peacock looked at her uncomprehendingly. She bit her lower lip and said quickly, "I mean tonight at Mama Jean's." Her eyes filled with tears.

"I'll be back later, but I have to go to the office first." But he knew she wasn't asking about tonight. They knew that he came from another world, and one that must seem to them far more attractive, to which he could return.

He had not told them his reason for wanting to go back to the office. He had to call the national office with a report of the evening's events and he did not want them to hear him reporting and describing their loss to unknown people.

Before he had begged and pleaded to be put on the organizing staff he had worked on the public relations staff in
the national office. He had written hundreds of coldly factual
reports of burnings, bombings, and murders. And the "state-
ments," how many of those had he written, carefully worded,
expressing rage, but disciplined controlled rage, phrases of
grief balanced by grim determination, outrage balanced by
dignity, moral indignation balanced by political demands.
Every time it was the same, yet behind those phrases, the
anger and the sorrow and the fear were real. So we become
shapers of horror, artists of grief, giving form and shape and
articulation to emotion, the same emotion, doing it so often
that finally there is nothing left of that emotion but the form.
    He reached the Freedom House and placed the call. Before
it was completed Raf called through the door. Peacock let him
and his companions in.
    "The womens said we wuz to come stay with yo'." Raf ex-
plained. "We got some mens watching the café." Peacock
watched them file into the office, gaunt men roughly dressed
in overalls and Army surplus boots, as he was. One of them,
an older man with balding gray hair and a creased face came
up to him. Peacock did not know him. The man took his
hand in a horny calloused grip.
    "Ah knows ah ain't bin to the meetin's. Ah call myse'f
keepin' outta trouble. Ah says them Freedom folk, they mean
to do good, but they ain't from roun' heah, somethin' happen
they be gone an' lef' us'ns in the mess. Ah wuz 'fraid, ah ain't
shame to say hit. But ah seen yo' wit the laws tonight an' ah
says, let the fur fly wit' the hide. Ef thet young feller kin do,
ah kin do too. Ah's heah to do whatevah is to be did." Peacock was like an evangelist suffering from doubt in the face
of a convert. He had heard those words before. Each time it
had been a new and moving experience to see a man throwing off his burden of fear and hesitance and finding the courage to step forward. But this time the responsibility seemed

too much. What was the man expecting? Reassurance, praise? The phone temporarily rescued him.

The connection was a bad one, and it was as though his voice and not another's, echoed hollowly back into his ear. "June 16th, Bogue Chitto, Miss. . . ." Peacock was staring into Richie's shock-glazed eyes. ". . . A Negro civil rights leader was killed in the blast that destroyed his home. His wife and two children were unharmed . . ." Peacock saw Miss Vickie's rigid sleepwalker's face . . . "Resentment is high in the Negro community. A crowd formed in front of the house, but the local representative of the Nonviolent Council persuaded the crowd to disperse peacefully . . ." The voice went on and on. Raf and the other men were watching him as though he had stepped into a new identity that they did not recognize.

"No," Peacock said, "I have no statement."

"But we should have something from the local movement. You are project director."

"Look, if you want a political statement, write it, that's your job. All I can say is I'm sorry." Peacock hung up the phone and sat cradling his head in his arms. He knew the office would call back. Tomorrow the networks would be in town, so would politicians, leaders of various organizations. For a few days the eyes of the country would be focused on the town and everyone would want to be included. He wanted no part of it. The secret fear of every organizer had become reality for him. How do you cope with the death of one of the people you work with?

The phone rang again. Peacock knew before he answered it that it would be Truman. Big, shaggy, imperturbable, bear-like Truman. He was the chairman and was always scrambling to keep the organization afloat, to keep the cars running, the rent paid. Before he had become administrator, he had worked in the field. He would be calling with a program to "respond" to the bombing.

"Hey, Travis, how you doing, you all right?"

"Yeah, Truman, I'm all right."

"Look, in the next couple days you are going to need help. Would you like me to come down?"

That was a normal question, but Peacock suddenly felt a need to lash out. "What do you want to come for, the publicity? To be in all the pictures, to project the organization?"

"I know you are upset, man, but I think you should apologize."

"I'm sorry, man. You know I don't mean that." No, he couldn't afford to mean it because it was too close. God, they were forcing us to be just like them. Then Truman started outlining the program. Peacock listened silently. Then he interrupted. "Stop, Truman, stop. You want to stage a circus. I can't ask the family to subject themselves to that."

"Look, Travis, I know how upset you must be. But we have to do it. Where is the money to come from to build back the house, to educate the kids? We've gotta launch a national appeal and the family must be there."

"Yes, I'm upset. If I hadna come here . . ."

"He might still have been killed. He was organizing before you came."

"But it was me who told him to go register. I went to that courthouse with him, not you."

"Travis, I know it's tough, but it's what happens in this kind of a struggle. We've got to live with it. You got to keep telling yourself that we don't ask anyone to do anything that we don't do ourselves. You gotta remember that. You or Ray or Mac could have been in that house."

"For God's sake, Truman, don't lobby me. I know the line."

"Listen. . . . You say you want to respect the family's privacy. So do I. But what's your responsibility? The only way to stop these bombings is to make them public. Yeah, we gotta exploit it. Yeah, we gotta have the family crying on national TV. The cat's dead and nothing can undo that, but we have a responsibility to use his death against the people that killed him."

"I don't want to argue politics. That's not the issue," Peacock said.

"Travis, how can you say that? It is already an issue. And we, whether we like it or not, have to take it from there."

Peacock agreed with Truman but he could no longer respond to that category of practical, pragmatic realities.

"Besides," Truman was saying, "even if we wanted to keep everything simple and pure we can't. If you think that the other organizations won't be in town tomorrow morning, then you are crazy. You call it a circus; well, it's going to be one with or without us. Just came over the wires that Williams is calling for a hero's burial in Arlington, a mourning train to Washington, all under the auspices of *his* organization. We can sit aside and refuse to participate or get in there an fight . . ."

"Yeah," Peacock said, "fight for the corpse. Fight for the corpse and raise some money?"

"Yeah, Peacock. That too." Truman was angry now. "You know how many folks been fired that we are carrying on the payroll? When those people off your project got arrested two weeks ago, where did you call to get the thousand dollars bond? You know people only send us money when they feel guilty. And that's the same as saying when someone gets killed. What the hell do you expect us to do?"

"It's true, but it's not right. Man, all I can see now is that little house blown to hell. And that lady just sitting and staring . . . Man, I just don't know."

"Look, I know what you're going through, but if you feel that you can't organize in the situation right now, I understand that. If you want to go someplace for a while . . ."

Peacock saw what was coming. He would go off to "rest" someplace, and someone else would come in. Someone who, without his guilts and hesitations, could milk the situation for the most mileage. He was furious precisely because something in him wanted to leap at the chance. "You really think I would do that? Run away now? Screw you, Truman!"

"It may be wrong. In fact it is . . ." Peacock heard a weary sigh, ". . . but man, I don't see how else we can operate. Get some sleep, man. Tomorrow you will feel different about what has to be done when the vultures swoop down. You decide then how to operate."

"Thank you," Peacock said.

"One last thing, man. Maybe I shouldn't even say this but . . . ask yourself this question. Suppose it was you who had got it, what would you want us to do? What would you expect us to do? Then ask yourself if Jesse Lee Hightower was a lesser man than you. Freedom."

"Freedom," Peacock said and hung up.

Peacock crossed over to the door, opened it and stood looking down on the sleeping town. Later today it would be overrun. Camera crews, reporters, photographers, dignitaries. Across the country guilty and shocked people would be writing to Congressmen. Some would reach for checkbooks. And the checks would go to the first name they read in the papers, the first face they recognized on the screen. Some labor leader would announce a Hightower relief fund and kick it off with a munificent contribution. Others would follow, even unions which somehow managed to have no black members. And the churches would send collections. Some conscience-stricken soul would make the rounds of his suburban community where no black folk lived. The resulting check would somehow reflect that fact. In Washington, Jesse Lee's fate would be officially deplored and an investigation ordered. And in the middle of all this, the meaningful thing would be to try to get enough to keep going for another six months. He was known and trusted by the family and the community. They would be asking his advice on every proposal, at every development. He could stage-manage the entire proceedings for maximum effect, package the pain and the loss to ensure the greatest "exposure."

They were talking about a hero's burial. Well, he had seen the last one. He remembered the fight about which organization had priority, whose leaders would have the right to walk on the right of the bier where the cameras were set up. He remembered the night before the funeral. The "hero" lay in state, his coffin set up in the center of the room draped with a wrinkled American flag smelling of moth balls. At a table by the door an old woman sat selling memberships, buttons and pamphlets to the people who filed in. Outside, proselytes of all kinds sold or gave away their particular version of the truth. The people bought their memberships and filed past that rumpled, dingy flag.

Somehow a man's life should be reflected in the final ceremony at his death. Jesse had been a simple man, and honest. That had been his way in the world and that was how he should go out. Peacock turned and walked back into the room.

"Travis, Travis. Whut happen?" Raf sprang to his feet and was peering at him anxiously.

"I . . . I'm all right, what's the matter?"

"Wal," Raf said, "effen yo' seen yore own face jes' now hit woulda set yo' back, too. Yo' bettah take a taste." Peacock drank deeply, the hot liquor bringing tears to his eyes.

"We wuz jes' figurin'," Raf said, "whut is we gon' do now, Travis? Ah mean the movement heah in Bogue Chitto?"

Peacock sat down and shook his head. He passed his hands over his face, massaging his eyes. He shook his head again. But when he looked up the men were still looking at him questioningly.

"Well," Peacock said, "be a lot happening real quick during the next few days. Here's what I think . . . We got to start with that meeting tomorrow . . ." Peacock talked, the men listened, nodding from time to time. He kept looking at his watch. When morning came he had to go back to be with the family. Funny he hadn't thought of it before, but Miss Vickie had a great face. Be great on a poster or on TV. . . .

CLAUDE BROWN

Harlem Revisited

From Manchild in the Promised Land

The year 1965 marked the publication of the autobiography of a child in the "promised land" of Harlem, that area of New York City into which a generation of Southern Negroes had poured during the decade that followed the Depression. CLAUDE BROWN was born in 1937 into what he has referred to as the "dirty, stinky, uncared-for closet-size section of a great city." At eleven he was sent to Wiltwyck School for emotionally disturbed and deprived young boys, having been since he was nine a member of several gangs of thieves and street fighters. After two years at Wiltwyck, he was sent to Warwick Reform School. His school, street, family and gang life are graphically pictured in his remarkable autobiography, *Manchild in the Promised Land*, called by one critic not only "a moving personal testimony but social evidence of some importance." He later graduated from Howard University and went on to law school.

I haven't lived in New York for some time now, but from time to time I still go back to Harlem to see if the streets are the same, to see if I recognize any of the faces of the junkies along Eighth Avenue, to see if I can recognize any of the slang terms that they're using. It seems as though the changes now are even faster than before.

Sometimes I walk along the street and look at the luxury apartment houses they are building in Harlem and wonder who lives there, what kind of people.

I recall once having met an elderly white man who said he had lived in Harlem around the turn of the century. He told me that he remembered Harlem when the Alhambra Theatre, on 126th Street, was a vaudeville theater. I thought that was really something, because the Alhambra Theatre was far from being a vaudeville theater in my lifetime. My strongest memory of the Alhambra Theatre was standing outside pouring some buttermilk down Danny once when he had taken an O.D. I could never imagine it having once been a vaudeville theater. Then, there are so many things about Harlem that I could never imagine.

I could never imagine the Black Muslims starting riots on 125th Street, but they tell me that they've done it. I could never imagine Alley Bush being in jail accused of murder, but they tell me that he's there.

There are so many things about Harlem that have changed, and they don't seem possible for Harlem. I suppose no one who has ever lived in a Harlem of the world could ever imagine that it could change so drastically and yet maintain so much of its old misery.

Not too long ago, some junkies broke into my folks' house and stabbed my mother. I panicked. When I heard about it, it seemed as though I just forgot everything else in the world. All I knew was that something had to be done about it. Exactly what, I didn't know.

I remember walking the streets, night after night, for nearly two weeks. All night long, I just walked the streets and looked in dope dens and other places where junkies hung out. I

remember meeting Rock, who was usually in jail, down on
129th Street. It was surprising to see him so changed, so clean
and still so young looking and talking the way he was talking. I told him that I was looking for a junkie named Skippy.

Rock said, "Yeah, I heard about it, Sonny. Just about
everybody's heard about it, but, man, I didn't know it was
you and your moms."

"Yeah, Rock, I wish it wasn't."

"Yeah, well, Sonny, I hope you're not ready to do anything crazy, man."

"Crazy like what, Rock?"

"Well, you know, Sonny, I've been out on these streets
about nine months, man. The one thing I've noticed is that
Harlem's changed. Man, it's changed a hell of a lot."

"How do you mean that, Rock?"

"You remember when we were comin' up, man, if a cat
messed with you, you could get your piece and go looking
for him. And if he heard that you were lookin' for him, he'd
get his piece and start looking for you too."

"Yeah, Rock, I remember."

"Well, man, it ain't like that no more, Sonny. It's just not
the way it was when we were comin' up."

I looked at him, and I said, "Yeah, I sort of had that feeling." I knew that Rock was going to offer some advice and
that I was going to listen. Rock was street-wise. He knew
about hurting people and even about killing people. I wasn't
sure that that was what I wanted to do, but at the same time,
I wasn't sure that it wasn't what I wanted to do. So I listened
to him.

Rock went on. He said, "Yeah if a cat hears you're gunnin'
for him now, man, these niggers'll run to the police. You
know?"

I said, "Yeah."

"Sonny, if you've got anything on you, baby, your best bet

would be to get rid of it in a hurry, because, for one thing, just about everybody in Harlem knows you're lookin' for the nigger."

"Yeah, that's probably true, Rock."

"And another thing, Sonny. You ain't got no business on these streets gunnin' for somebody, huntin' somebody down. Look here, why don't you just let me find him?"

"Rock, you know better than that."

"I'll probably run across the cat anyway."

"What makes you think that you'll do that?"

"I see quite a few junkies, Sonny. Eventually, they all come lookin' for me."

"No wonder you're so clean."

"Yeah, baby, that's the way it is." Then he said, "You can't give up the hunt, huh, Sonny?"

"No, Rock, I can't do it."

"Look, if you can't do that, why don't you just let me come along?"

"No, Rock, thanks for the offer, but I can't do that either." I just wasn't sure that I wanted somebody like Rock along with me, somebody as cold as him. I knew I wanted to hurt this cat when I found him, but I didn't know just how badly I wanted to hurt him. I knew that there was no controlling Rock. I guess I just never forgot the way that boy flew off the roof on 147th Street, or that gang fight on 148th Street. I told him that it was something I felt I had to do by myself.

Rock said, "Okay, Sonny, I can halfway understand that. But, look here, why don't you let me give you a little advice on it?"

"Sure, Rock, maybe you can tell me where to find him?"

"I wish I could. If I could, Sonny, you wouldn't have to find him."

"Yeah, well, thanks anyway."

"Sonny, look, whatever you've got on you, why don't you

put it down and just take this roll of pennies from me and do whatever you're gon do with that?"

"With a roll of pennies?"

He said, "You could do a whole lot with a roll of pennies, man."

I sort of laughed at this.

"Look, Sonny, this is not the Harlem that we grew up in."

I said, "Yeah, man, I had that suspicion a few times."

"Sonny, I'm not jokin'. You've got to face it, man. You can't be doin' that old kind of shit no more. What you got to do today if a nigger mistreats you is catch him, break his hands, break his legs, or something like that. That's what you got to do."

"I think you're right there, Rock, I really think you're right."

"Well, if you really thing so, man, let me come with you, just to cool you. I think you ought to have somebody with you, somebody whose moms is not involved in it."

I said, "Yeah, Rock, I wish I could, man, but I just can't do it. You know?"

"Yeah, man, I know, but, anyway, good luck."

I never saw Rock again after that. He got busted again, and he was a three-time loser.

I never found Skippy either. The police found him. That was surprising, that the police would really find somebody—that they'd really look for somebody for two weeks—for having hurt somebody else in Harlem. I guess Harlem was changing.

Every time I see Danny, he makes me want to look back into the past and wonder if it was real, if it all happened. The last time I saw Danny, it was on 125th Street. I bumped into him, and we stopped and talked for a while. He had two little kids with him, a boy about three and a girl about four or five. I asked him whose kids they were. I thought they were

his niece and nephew or something. He said, "Mine, man."
I said, "Damn." It didn't seem real. I said, "Has it been
that long?"

"Yeah, Sonny, it's been that long. I'm really in that father
role now, man. I take the kids to church on Sunday, even.
Why don't you come and join us sometime, man?"

It almost frightened me. It seemed like the world was
changing too much for me. I said, "Look, Danny, I'd feel real
out of place in church, man, even still. But, look, the next
time you go to church, man, you say a prayer for me."

"Yeah, Sonny, we all will, man. My moms keeps tellin' me
that it was all an answer to her prayer. Every time I take
the kids by and we have dinner there or she comes by my
house for dinner on Sunday, she says grace, man. She comes
up out of it with a little smile on her face, looks at the family,
and says a little, 'Thank you, Lord.' I don't know. I use to
think it was crazy at one time, Sonny, but now, man, I'll tell
you the truth, I really don't know."

"Yeah, Danny, I don't know either. Something's happened
to people and things. Life seems to have changed."

"Yeah, Sonny, I guess maybe it's for the good, man."

I looked at Danny's little boy, and I said, "What'd you say
his name was, Danny?"

"His name is Melvin, man."

"I wonder if he'll play hookey when he gets to school?"

Danny said, "Hell, he better not, 'cause I'll beat his ass and
take him to school every mornin' and wait right there for
him."

"Yeah, Danny, I bet you will. I bet you know the value of
school, more so than most people."

Danny and I talked about people who had come up in the
neighborhood. It seemed as though most of the cats that we'd
come up with just hadn't made it. Almost everybody was
dead or in jail. But I got the feeling that the worst was over
for our generation. The drug-plague wave had come, and we

were in its path. It just swept through, and then it was gone. It took a lot of people with it.

Danny asked me what had become of people I knew, "those young boys you use to hang out with," meaning Bucky and Mac and Tito and Alley Bush and Dunny. I told him that most of them had gone the same way, that they were in jail, the last I'd heard of them. Mac had settled down, but his brother Bucky was crazy and was still acting up. I'd heard he was doing five years for stealing a car.

Danny said, "Yeah, he always was a kind of crazy cat."

"Yeah, maybe he was."

"I read about Turk, man, in the paper. He's doin' good, making the entire neighborhood proud of him."

"Turk is number two in line for the heavyweight crown, man," I said.

He said, "Yeah, could you imagine that, man? I look around, man, I wonder if I was there. I see cats now, man, who are strung out, and they were strung out when I was strung out. It looks like they're gonna still be strung out for a long time to come."

"Yeah, maybe they're paying, Danny; maybe they're paying for some of the shit that you and I got away without payin' for."

"Sonny, I hope not, man. I felt as though I had done my sufferin'; I felt as though I had done enough sufferin' for me and for all the sins of all my ancestors. You know?"

"Yeah, Danny, sometimes I felt as though you'd done it too, like you'd suffered for everybody in the world."

Danny laughed and said, "Man, it wasn't that bad. Look here, Sonny, why don't you come by sometime, man?" He gave me his address and his phone number.

"Yeah, Danny, I'll do that."

"My moms always asks about you, man. She asks me if you've been saved yet."

I laughed. "Danny, tell her I've been saved, but I don't think it was by the Lord."

"Sonny, how's Pimp?"

"Pimp's changin', man. Or at least I think he is. The cat finished high school in the joint, got a diploma, and he's talkin' some good stuff. He writes a lot of poetry in the joint."

Danny smiled. "Yeah, man. I know how that is. The joint could make a cat deep sometimes, sometimes it'll make him real deep." We laughed.

I said, "Yeah, Mama says he'll be a real fine young man when he comes out, provided he doesn't become a faggot."

Danny laughed and said, "You know, Sonny, I think, man, with most cats, the stuff is all right in the joint."

"What stuff?"

"You know. Taking other outlets, deviating from normalcy. As a matter of fact, that's a normal way of life in there."

I said, "There's no real fear, man. She wouldn't say anything about it if she thought it were true."

"Yeah, I'd like to see that nigger. I remember the time when I talked to him about drugs and about drug life and about the stuff he'd have to go through. He only seemed fascinated by it, Sonny. It didn't frighten him. I knew, man, I knew that he was gonna be all right."

"How do you mean you knew he was going to be all right?"

"Because he understood it. I was certain that he understood everything that I was telling him, and at the same time, he had to do it on his own. There was somethin' in his eyes that kept tellin' me, 'Shit, if that's the way I'm gonna have to suffer and if that's what's waitin' for mc, I'm just gonna go on and meet it.' Pimp was a game little cat, Sonny, and somebody like that's got to make it, man. Those are the cats who always do."

"Yeah, Danny. I hope you're right."

* * *

I haven't seen Danny lately, but I've seen so many other people in Harlem. Most of the junkies around there now are young cats; they're younger than Danny and younger than me. I wish I could get out in Harlem in a truck with a loud-speaker on it, like the politicians do around election time, and just tell the story of Danny to some of the cats out there on the streets nodding and scratching—and maybe tell the story about Turk, the stuff he came through, and the achievements he made despite it all.

I'd like to show them that despite everything that Harlem did to our generation, I think it gave something to a few. It gave them a strength that couldn't be obtained anywhere else.

The last time I walked up 145th Street, I remembered the little boy and the dog with the black spot over his eye, and the boy standing in front of me and saying, "I want to be like you." I thought. Well, maybe now I wouldn't be so embarrassed about it all. But I thought that there were a lot of guys around there who would have been a better example, guys like Turk and Danny. There were a few cats who'd made it pretty big.

It was unbelievable to think about Tony being dead, having died before he'd had a chance to realize the things he was struggling for. He had tried so hard. It was unfair of life not to hold on to him a little longer.

Every time I visit Greenwich Village and pass by the old place where we used to hang out—where we hid from Harlem during the uncertain period—I remember that there was somebody else who had wanted to make it too. I always have the feeling that I have to make it for both of us. I remember the times when we got high and walked around the streets in Harlem and planned to save the neighborhood one day. It was really some dream.

It seemed to me that somebody or something else had also had a dream, somebody or something else that I hadn't even been aware of. This dream was there, and slowly but surely, it was coming true. Somebody had had a dream that all Harlem would be completely changed in about ten years.

It seemed as though most of the old tenements have gone. I can hardly recognize Lenox Avenue any more. A whole section of Lenox Avenue where there used to be a lot of drug dens—from 132nd Street to 135th Street—is gone. Now they've got big apartment houses. Only now does it seem to be becoming more of everybody's Harlem.

Al Betts was talking about moving back to Harlem. He said they had some fabulous houses in Harlem now, and this was where his heart was anyway. He'd always wanted to live there, but he couldn't get a decent apartment. Now that it was possible to live there respectably, he felt that he could go back there and really be happy.

I told Al Betts I could hardly wait to get back myself.

The last time I saw Reno was on the streets in mid-Manhattan about four years ago. Reno looked much older. Maybe it was the hard life. He was walking fast, looking nowhere, and seeing everything. So I knew he had to be jostling, still.

He acted as though he hadn't seen me. I waited for a while to see if he was in the middle of a trick. After I watched him walk down the street for a half a block, I caught up with him and spoke to him. He turned around, almost too fast, when I said, "Hey, Reno."

He said, "Hey, Sonny, how you doin'?" But he was kind of cold.

"Oh, I'm doin' fine, man."

"Yeah, I haven't seen you around lately, man. I've been asking about you, and nobody seems to know where you cut out to."

"Well, I left town, man."

"Yeah, I heard. Is there anything to that rumor, man, about you goin' to school?"

"Yeah, Reno, it's something different, something to do."

Reno threw up both hands, as if to say, "Wow, what a change!" He sort of backed away from me. Then he smiled and said, "Sonny, I always knew you had somethin' like that in you, man. I'm kind of glad that you went on and did it."

"So am I, Reno, because I felt as though I wasn't goin' anyplace in Harlem. I wasn't doin' anything."

"Yeah, that's understandable, Sonny."

I said, "What are you doin' for yourself?"

"Well, you see where I'm at, Sonny. It's the same old thing with me, man. I guess I'm too old to ever change my game, you know?"

"Man, why don't you stop talkin' that nonsense, Reno. I always figured you for a cat who would go places and do things, a whole lot of things."

"Yeah, Sonny, maybe I could go to college, huh? Yeah, but what would I do there, man, but screw all the fine young bitches they got there until they threw me out or somethin'?"

"Yeah, I'll bet." I'd always felt that Reno really had something on the ball. But this is the way it was. He'd resigned himself to the jostling life a long time ago. I had the feeling that he resented me for not resigning myself to a life of petty crime.

He asked me, "Sonny, what you doin', man?"

"I told you, man, knockin' about in school."

"Yeah, but what you studyin', man? You must be into somethin' down there."

"I haven't made up my mind yet what I'm gonna get into."

"Well, do me one favor, man."

"What's that?"

"Now, baby, don't go down there and come back the Man. That'd be some real wicked shit. All the stuff we been through together, if you became the Man and busted me or any of the cats around the neighborhood, that shit would really hurt, man."

"Yeah, I guess it would, Reno." I laughed. I said, "Yeah, imagine me becoming the Man. Even I wouldn't know how to take it."

"That's good. That's good, man. You want to get high, Sonny? I'm not doin' anything now."

"I thought you were takin' care of business."

"Man, shit, that can wait. There's a lot of time for business. I don't see you every day. Who knows? I may need you for somethin' one day. You go down there and you become a big-time lawyer, big-time doctor, big-time teacher, big-time anything. Just don't become a big-time preacher, Sonny. I just can't use you if you go and do somethin' like that."

"I think that's another thing you won't have to worry about, Reno."

"Come on, Sonny, let's get high."

"No, Reno, I don't get high any more."

"Damn, man. They really turned you around at that place, huh?"

"I stopped gettin' high before I went down there, man."

"Oh, yeah, that's right, I remember. You want a drink, man?"

I felt sort of compelled to take it because it was a second offer, a second attempt by Reno to maintain the old friendship. Reno and I went into one of the bars on Forty-third Street and had a couple of drinks. I could tell that the liquor didn't agree with him.

He started telling me about how he wished he had gotten out of Harlem. I said, "Yeah, there are other things to see, but as far as education goes, I don't think any place offers a greater one than the Harlem streets, man, right here." I told him I had found out since I had been in school that the things that were most educational were those I'd learned outside the classroom.

He said, "Yeah, Sonny, I can dig that, man. I learned a whole lot of shit out here. The hippest cats I've met, man, were the cats who just came up in the streets. But we still don't make it to college. I'm kind of puzzled at that stuff you did. I still don't know what's behind it, but knowing that it's you, baby, it's got to be all right. It's got to be somethin' to it."

"I wish I could throw some light on it, Reno, but I'm not sure what it's all about myself. I just looked up one day and found me in this groove. That's how it's been with me all the time, Reno. I have admired you from way back, man, because of all the stuff you showed me, not only the stuff you knew, but the way you just made decisions, man, on a snap, and said, 'If I hit, I'll make it. And if I miss, fuck it.'

"Reno, I remember the first time you took me downtown to cut me into the Murphy. I asked you, I said, 'Look here, man, tell me just what happens.' Then you started runnin' it down to me. You said, 'It's simple, Sonny, really. If everything goes off like we plan, we'll each have a good two hundred dollars in our pockets by the time we come back uptown. And if it doesn't go off like we plan, we'll probably be in jail. It's as simple as that.' Reno, that was one of the first times in my life that I didn't mind goin' to jail, that I felt I was ready to go to jail. I admired you for bein' able to assume that attitude, man. I was certain that the things you'd done in street life had given it to you. I saw it as a maturity, man, that I strived for a long time after that."

He said, "Oh, man, come on. Don't bullshit me, Sonny."

"No, man, I'm not stuffin'."

"That's funny, but, believe it or not, Sonny, I've been to college, man! I've been there too. Only, I've been to a different college."

"I'm not readin' you yet, baby."

"Yeah, Sonny. The time I did in Woodburn, the times I did on the Rock, that was college, man. Believe me, it was college. I did four years in Woodburn. And I guess I've done a total of about two years on the Rock in about the last six

years. Every time I went there, I learned a little more. When
I go to jail now, Sonny, I live, man. I'm right at home. That's
the good part about it. If you look at it, Sonny, a cat like me
is just cut out to be in jail.

"It never could hurt me, 'cause I never had what the good
folks call a home and all that kind of shit to begin with. So
when I went to jail, the first time I went away, when I went
to Warwick, I made my own home. It was all right. Shit, I
learned how to live. Now when I go back to the joint, anywhere I go, I know some people. If I go to any of the jails
in New York, or if I go to a slam in Jersey, even, I still run
into a lot of cats I know, It's almost like a family."

I said, "Yeah, Reno, it's good that a cat can be so happy
in jail. I guess all it takes to be happy in anything is knowin'
how to walk with your lot, whatever it is, in life."

Reno put out his hand for me to give him five, and I
slapped it. "Sonny, you want another drink?"

"No, man, I'm movin', Reno. I 've got to be someplace."

"Yeah, well, me too. I got to get ready for somethin', get
ready to get me some money, or either get ready to do some
time."

I tapped him on the shoulder and said, "Good luck, Reno."

"Later, baby. I'll see you around."

I had the feeling that Reno had managed to become one of
the happiest people in Harlem. I felt very close to Reno. People used to say that friends were "as thick as thieves." Maybe
I had a thief's affinity for him. He had taught me a lot.

Reno was somebody right from the streets. I think he took
to me because he saw me as somebody from the streets, somebody who hated to see the sun go down on Eight Avenue,
who would run up on Amsterdam Avenue, follow the sun
down the hill, across Broadway, to the Drive and the Hud-
son River, and then would wait for the sun to come back. I
guess Reno thought he'd found somebody who was destined
to be in the streets of Harlem for the rest of his life.

I felt as though I had let him down. I was saying, "Look, man, we aren't destined. You just bullshitted yourself and messed all up." But I guess he hadn't, really. He'd just made his choice, and I'd made mine.

As a child, I remember being morbidly afraid. It was a fear that was like a fever that never let up. Sometimes it became so intense that it would just swallow you. At other times, it just kept you shaking. But it was always there. I suppose, in Harlem, even now, the fear is still there.

When I first moved away from the folks, it seemed as though I was moving deeper into the Harlem life that I had wanted to become a part of and farther away from what Mama and Dad wanted me to become a part of. I think, as time went on, they both became aware that the down-home life had kind of had its day. But they didn't know just what was to follow, so how could they tell me?

I didn't realize it until after I had gotten out, but there were other cats in Harlem who were afraid too. They were afraid of getting out of Harlem; they were afraid to go away from their parents. There were some cats who would stay at home; they wouldn't work; they wouldn't do anything. I didn't see how they could do it, but they seemed to manage. They just didn't feel anything about it, but it was pretty evident that they were afraid of not being able to turn to their parents when things got rough. And they were afraid of getting out there and not being able to make it.

When I moved up on Hamilton Terrace, I suppose I still had my fears, but it was something. I was a move away from fear, toward challenges, toward the positive anger that I think every young man should have. All the time before, I thought I was angry. I guess I was, but the anger was stifled. It was an impotent anger because it was stifled by fear. I was more afraid than I was angry. There were many times when I wondered if Rock would have hurt anybody if he hadn't been in Harlem . . . or if Johnny Wilkes would have been so mean if he hadn't been in Harlem. I was afraid of what Harlem could bring out in a person. When I decided to move, I was trying to get away from the fear.

Everybody I knew in Harlem seemed to have some kind of dream. I didn't have any dreams, not really. I didn't have any dreams for hitting the number. I didn't have any dreams for getting a big car or a fine wardrobe. I bought expensive clothes because it was a fad. It was the thing to do, just to show that you had money. I wanted to be a part of what was going on, and this was what was going on.

I didn't have any dreams of becoming anything. All I knew for certain was that I had my fears. I suppose just about everybody else knew the same thing. They had their dreams, though, and I guess that's what they had over me. As time went by, I was sorry for the people whose dreams were never realized.

When Butch was alive, sometimes I would go uptown to see him. He'd be sick. He'd be really messed up. I'd give him some drugs, and then he'd be more messed up than before. He wouldn't be sick, but I couldn't talk to him, I couldn't reach him. He'd be just sitting on a stoop nodding. Sometimes he'd be slobbering over himself.

I used to remember Butch's dream. Around 1950, he used to dream of becoming the best thief in Harlem. It wasn't a big dream. To him, it was a big dream, but I don't suppose too many people would have seen it as that. Still, I felt sorry for him because it was his dream. I suppose the first time he put the spike in his arm every dream he'd ever had was thrown out the window. Sometimes I wanted to shout at him or snatch him by the throat and say, "Butch, what about your dream?" But there were so many dreams that were lost for a little bit of duji.

I remember Reno used to say that all he wanted was two

bars in Harlem and two Cadillacs. It sounded like something that was all right to me. I used to envy Reno for his dream. When he first told me, I thought to myself, Wow, if I could just want two bars and two Cadillacs. I was hoping all the time that he'd make it. Once I asked him, "Reno, what's the two Cadillacs for, man? You can only drive one at a time."

He said, "One I'm gon get for my woman."

I said, "Oh, then the other one'll be hers."

"No, man, you can't expect but so much out of a bitch, not any bitch, I don't care how good she is."

"Uh-huh. So what?"

Reno said, "Every time a bitch fucks up, I'm gonna just cut her loose and get another one. Every time I get a new bitch, the other Cadillac's gon be hers. You dig it?"

"Yeah, I dig it. It sounds like a pretty hip life."

"I don't know, man, but that's what I want to do, Sonny."

"Yeah, Reno, I guess that's all that matters, that a cat does what he wants to do."

I used to feel that I belonged on the Harlem streets and that, regardless of what I did, nobody had any business to take me off the streets.

I remember when I ran away from shelters, places that they sent me to, here in the city. I never ran away with the thought in mind of coming home. I always ran away to get back to the streets. I always thought of Harlem as home, but I never thought of Harlem as being in the house. To me, home was the streets. I suppose there were many people who felt that. If home was so miserable, the street was the place to be. I wonder if mine was really so miserable, or if it was that there was so much happening out in the street that it made home seem such a dull and dismal place.

When I was very young—about five years old, maybe younger—I would always be sitting out on the stoop. I remember Mama telling me and Carole to sit on the stoop and not to move away from in front of the door. Even when it was time to go up and Carole would be pulling on me to come upstairs and eat, I never wanted to go, because there was so much out there in that street.

You might see somebody get cut or killed. I could go out in the street for an afternoon, and I would see so much that, when I came in the house, I'd be talking and talking for what seemed like hours. Dad would say, "Boy, why don't you stop that lyin'? You know you didn't see all that. You know you didn't see nobody do that." But I knew I had.

JOSEPH F. PUMILIA

Niggertown

JOSEPH F. PUMILIA is a law student at the University of Houston and writes that his story, which was a prize winner in the nationwide STORY College Creative Awards contest of 1970, "deals with one aspect of the immediate future, instead of a more distant future—a sort of miniature *1984* or *Brave New World*." He is a white author, a member of the Houston Science Fiction Society. Regarding the black Christ in the back of the car, he says, ". . . the statue of Christ as a Negro indicates the universality of his message. . . . Also it symbolizes the racial character of the city, and the putting aside of the 'white man's God' (which is only a distortion anyhow), and an attempt to make prayer seem less like begging favors from a Great White Massah."

The large statue of the black Christ bounced in the back seat as we drove through the inner part of the city, where the streets were filled with shoppers, all black. The faces in the other cars were black too. There were only black people coming out of and going into Foley's and Woolworth's. A lot of the kids wore shirts with slogans and symbols, and some of these had red stripes on their right cheeks.

Here and there I caught a glimpse of a white face; they belonged mostly to well-dressed men, probably lawyers like my-self, or businessmen who were making arrangements for the few remaining whites to sell out. Everybody else was Negro. Some of them wore colorful robes and wraparounds, and a few sported gaudy feathers in their cloudy black hair. They looked like extras for a Tarzan epic. The clean-cut blacks in business suits generally avoided these, like I used to avoid hippies.

The Reverend indicated one of the red-striped kids. "Street gangs," he said. "City's trying to keep them down, but as long as they don't do anything in front of anybody we can't touch them."

He drove up to the city hall. It was surrounded by scaffold-ing, and workmen were redoing it in black marble.

"You don't mind if I stop here a minute, do you?" he asked.

"No. It's okay. How long will you be?"

"Won't take a minute."

After he parked the car and excused himself, I put on the radio for the noon news. There were mostly soul stations, but there was one wholly devoted to news. They were all black-controlled, as were the local TV affiliates. The news led off with foreign affairs, largely African, skimming lightly over national affairs, except for a criticism of the latest civil-rights legislation.

I cut off the radio, got out of the car, and bought a paper from a machine. I got back inside, but before I could read anything I discovered I was not alone.

A group of lanky kids were leaning all over the car, sitting on the trunk and hood. A bony black face I recognized ap-peared in the window. It wore the red stripe.

"You know where you're going to end up, man? In the ovens. In the gas chamber."

"I have a choice?"

"No. You don't got no choice."

"Hey you, Raven," I said, "leave that wiper alone!"

The kid on the hood gave me an absurd pop-eyed look and let the wiper snap back against the glass.

Just then a cop who'd been making the rounds drove up. "Break it up," he ordered. "Get off the man's car."

"Who're you for?" demanded the kid. "The man or us?"

"All right, Raven," said the cop, "you know I'll run you in if you give me trouble. What would your daddy think?"

"I don't give a damn what he thinks." He turned away and the kid on the hood slid off, and the rest of the group followed them down the street, looking back at me, walking backwards, and making obscene gestures.

"Are you going to be long?" the cop asked, his dark face looking into the car.

"I'm waiting for the Reverend Smith," I told him.

The cop recognized the name. Then he saw the Reverend's black Christ in the back seat. He started to turn away, then came back and said, "Aren't you Cameron, that lawyer?"

"One and the same."

He looked at me and grinned slightly. "You know, I have to laugh when I think about that case."

"The Trueson case," I prompted.

"Yeah," he said, his smile gradually fading into an official deadpan. "Well, try to stay out of trouble." He drove off, stopped at a car four spaces down and ticketed it.

George Trueson, a white man, had been refused entry into a restaurant owned by a Negro. Trueson had originally owned the restaurant. He had sold it to a Puerto Rican and had left town, along with most other whites. The Puerto Rican had been pressured into selling by a Negro boycott. Trueson came back to town one day on business and stopped for lunch at his former restaurant. The new owner refused to serve him.

Trueson was pretty mad. He claimed his civil rights had been violated and got the Attorney General to authorize a suit by the United States. The restaurant owner was found guilty, but was fined the minimum and was promptly reimbursed by a neighborhood collection. Undoubtedly the court had been influenced by the fact that it had found Trueson guilty of violating the same law some years before. I defended Trueson in the first suit, the new owner in the second.

The Reverend came back. "Hope I didn't keep you waiting."

"Not at all."

He launched the car into the stream of traffic. We drove past the park where some sort of rally was in progress. There was much shouting and waving of placards. I could see that the pseudo-Greek statues adorning the park had all been painted black.

I unfolded the paper in my lap. It was the daily *Uhuru* and was pretty much a written version of the newscasts. There was a short item that caught my eye. It stated that an effigy of a member of the white race had been found in an unused cage at the zoo. The article decried this sort of rowdyism and hoped it wouldn't happen again. It said people should look for more constructive ways to express dissent and referred the reader to an article about the rally in the park.

I scanned the sports section and read about the top black athletes. The adjacent comics section had a strip about a black Mary Worth.

We'd left the heart of the city. The few buildings remaining were old-style structures, but they were colorfully decorated by amateur artists. Ancient brownstones and nondescript warehouses and shacks glowed with bold color, reminding me of Miró's transfiguration of a trash heap in "Still Life with the Old Shoe." Some buildings were adorned with portraits of past and current black leaders or scenes from black history. When we paused for a red light I saw a powerful black angel casting from the city a white Adam and Eve; a new mythology was arising.

Outsiders called the city Niggertown. It was one of the first in the country to go completely black. The situation was the result of long-standing trends and prejudices, and after the white middle class left the center of the metropolis for the suburbs, Negroes moved in to fill the vacuum, which grew more voracious as the remaining whites felt compelled to move away. The suburbs were satellite cities with all the comforts of civilization; there was little reason to go into the city proper at all. Finally the white politicians went where the white voters were, leaving a political vacuum for the blacks to fill.

One day we woke up and saw the whole city was black. The slums went up in flames. "A new Rome," proclaimed volume one, number one of *Uhuru*. "The slumlords did it," they said, pointing to the flames. The black mayor promised better houses at lower costs. He kept his word. He promised more blacks on the police force. The white cops had already obliged him by leaving town.

A few whites stayed on, mostly local businessmen and church groups. They tended to cluster together. The newspapers were the last to turn black. One day the editor took a look at the assistant editor, the office staff, the delivery boys; when he found out he was the only white man in the company he moved out. I know that editor; he runs a weekly in the suburbs; he says he's going daily soon. The owner of the paper sold it at a handsome profit to local blacks; nobody's sure where the money came from.

Only thing is, the suburbs and satellite cities too are beginning to blacken around the edges.

"We agree," editorialized *Uhuru*, "that there should be no intermarriage between the races, and that white parents should not be forced to put their children in predominantly black schools. Fortunately, the racial boundaries in our area are distinct, so that if we escape the federal government's misguided paternalism and race-mixing programs. . . ."

Our car whizzed around a large truck. I watched the startled driver disappear behind us. Then the Reverend curved swiftly into a private drive and skidded to a halt. "Here we are," he said.

I exhaled heavily, mopped my face, and got out of the car. The Loomis mansion with its pseudo-New England façade stood embedded in a semiforest of sinewy oaks. A moving van was parked in front of it, and men were filling the van with tasteful and expensive furnishings.

A well-dressed woman with tight facial skin met us at the door. She was Mrs. Loomis. She went to find her husband while we waited in a stripped, musty-smelling living room.

"A nice house," said the Reverend. "Our people will be very happy here."

A few minutes later, Loomis himself showed up. He was tall, thin, bald, and wiry, and he wore fogged-up eyeglasses perched on a fleshy ledge above his nose. He was sweating and his sleeves were rolled up. He saw the Reverend and said, "*You,*" in a scornful, breathy voice.

The Reverend's eyes narrowed.

"Smith. Who'd have thought *you* would be the Smith, with all the Smiths there are in the world."

"Gentlemen," I interposed, "is there something I should know? I was under the impression you were both willing parties to this transaction."

"That man," said Loomis. "His son is a guerilla, a terrorist. I had him arrested for vandalizing my property."

"Yes, sir," said the Reverend humbly—too humbly. He was being sarcastic. "You were quite right. He got what he deserved."

"Probation!"

"And also an accounting. You received my check for the damage and fine?"

"He should have been jailed."

"The court"—said the Reverend.

"The court! Black courts! No white man can get justice in

black courts. They're even making laws now—the courts, Congress, everywhere!"

The Reverend scowled and pulled out an envelope.

"I have the necessary papers," I said. "Perhaps we can find a table."

Loomis jerked his head to one side and led the way through a door into a roomful of crates. We used a packing crate as a table, and the papers were signed with much heavy breathing and no ceremony. Loomis took the check with a quick grasp. It was for a large sum, paid in the name of the Freedom Church of Christ Jesus.

"When will you be off the premises?" asked the Reverend.

Loomis paused a long moment, letting his temper rise, and said, "Just as soon as I damn can, you son of a bitch!"

The Reverend quivered slightly like a plucked wire. "That is satisfactory. We'll pray for your soul, Mr. Loomis, for in your own way you have contributed to the work of the Lord."

"Get out of here, nigger."

I snapped my briefcase shut and followed the Reverend out. Loomis called after me, "White nigger."

"You say it, Loomis. You just can't see there's no dividing line."

"You know which side your bread's buttered on, don't you? What do you think will happen when you aren't needed any more?"

The Reverend, sitting rather rigidly behind the wheel, was stoically observing the van crew. "Damn that man," he muttered, clenching the wheel. "God forgive me, but damn him."

The car bolted out of the gate and into the street. We drove back by another route, through a residential area. The yards were bristling with FOR SALE signs and cars with black families were cruising slowly along the curbs eyeing the houses.

"The promised land?" I asked wryly.

"They think so, but they're wrong."

"You should have let me handle the sale."

"I had to be there."

We drove back into the city proper, passing the other side of the park. The big group was still there, but it was moving out, led by a shouting few. They crossed the street in front of us and the Reverend's car came to a halt. These blacks seemed to have some goal in mind. Some of them carried ropes.

"Where do you suppose they're going?" I asked.

"Those are ropes they have. We'd better go along."

We abandoned the car and followed behind the mob. They left the park, crossed another street, and headed back toward town. I spotted Raven nearby and caught him by the shoulder.

"What's going on?"

He grinned. "We're gonna hang a honky," he said, pulling away.

"Who?" demanded the Reverend. He came around me and seized the boy. "William, tell me who!"

Raven avoided his glance, and I saw the mob march boldly down the street, chanting joyously. Cars were pulling aside for them. The Reverend slapped the boy.

"Tell me!"

Raven broke free and ran into the mob.

The Reverend trembled, fists clenched. "My own son," he said in a defeated voice.

I left him there and ran ahead, looking for a phone. Finally they spotted their quarry. They tied their ropes together and weighted the ends. They slung them around the supports of a beaming *Colonel Sanders* sign atop an eating establishment and began to pull. The owner of the shop came running out, saw what they were doing, laughed, and took hold of the ropes too.

The supports gave way. The benign antebellum whitegoateed Colonel came crashing down and shattered on the pavement. A mighty cheer thundered up.

I found myself damp with sweat. Somehow it had been almost as bad as a real lynching. But then that's the reason for symbolic sacrifices: nobody gets hurt but you feel just as good afterward.

I found the Reverend walking up the street. He'd seen the whole thing. "For a minute," he said, "I lost faith in my own son. I thought he'd become like—I don't know."

"Come on. I'll drive this time."

I drove to my office and turned the car over to him. "I'll give you a call tomorrow." I watched him drive away.

Susie was at her desk, typing.

"How'd it go?" she asked.

"Don't ask," I said. I took her calendar pad and flipped it to Monday. Sit in on city council meeting; discuss influx of Puerto Ricans into lower rent areas causing Negroes to move out. Pre-trial hearing. . . .

I watched Susie typing, her brown fingers flying over the keys. Susie was a tree with deep roots. She was a mixture of Negro, Puerto Rican, and white. Shake well before using, she tells her boy friends; and I thought about what Ben Franklin had said about hanging together or hanging separately. And I remembered the bottle of bourbon in the file cabinet under "B."

CHRIS FRAZER

Zydeco

CHRIS FRAZER is a young woman writer who, being part Cherokee Indian, says: "I have a special interest in all minority group relations. My story was based on an actual incident and I feel it presents a hithero unexplored aspect of ghetto life." The story won a STORY College Creative Award cash prize in the 1970-71 nation-wide competition of writers in the colleges of the United States and Canada. She was then a student at the University of Delaware majoring in American history and American literature, with special reference to native cultures and the historical progression of the trans-Mississippi frontier. She was born in 1950.

They burned up the street last night, I was telling Tone after we got out of school. He just shrugged his shoulders around and said, "Well, waddya expect t' happen?" We went down to see the burned-up place, not because it was anything special, but more because it was the way my brother and me always went in the afternoon. Everything had been eaten up by the fire, the store windows were gray with smoke, the sidewalks all pocked, and more pavement loose than usual. A lot of kids were walking down the same way. We all gathered together and talked about the burned-up street.

"What did they use, huh?" a mule was asking Tone.

"Flame th'ower, what else? Like they used on 'Combat'," Tone told him, but he was looking at me.

"They didn't use no flame th'ower," Jeep laughed. "I didn't hear it, I woulda heard it, if it'd come."

"What's them tracks on the street, huh? What's them big griddy holes?" Tone pointed to the dug-out path down the center of the street.

"I still didn't hear it."

"Course not. How could ya hear it, when you was hidin' in the john?"

Jeep looked angry and said real loud, "I wasn't hidin' in the john, man, you know that."

"Under your mamma's bed, then," Tone told him, then pulled at my arm. "Come on, there ain't nothin' here t' see."

"I wasn't hidin' under no bed—" Jeep said as we were walking away. I knew him to be a mean kind, so I told Tone:

"Watch that Jeep, he's the one's gonna be wantin' t' get back at you for puttin' him down."

"What's he gonna do t' me? Nothin' he could do'd scare me." Tone kept kicking at the side of the pavement, crumbling the corner of the sidewalk into the gutter. I wasn't really worried about Jeep getting him back, because Tone could always take care of himself. It was that way most of the time, Tone taking care of himself and taking care of me too. He said that was what girls had older brothers for.

"Why'd they hafta burn up the street?" I asked him.

"Y' know they're gonna burn up the street when anyone starts messin' 'round. And there was alotta that las' night."

"They killed the two on the Charles Street beat, didn't they?"

"Yeah, Officer Mack an' t'other. Shot 'em like dogs," Tone told me calmly. He wasn't happy or sad about it, just telling me how it was.

"But why'd—"

"Now doncha remember when Joey Kas got shot las' week-end, they said they was gonna get Officer Mack, 'cause he did it."

"But they didn't hafta burn up the street."

"You liked that street the way it was or somethin'?"

"No, but it jus' seems——"

"Then quit it, huh? You're gettin' stupid."

I didn't want to go home then, so I told Tone I'd see him in a while. He wanted to know where I was going and I made up a story about going to see Lettice around the corner, be-cause Tone wouldn't like what I really wanted to do. I did go around the corner, but instead of going up to Lettice's, I cut between the building alleyways. This is the fastest way to get from Charles Street to Murdock without anyone seeing you, and I'm still little enough to squeeze between the row houses. Over at Murdock, I checked the corner out to be sure no one saw me, then I ducked into the cellar that the Libera-tion Army uses as headquarters.

Everything was crazy—torn up and all empty—because they had busted the headquarters after they burned up the street. I went back through the double doors that usually had two armed studs standing guard, looking around for someone in the office. A pot of coffee boiled on the hotplate and a cup stood ready. So someone had to be around, but they probably wasted when they heard me.

"Hey," I called out, "hey, anyone here—"

"Hey, yourself. Whatcha doin' here?" Zydeco stepped out of the doorway that led onto Severall Street and put his piece down on the counter. He was ragged and dirty and his shirt had smokestains all over the front. I started across the room, but he said quickly, "Wait! Anyone with you?"

"No, I come by myself."

"All right." He sat down on a stool next to the counter. "Pour me that coffee, wouldja?" He kept his hand loose by his side, like he was ready to grab up the piece should anyone

else come through the doubledoors. I got him the cup and
handed it to him. Even if his hands were as steady as ever
taking the coffee, I could guess that he was shaking inside.

"What the hell'd you come over here for? Someone coulda
followed."

"I went through the alleys."

"Huh." He stuck a finger into the cup to test how hot the
coffee was. "Got any cigarettes?"

I found them in my coat pocket, the ones I'd smoke in the
washroom with my girlfriends between classes.

"Thanks," Zydeco took the cigarettes and lit one. "You
want?"

"Yeah." I took a cigarette for myself and he laughed at me.
"You look funny smokin' that, with your baby face hangin'
out."

"I'm old 'nough."

"Sure you are. Now why'd you come?"

"I had to see what happened t' you. Someone tol' me at
school you was shot, maybe dead. If you was shot, I was gonna
get you help."

"An' if I was dead?" he asked.

"I dunno. Tell Mamma, I guess. She'd wanna see you was
buried right."

Zydeco reached out his free hand and rubbed at the side of
my head. "You're the only one of 'em that'd do that, come
an' see if I was still alive." He drank a little sip of the coffee.
"It was a nice thing t' do, babyface. But if they'd followed
you, I'd be up shit's creek with a bullet in my ass."

Mamma said he'd always been up the creek, since the day
he came to live with us when his own mother died. Zydeco
was very big on the street, he'd been up to the Boy's Home
three times since he was twelve. Twice for fighting in gangs
and once for selling gage. That last time he came back, this
past year, he changed a lot. Zydeco wasn't ever a mean sort,
just touchy and no one could ever push him around. But now

CHRIS FRAZER   [366

he was mad; he started running with all the others in the
Liberation Army. Tone said I should have nothing to do with
him, because the Man would be on me for hanging out with
that kind. I never listened because Zydeco was my cousin and
I didn't think it right to cut off your relatives like that.
    "How bad is it for you?" I asked.
    "How bad? They got a A.P.B. out on me, money on my
head." Zydeco was laughing about it. "Hell, they'll be comin'
outa the sewers t' get me, get that bread. I gotta get outa here,
but I don't have a way."
    "An' the others?"
    "Dunno 'bout some," he said, his voice very low and slow,
"Billy Kay got it with me, I carried him 'cross the street an'
he died in front of Tanker's store—think of it! Dyin' in front
of a liquor store. They got Jake an' Boo an' Sam an' Toby
uptown. If Toby ever lived that far. They jus' shot his eyes
outa his face."
    "You get hit?"
    "Scratched, that's all. I got to Myra's, that's where I hid,
she put some cover on me, gave me all her money. That's only
fifty bucks."
    "How 'bout Corey?" Except for Billy Kay, he was Zydeco's
best friend.
    "He's runnin' free, f' all I know."
    "I could find him for you."
    "You do no such thing. They take a look at you, shoot you
down quick as nothin'."
    "I know I could find him. His sister's a friend of mine, she
might know where he is."
    Zydeco shook me hard. "Look, they shot a sixteen-year-ol'
kid las' weekend for cussin' at a pig. They'd shoot you too f'
tryin' t' find Corey."
    "It's nothin'. I'm goin' t' see my friend, that's all. If I jus'
happen t' run into Corey, that's no fault of mine."

"You know," he said, "you got more sense than anybody in the whole family. You got more sense than me."

"All right, then, I'll go."

"All right."

"I'll be back in a while." I started to go for the door. "You want me t' bring anythin' back with me?"

"Food'd be nice, an' some other clothes."

"Dunno where I'd get clothes big 'nough, borrowin' 'em," I said. "Gimme money an' I'll buy you some."

He handed me one of Myra's ten-dollar bills. "Watch out, huh? If anythin' happens, don't come back here. Don't risk it."

"I'll see ya in a while."

Corey's sister lives four blocks over, so I took the alleyways to save time. As I came out on Brownhill Avenue, I could hear sirens in the next block and they scared me. Taking the steps two at a time, I was out of breath by the time I'd climbed four flights to the right room.

"EvaMarie, you home?" I shouted and pounded on the door. Everything was very still inside, like no one was there. Or people were there and they didn't want anyone to know.

"Who is it?"

I shouted in my name, then EvaMarie opened the door as far as the chain would let. "Whatcha want?"

"Trouble, you know, there's trouble."

"What trouble?"

"Where's your brother, EvaMarie?"

"Haven't see him in a long time, holy God knows I'm tellin' you the truth," she said.

"That's a lie. Is he here now?"

"Whatcha lookin' for Corey about?"

"My cousin's in a lotta trouble too, he needs Corey t' help him. Maybe Corey needs Zydeco t' help him too."

"Wait here." She shut the door and I could hear her walking back into the room. In a few minutes, she opened the door wide enough for me to come in. "Anyone out there?"

"No one follows me, you know that." I was looking around the room for Corey, but I didn't see him.

"It's all right," EvaMarie called out, and Corey came from the kitchen. He didn't have a shirt on, his right shoulder was all wrapped up in bandages, and his face was battered in. In one hand he had his jackknife.

"Zydeco, where is he?"

"Back at headquarters. He's scratched, but that's all. He needs a way out. You hurt bad?"

Corey rubbed a hand across his eyes. "In m' lung. Zydeco got any bread?"

"Fifty—forty dollars."

"Ain't nothin'." He sat down on the sofa. "But I gotta way, if the dude comes through. You tell Zydeco if he gets here by ten, an' the dude comes through, he can get out with me."

"All right," I nodded at him. Then I thought about the clothes. "EvaMarie, is your cousin Richie here?"

"Yeah, whatcha want him for?"

"I gotta buy Zydeco some clothes an' I don't know nothin' 'bout his size. Richie's 'bout as big as him, he can buy 'em for me. 'Sides I need someone t' cover for me, 'cause I wanna get him a coat an' I can't 'ford t' pay for it."

"Sure, Richie'll help you." EvaMarie went back to find her cousin and I watched Corey. He didn't look well enough to go anywhere. Besides his eyes had a glazed-over look you get when you've been popping handfuls of reds. Him up on reds and shot in the lung wasn't the best way to get out of anything. Soon enough EvaMarie came back with her stupid cousin. It took her about ten minutes to explain what I wanted him to do.

"Ten o'clock, Zydeco'll be here," I told Corey as we left to go to the secondhand store. Richie kept muttering to himself, it was getting on my nerves, so I told him to shut up.

"Talk t' me like that, I won't buy your clothes f' you."

"All right, I'm sorry. Jus' hurry up, will ya?"

We went into the store and Richie started talking to the man, telling him about the shirt and pants he needed. It was lucky for me no one else worked there, and that the coats were near the door. When the man had his back to me, I picked out the biggest overcoat on the pile and lighted out the door with it. In about an hour, it seemed, Richie came out of the store. I grabbed the bag from him, took the change from the ten and gave him fifty cents for his trouble and to keep him quiet. Then I was back through the alleyways again.

Zydeco stood by the door, waiting for me. He was surprised to see the coat. "How'd you get that?"

"Ripped it off. You be at Corey's ten o'clock, he says there's a way out."

"How'd you expect me t' get outa this place an' not be seen?"

"Go through the alleys like me. You can do it sideways, your shoulders're too broad t'let you do it frontways."

Zydeco was looking at the clothes. "Jesus God, aren't they ugly?"

"Guess so."

"Can't 'spect to get outa this place lookin' like the baddest dude on the street. How's Corey?"

"Shot in the lung. An' I think he's been eatin' pills all day."

"Damn good way t' go. Hey?" he said as I started for the door. "Where're you goin' now?"

"I can't stay here long, gotta get back for dinner or Mamma'll raise hell."

"It's gotta look funny, you keep poppin' in an' outa here."

"Look, she'll lemme out after I eat," I told him and I left.

Supper was a meal and a half, because Mamma still had meat left over from Sunday to go along with the red beans and rice. I told her how EvaMarie and me were working on a history paper together and how I wanted to get a good grade, so I'd have to go over to her place after dinner. She was pleased about me wanting a good grade, but not at all happy about me going out at night.

"Aw, I' been goin' out at night f' years now, an' nothin's ever happened."

"Well, after the troubles we had las' night, I don't want you goin' out alone. Tone can walk you over—you're friendly with EvaMarie's cousin, aren't you, Tone?—an' walk you back again."

"It isn't necessary, Mamma. I can do it alone."

"You don't argue with me. Tone's gonna walk over with you."

There wasn't any use in fighting her. If I did she'd keep me in all night. So I let Tone come along, figuring how I was going to get back to Zydeco with my brother watchdogging me. Mamma told us to be sure and come back by curfew time. We went out of the building, started down the street, watching the squad cars driving round the block over and over again.

"Must be 'spectin' somethin' to happen," I said to Tone.

"Or they're lookin' for someone they didn't get las' night."

I let that pass and told him, "We gotta stop at the grocery store."

"Don't EvaMarie's people have food or somethin'?"

"Never mind, I jus' gotta stop."

I went inside and Tone waited by the pinball machine at the door. With what was left of Zydeco's ten bucks, I bought a tin of meat and some bread. Then I was thinking about him getting out of town, so I bought a razor, some blades and a little can of cream. He wouldn't be so easy to identify if he shaved off his beard and moustache.

"I thought EvaMarie lived in Brownhill," Tone said as we cut down from Charles Street to the headquarters.

"She does, we're jus' goin' somewhere else first."

"Where else?"

"Don't matter, you'll see when we get there," I figured that telling Tone would only be trouble, so I just thought I'd surprise him.

We kept cutting through alleyways and Tone was complaining, "Doncha like the streets or somethin'?"

"With all them patrols on the streets, we might get stopped. This saves time."

"You in lotta hurry t' get somewhere."

"Yeah," I said, "an' your talkin' is slowin' us down." He was quieter after that.

When we came out onto Murdock, I was looking all around for people who might see us. Tone grabbed my arm, "I know where this is!" he said in a sneaky way.

"Smart, aren't you? Yeah, this is Murdock Street. Come on." I jerked away from him and ran across the street to the door of the headquarters. Tone hopped right behind me, getting really mad.

"Whatcha doin' in this place? I tol' you it was trouble t' mess with these shits."

Then Zydeco pulled the door open all of a sudden and stood facing Tone and me, with his piece up in his hand. "Shut up, boy, an' get in here quick!" No one ever argues with Zydeco, so Tone scooted in behind me and Zydeco shut the door.

"Here's the food," I said as he took the bag.

"What's the damn razor for?"

"So's you can shave off your beard an' they won't know you so easy."

"Cut my hair too. You think pigs're gonna stop to check if I'm shaved or not?" Zydeco said as he pried the lid off the tin of meat.

"Maybe so, maybe not. Better if you shave an' see."

We followed him into the back room, Tone holding his hands at his sides, his face all tight and angry. He wanted a chance to say something to Zydeco, but he wasn't getting one.

Zydeco just acted like he wasn't there, walking back and forth, eating the meat and bread, drinking coffee and talking to me.

"Ten o'clock, you said. Who's gonna get us out?"

"I dunno, I jus' know the time."

"In the lung, huh?"

"Yeah, in the lung."

"Well, you better stay here 'til I leave, 'cause I don't want no one gettin' suspicious of all this comin' an' goin'."

Tone jumped in there, "You can't make me stay here. I'll go when I wanna go."

"Kid, you go when you want. But if you tell anyone what you seen, it's your sister's gonna be hurt when they come to get me." Zydeco didn't even look at Tone when he was talking to him, he acted like he cared that little what my brother did.

"She's comin' with me."

"No, I'm stayin' here 'til I see Zydeco off," I said to Tone.

"You're stupid, you're really dumb, y' know there's men all over here an' they'll get him an' they'll be shootin' at you too," Tone was shouting at me.

"Shut up," Zydeco said in his softest voice, the way someone once told me he always talked when he was going to vamp someone really bad. "You're the stupid one. Get outa here, I sure as hell don't want you 'round."

Tone shook his head. "I'm stayin' if she's stayin'. Someone's gotta look out for her."

I was all ready to yell at Tone myself, but Zydeco said first, "Nothin's gonna happen, y'think I'd let anyone get t' her? Hey, have one of your cigarettes, baby face." He smiled and handed me the pack. "Besides, considerin' what she's done today, I'd say she can do a good job of lookin' out f' herself."

It seemed that Tone needed the cigarette more than me, so I gave it to him. Zydeco went into the washroom to shave off his beard and moustache.

Tone asked me if I'd been coming here for a long time,

then lying to him about it. I told him the truth, then explained about that day, wondering what had happened to Zydeco. Then I told him about getting the clothes and EvaMarie's brother and all that.

"Think you're pretty bad, doncha?"

"Don't think I'm bad at all, jus' doin' somethin' f' my cousin. Y' oughta be willin' t' do the same thing," I said.

"Not for that shit."

"You wouldn't call him that t' his face."

"I would an' I'll do it. He's nothin' but a shit, gettin' messed up with these other shits an' gettin' people shot an' streets burned up an' messin' everythin' up f' the rest of us," Tone told me and he didn't bother to lower his voice, so I guess he didn't mind that Zydeco could hear every word he said.

In a bit Zydeco came out of the washroom all shaved, it made him look a lot younger. I always think of him as really older than me, but he's only nineteen or so. With the beard, he looked almost twenty-five, but now he just looked like he was, four years older than Tone and five years older than me. He rubbed at his face and put the razor down on the counter.

"Think I'm a shit, huh?" he said to Tone.

"Yeah, I think you're worse'n nothin'."

"You know what I think of you?"

"Don't really care," Tone told him.

"I think you're a toad, somethin' I'd step on, but it's not worth the trouble of gettin' my shoe dirty," Zydeco said. I'd heard him talk like this once before, to one stud in the Liberation Army who'd messed with a kid on the street. It was scary because after he'd called the stud some names, Zydeco had practically taken his head off. I was a little afraid he was going after my brother too.

"You pretend t' be real worried 'bout your sister," Zydeco kept talking, "but you're really worried 'bout yourself. Worried that other people's gonna say 'bout you. You wanna keep everythin' cool, make sure you never get hurt, never see any kinda change, never get better an' never get worse. Toads like you fuck this world up for the rest of us."

Tone stared at him, not saying a word because I think he was scared too. Some of what Zydeco said was true, of course, Tone did worry a lot about what people thought of him. But I knew he wasn't that bad, so I said that to Zydeco, hoping to cool him off. He laughed at me.

"Scared I'm gonna go down on him, huh? You gotta be the mos' loyal person I've ever met. Him an' me, we're two different things. So you help me out an' you defend him t' me."

We were all quiet then, me wondering how Zydeco and Corey were going to get out, Tone probably trying to think of something to get back at Zydeco with, Zydeco just staring at the clock on the wall. The clothes fit him pretty well, even if they were ugly. When he got the coat on, it would cover up a lot, like the pants being too big and the shirt being too tight. About seven-thirty, there was a hard thump from the other room as the front door got thrown open. Zydeco said instantly:

"Get the hell down in that corner!" and he pushed me against the wall, running into the front room and shoving the cartridges into the piece.

Something fell hard, then a minute later Zydeco came back into the room truly carrying Corey in his arms like a baby. He put him down on the floor gently and knelt beside him. Corey didn't have a coat on, there was a lot of blood over the front of his shirt. He kept sucking in air fast, but it didn't seem to be doing him any good. It was like he was choking. Tone and me got out of the corner and went close to the both of them. Corey was trying to talk.

"Goddamn Richie . . . let one word drop y' know . . . pigs all over the streets, I got the hell out but they got me again . . . tore it loose, bleedin' all over . . . can't get air, can't get no air . . . Hey, man!" He grabbed Zydeco's hand in both of his,

"Hey man, what's comin' here, mebbe you tell me, see, tell me now. . . ."

That was crazy kid talk, zydeco-slang, the way we talk when we're all in a group feeling good, or when we're lonely and want to feel good again. When he was a kid, that was the only way Zydeco would ever talk, so that's how he got his name. Now he was talking that way back to Corey.

"Yeah it's comin' down now mebbe, but we see what's gonna come in some time later on, you see, baby, don't worry 'bout not one thing."

"I not comin' not comin' nowhere, but you gotta waste y' see, so here is what for you: go up pier-side 16, Zydeco hear me, up there's easy way you gettin' outa this sorry shitstorm, quick an' oh, so quick an' easy, see?"

"Yeah an' you comin' too."

"No, man, not comin' not this way, I got made down—you see, pier-side 16, get wastin' now an' be free—"

"Don't gimme that scam, I'll carry you out, ridin' easy on my back mebbe."

"Get the hell outa this, Zydeco, quick now, see? An' gone an' gone away free." Then Corey dropped Zydeco's hand, coughed some blood over Zydeco's pantleg, moved his head, then didn't move anymore.

"You better do what he said," I told Zydeco, " 'cause they'll be here soon."

"Yeah, gotta get wastin'." He stared at Corey. "Nothin' else t' do."

"Be careful, keep t' the alleyways."

"I'll be careful as I can, baby face." He rubbed at the side of my head one more time, then he put on the coat, stuck the piece in his right pocket and went out the back door onto Severall. Tone stood up, staring at Corey the way Zydeco had.

"We gotta go too," I told him.

"This ain't any good at all," Tone told me, "no good at all."

"Yeah, it's no good, I know that. Come on." We went out into the street, cut into an alleyway and were deep in the buildings before we heard the sirens.

"Where's he gonna go, huh?"

"Maybe Mexico, I dunno. I didn't ask him."

"Wonder if he'll ever come back."

"Don't think that'd be a smart thing t' do," I said, but hoping that Zydeco did come back sometime.

I was expecting an army to be waiting for us, but Charles Street was real quiet and still. Tone and me walked along slow, him kicking at the sidewalk the way he always does. He was worried about something, and soon enough he said:

"I don't think I'm a toad, d'you think I'm a toad?"

"No, you're not a toad at all. Wouldn't have a toad for a brother."

He liked that, so he said, "I got a quarter, you wanna soda?"

"Sure, if you're gonna buy it f' me."

"Yeah, I'm gonna buy it f' you."

ELDRIDGE CLEAVER

To All Black Women, From All Black Men

From Soul on Ice

ELDRIDGE CLEAVER, a black man who has spent "eight out of thirty-four years in various prisons in the United States" and who, since November 27, 1968, has been living in Cuba or Africa as a refugee from a court decision ruling that he must return to prison for violation of parole, was born in 1935 in Wabbaseka, Arkansas. He is the son of Leroy Cleaver, a dining-car waiter, and Thelma Cleaver, a janitress. He attended a junior college but says he did most of his studying in California prisons, from one of which he was released following the writing of his autobiography, *Soul on Ice*. He ran for the presidency of the United States in 1968 on the Peace and Freedom party ticket and has been identified with the Black Panthers as Minister of Information. He is married to a California civil-rights lawyer, Beverly Axelrod, who obtained his release from Folsom Prison after nine years. His *Soul on Ice*, from which this excerpt is taken, has been considered by at least one critic (Maxwell Geismar) as "one of the discoveries of the 1960s. . . . As the volume opens on the theme of love, so it closes on it," he points out. "Eldridge Cleaver never misses the sexual core of every social (or racial) phenomenon."

Queen–Mother–Daughter of Africa
Sister of My Soul
Black Bride of My Passion
My Eternal Love

I greet you, my Queen, not in the obsequious whine of a cringing Slave to which you have become accustomed, neither do I greet you in the new voice, the unctuous supplications of the sleek Black Bourgeoise, nor the bullying bellow of the rude Free Slave—but in my own voice do I greet you, the voice of the Black Man. And although I greet you *anew*, my greeting is not *new*, but as old as the Sun, Moon, and Stars. And rather than mark a new beginning, my greeting signifies only my Return.

I have Returned from the dead. I speak to you now from the Here And Now. I was dead for four hundred years. For four hundred years you have been a woman alone, bereft of her man, a manless woman. For four hundred years I was neither your man nor my own man. The white man stood between us, over us, around us. The white man was your man and my man. Do not pass lightly over this truth, my Queen, for even though the fact of it has burned into the marrow of our bones and diluted our blood, we must bring it to the surface of the mind, into the realm of knowing, glue our gaze upon it and stare at it as at a coiled serpent in a baby's playpen or the fresh flowers on a mother's grave. It is to be pondered and realized in the heart, for the heel of the white man's boot is our point of departure, our point of Resolve and Return—the bloodstained pivot of our future. (But I would ask you to recall, that before we could come up from slavery, we had to be pulled down from our throne.)

* * *

Across the naked abyss of negated masculinity, of four
hundred years minus my Balls, we face each other today, my
Queen. I feel a deep, terrifying hurt, the pain of humiliation
of the vanquished warrior. The shame of the fleet-footed
sprinter who stumbles at the start of the race. I feel unjusti-
fied. I can't bear to look into your eyes. Don't you know
(surely you must have noticed by now: four hundred years!)
that for four hundred years I have been unable to look
squarely into your eyes? I tremble inside each time you look
at me. I can feel . . . in the ray of your eye, from a deep hiding place, a long-kept secret you harbor. That is the un-
adorned truth. Not that I would have felt justified, under the
circumstances, in taking such liberties with you, but I want
you to know that I feared to look into your eyes because I
knew I would find reflected there a merciless Indictment of
my impotence and a compelling challenge to redeem my
conquered manhood.

My Queen, it is hard for me to tell you what is in my
heart for you today—what is in the heart of all my black
brothers for you and all your black sisters—and I fear I will
fail unless you reach out to me, tune in on me with the
antenna of your love, the sacred love in ultimate degree which
you were unable to give me because I, being dead, was un-
worthy to receive it; that perfect, radical love of black on
which our Fathers thrived. Let me drink from the river of
your love at its source, let the lines of force of your love seize
my soul by its core and heal the wound of my Castration,
let my convex exile end its haunted Odyssey in your concave
essence which receives that it may give. Flower of Africa, it
is only through the liberating power of your *re*-love that my
manhood can be redeemed. For it is in your eyes, before you,
that my need is to be justified, Only, only, only you and only
you can condemn or set me free.

Be convinced, Sable Sister, that the past is no forbidden
vista upon which we dare not look, out of a phantom fear

of being, as the wife of Lot, turned into pillars of salt. Rather the past is an omniscient mirror: we gaze and see reflected there ourselves and each other—what we used to be, what we are today, how we got this way, and what we are becoming. To decline to look into the Mirror of Then, my heart, is to refuse to view the face of Now.

I have died the ninth death of the cat, have seen Satan face to face and turned my back on God, have dined in the Swine's Trough, and descended to the uttermost echelon of the Pit, have entered the Den and seized my Balls from the teeth of a roaring lion!

Black Beauty, in impotent silence I listened, as if to a symphony of sorrows, to your screams for help, anguished pleas of terror that echo still throughout the Universe and through the mind, a million scattered screams across the painfull years that merged into a single sound of pain to haunt and bleed the soul, a white-hot sound to char the brain and blow the fuse of thought, a sound of fangs and teeth sharp to eat the heart, a sound of moving fire, a sound of frozen heat, a sound of licking flames, a fiery-fiery sound, a sound of fire to burn the steel out of my Balls, a sound of Blue fire, a Bluesy sound, the sound of dying, the sound of my woman in pain, *the sound of my woman's pain,* THE SOUND OF MY WOMAN CALLING ME, ME, I HEARD HER CALL FOR HELP, I HEARD THAT MOURNFUL SOUND BUT HUNG MY HEAD AND FAILED TO HEED IT, I HEARD MY WOMAN'S CRY, I HEARD MY WOMAN'S SCREAM, I HEARD MY WOMAN BEG THE BEAST FOR MERCY, I HEARD HER BEG FOR ME, I HEARD MY WOMAN BEG THE BEAST FOR MERCY FOR ME, I HEARD MY WOMAN DIE, I HEARD THE SOUND OF HER DEATH, A SNAPPING SOUND, A BREAKING SOUND, A SOUND THAT SOUNDED FINAL, THE LAST SOUND, THE ULTIMATE SOUND, THE SOUND OF DEATH, ME, I HEARD, I HEAR IT EVERY DAY, I HEAR HER NOW . . . I HEAR YOU NOW . . . I HEAR YOU. . . . I heard you

then . . . your scream came like a searing bolt of lightning
that blazed a white streak down my black back. In a cowardly
stupor, with a palpitating heart and quivering knees, I
watched the Slaver's lash of death slash through the opposing
air and bite with teeth of fire into your delicate flesh, the
black and tender flesh of African Motherhood, forcing the
startled Life untimely from your torn and outraged womb,
the sacred womb that cradled primal man, the womb that
incubated Ethiopia and populated Nubia and gave forth
Pharaohs unto Egypt, the womb that painted the Congo black
and mothered Zulu, the womb of Mero, the womb of the
Nile, of the Niger, the womb of Songhay, of Mali, of Ghana,
the womb that felt the might of Chaka before he saw the
Sun, the Holy Womb, the womb that knew the future form
of Jomo Kenyatta, the womb of Mau Mau, the womb of the
blacks, the womb that nurtured Toussaint L'Ouverture, that
warmed Nat Turner, and Gabriel Prosser, and Denmark
Vesey, the black womb that surrendered up in tears that
nameless and endless chain of Africa's Cream, the Black
Cream of the Earth, that nameless and endless black chain
that sank in heavy groans into oblivion in the great abyss,
the womb that received and nourished and held firm the seed
and gave back Sojourner Truth, and Sister Tubman, and
Rosa Parks, and Bird, and Richard Wright, and your other
works of art who wore and wear such names as Marcus Garvey
and DuBois and Kwame Nkrumah and Paul Robeson and
Malcolm X and Robert Williams, and the one you bore in
pain and called Elijah Muhammad, but most of all that nameless one they tore out of your womb in a flood of murdered
blood that splashed upon and seeped into the mud. And
Patrice Lumumba, and Emmett Till, and Mack Parker.

O, My Soul! I became a sniveling craven, a funky punk,
a vile, groveling bootlicker, with my will to oppose petrified
by a cosmic fear of the Slavemaster. Instead of inciting the
Slaves to rebellion with eloquent oratory, I soothed their

hurt and eloquently sang the Blues! Instead of hurling my life with contempt into the face of my Tormentor, *I shed your precious blood!* When Nat Turner sought to free me from my Fear, my Fear delivered him up unto the Butcher —a martyred monument to my Emasculation. My spirit was unwilling and my flesh was weak. Ah, eternal ignominy!

I, the Black Eunuch, divested of my Balls, walked the earth with my mind locked in Cold Storage. I would kill a black man or woman quicker than I'd smash a fly, while for the white man I would pick a thousand pounds of cotton a day. What profit is there in the blind, frenzied efforts of the (Guilty!) Black Eunuchs (Justifiers!) who hide their wounds and scorn the truth to mitigate their culpability through the pallid sophistry of postulating a Universal Democracy of Cowards, pointing out that in history no one can hide, that if not at one time then surely at another the iron heel of the Conqueror has ground into the mud the Balls of Everyman? Memories of yesterday will not assuage the torrents of blood that flow today from my crotch. Yes, History could pass for a scarlet text, its jot and tittle graven red in human blood. More armies than shown in the books have planted flags on foreign soil leaving Castration in their wake. But no Slave should die a natural death. There is a point where Caution ends and Cowardice begins. Give me a bullet through the brain from the gun of the beleaguered oppressor on the night of seige. Why is there dancing and singing in the Slave Quarters? A Slave who dies of natural causes cannot balance two dead flies in the Scales of Eternity. Such a one deserves rather to be pitied than mourned.

Black woman, without asking how, just say that we survived our forced march and travail through the Valley of Slavery, Suffering, and Death—there, that Valley there beneath us hidden by that drifting mist. Ah, what sights and sounds and pain lie beneath that mist! And we had thought that our hard climb out of that cruel valley led to some cool, green and peaceful, sunlit place—but it's all jungle here, a wild and savage wilderness that's overrun with ruins.

But put on your crown, my Queen, and we will build a New City on these ruins.

JULIUS LESTER

The Mud of Vietnam

From Search for the New Land

JULIUS LESTER, born in St. Louis, Missouri, in 1939, is a graduate of Fisk University and now lives in New York City where he teaches a course at the New School for Social Research, dealing with the history of Black Resistance. He has written extensively on political and racial matters for various publications and for a time was a member of the Student Non-Violent Coordinating Committee. He has also hosted a weekly black television program. He is the author of the books *Look Out, Whitey! Black Power's Goin' Get Your Mama!* and *To Be a Slave, Revolutionary Notes* and *Search for the New Land,* from which this excerpt is taken.

. . . I remember walking by a construction site in Uppsala, Sweden, and as my feet touched the gravel I remembered all the gravel roads I had ever been on and the fields that surounded them and I was painfully aware that the gravel roads of Sweden had little meaning for me. The gravel roads of the South have been impressed into the earth by black feet and black feet are my feet and walking on those roads I know that I am walking in my own footsteps. I can see the feet inside the shoes that have traveled these roads, feet with corn plasters on the toes, feet whose skin is dry and wrinkled, running feet, hurting feet, feet that need to be thrust into a bucket of hot water in front of a potbellied stove, feet that did not know shoes until they were six or seven years old, feet that have curled the mud between the toes and left their imprint in the dust.

The earth is not the same everywhere because of the feet that mold it and the hands which hold it. The earth of Western Europe is a machined earth, a rubber-tired earth, not like the earth of Spain, Portugal, parts of Italy, not to mention Poland and beyond. I didn't understand the earth of Sweden, except where remains of Viking castles still stood. Those were footsteps I could walk in.

I fell in love with mud in Vietnam. It was so good to get out of Hanoi and walk up muddy muddy roads in early morning mist and I could feel so much of those fields and those people. I knew them, because of the early morning I walked up the steep muddy hill at Cousin Jessie's in Mississippi and it was so muddy I slipped several times on the slippery-as-ice mud and there was this mule eyeing me rather hostilely and the rain was coming down and I walked up the hill and climbed over a barbed wire fence and on through a field until I came to this sloping hill where all of my father's kin are buried and in the distance, almost obscured by the rain, the hills of Mississippi.

The
mud
of
Vietnam
is
woman-thigh
deep
with backs bent,
for muddiness is next to Godliness,

woman-thigh deep
in river mud at low-tide,
woman-hands
scooping mud to build
new dikes and
repair bombed ones;
woman-thigh deep
in the fields of
Hung Yen Province
carving slabs of
mud that will
be cut to
brick-size and
baked in kilns—
woman-thigh high
in water,
feet
deep
in
the
mud,
planting rice—
(with a quick
turn of the wrist
green stalks
are
thrust into the mud);
woman-thigh high
midst the delicate rice
hair (tied loosely
at the back of the head)
falling below the
hips
and
brushing the tops
of the
green
rice stalks.

Their
woman-ness
seems to grow from
the
mud
of
Vietnam
where they stand,
woman-thigh high,
woman-thigh deep.

I would like
to make love

woman-thigh high
woman-thigh deep

in
the
mud
of
Vietnam.

Vietnam. One cannot go there and come back the same. Particularly if you're black. To be in a country and not be surrounded by white people. What a joy. To be rid of that loneliness which comes from being constantly among a strange people who don't know anything about me and are convinced they do, a people who basically don't like me and say that they do. I look at white people and can see their little houses and lives and aspirations and it's like I don't exist. In Vietnam I felt completely free for the first time in my life, even though I couldn't talk directly to the people, didn't know the particulars of their lives and would never know them. Yet, I did know because their gentleness was mine, their mud was mine, and their enemy was mine. I did not need to hear from them, as I continually did, the facts of the war. Number killed does not mean much to me. Tonnage of bombs dropped does not move me. I know America and its capacity for evil would shame the Devil Himself. America places all of its confidence in its ability to destroy and kill and Vietnam places its confidence in people, as well it should. People are such fantastic creations, but in America we seldom have the opportunity to understand that, to feel it, to live it. But how can you destroy a people who have learned to carry a half ton of material on a bicycle, old women, old men, pushing bicycles loaded with bricks, mud, lumber and I didn't ask what else. How can you destroy a people who when a bomb is dropped in the center of their village leaving a crater thirty feet across and forty or fifty feet deep, either fill it, a bucket of dirt at a time, or simply pour water into it, a bucket at a time, and stock it with fish and then breed one and half tons of fish in the succeeding year. Driving through the city of Thanh Hoa that Easter Sunday after the planes had left for the day, I saw an old woman fishing out of a bomb crater, as if it were a lake that had been there since time immemorial. Everywhere I went in Vietnam I was given a ring made from the metal of a jet which was shot down in the area. They make medical tools from the metal of these jets. I was given a vase made from the casing of a thousand-pound bomb.

In Vietnam I learned what Man could be if given the opportunity. Even during a war, the Vietnamese exemplified a humanity I have never known. Yes, they're fighting a war, but you never forget that they are human beings fighting a war only because it has been forced upon them and if a people value themselves, they will defend themselves. In the dining room at the hotel, I flirted with the girls who waited on the tables, which isn't hard to do in Vietnam. Vietnamese women flirt outrageously, with that language of the face. One day there was an alert and we had to go to the shelter. As I went across the garden toward the bomb shelter I saw one of the waitresses running, helmet on her head, rifle in her hand, toward her position. I was stunned, because I had never dreamed that this petite young woman knew anything about guns. She felt me staring at her, I guess, because she stopped and looked at me and then blushed. Meanwhile the air raid siren is going, jets are swooping overhead, the antiaircraft guns are booming and this girl, rifle in her hand, blushes because I was staring at her. And there's no contradiction involved. Instead, that is the greatest exemplification of what it is to be revolutionary. In Vietnam I learned that the revolutionary is he who cries for those he has killed.

Revolution changes whole patterns of living and thinking. Once you get involved you start living right, as the old folks say. You know that you can't doodle on a piece of typing paper because the organization needs that piece of paper and a whole lot of people are depending on that piece of paper being used for getting out the word, not for some dude to sit up and doodle on. Once you get involved in revolution, you start to really care about people, how they feel, what they're going through and even if you can't do anything, you at least let them know that you know they're going through something and maybe that helps them endure it a little easier. But most people just throw that word around without letting it get into their lives, without letting it transform them. But the "I" which is me is more than my name, an identification tag used for social convenience. When "I" say that "I" am a revolutionary then "I" become You, if you will allow me, and You become "I." God, that's so hard. Most people won't let you inside them. We are educated to keep our "I" exclusive, to protect it and shelter it, but when we're afraid to let somebody else enter our selves, we don't live. We cling to our "I," which is like jumping from an airplane without a parachute. We cling to our "I" and like a poisonous climbing plant, it clings to us, making us so ugly, so incredibly ugly. Americans are the ugliest people in the world. Tight, hard faces. Eyes which broadcast mistrust. Beings which radiate fear of anything human. The young are different. Incredibly beautiful they are and I hope that they can retain it, let it grow. At least they're beginning to recognize that there are no institutions in the American Way of Life which encourage us to love one another and they are experimenting, trying to learn to love.

RITUAL

Standing with her eyes closed
and her feet close together,
a young woman allowed her
limp body
to be passed slowly
from hand to hand
by four men
standing in a small circle.
"The purpose is to see
how much we are willing
to trust ourselves
and
each other,"
said the leader.
Then,
each of the five participants
walked up to the others
one at a time,
touched them on the hands
or shoulders
and told them
"what I like most about you."

(*The New York Times*—July 24, 1968)

Sometimes that learning to love takes a courage most of us can't conceive of.

RITUAL—II

A young man
climbed over a five-foot-high fence
onto the grounds of the United Nations

last night
and
set himself on fire with gasoline.

Despite severe pain
from critical burns,
he apologized
for causing any inconvenience.

He gave no explanations of
why he had set himself afire.

(*The New York Times*—December 6, 1967)

The young are learning to love and to express that love. They are not afraid to reach out and touch another and know that that is good, that it is beautiful. It's so hard to do in America and people have to go through so many sick changes. They've been brought up to think of their bodies and feelings as ugly and no one, but no one, says anything about sex. How sick do you have to be to tell kids that a bird brought them. So once they discover their own body and someone else's body, some of them just freak out. And all they want to do is touch and feel and feel and touch. They can't get enough. But when you've been out in the cold all day, you want to get as close to the fire as possible when you come inside. The next generation will be much more casual, because this generation established the base camp.

Young blacks laugh at the struggles of young whites to free themselves. Yes, it is pathetic to read the ads in underground papers where people advertise for somebody and I would laugh, too, except for all the pain of loneliness which is really being advertised. And yes, I know, too, that those young whites are not free from racism, but at least they are conscious of so much that their parents have never known. Above all I know that those young whites can not be completely trusted. They can choose to go back home at any minute. But I want to trust them, to believe in them. They, too, are human and

I do not want to do to them what has been done to me. I can't ask other blacks, however, to forego the pleasure of hating. A part of me hates also. Sometimes, all of me, because they will never know, those young white kids, what it is like and I want to drown them in their whiteness. But, because they cannot completely know is no reason to deny them their right to humanity. They, too, are human and those I can love, I do and only hope that their numbers multiply with the rising of each sun.)

BY WHIT BURNETT

THE MAKER OF SIGNS, SHORT STORIES, HARRISON SMITH & ROBERT HAAS, 1934.
THE LITERARY LIFE AND THE HELL WITH IT, ESSAYS, HARPER & BROS., 1938.
IMMORTAL BACHELOR (WITH JOHN PEN), ROBERT BURNS NOVEL, STORY, 1942.

EDITED BY WHIT BURNETT

A STORY ANTHOLOGY (WITH MARTHA FOLEY), VANGUARD PRESS, 1933.
STORY IN AMERICA (WITH M.F.), VANGUARD PRESS, 1934.
THE FLYING YORKSHIREMAN, NOVELLAS (WITH M.F.), HARPER, 1938.
THIS IS MY BEST, 93 GREATEST LIVING AMERICAN AUTHORS IN THEIR BEST WORK, DIAL PRESS, 1942.
TWO BOTTLES OF RELISH, FANTASIES, DIAL PRESS, 1943.
THE SEAS OF GOD, STORIES OF THE HUMAN SPIRIT, J. B. LIPPINCOTT, 1944.
EIGHTEEN GREAT MODERN STORIES, AVON, 1944.
TIME TO BE YOUNG, STORIES OF YOUTH, LIPPINCOTT, 1945.
THE STORY POCKET BOOK, POCKET BOOKS, 1945.
AMERICAN AUTHORS TODAY, HIGH SCHOOL READER (WITH CHARLES SLATKIN), GINN & CO., 1947.
STORY: THE FICTION OF THE FORTIES (WITH HALLIE BURNETT, CO-EDITOR OF STORY), E. P. DUTTON, 1949.
THE WORLD'S BEST, 105 GREATEST LIVING AUTHORS IN THEIR MOST REPRESENTATIVE WORKS, DIAL PRESS, 1950.
STORY, MAGAZINE DEVOTED TO THE SHORT STORY, (WITH MARTHA FOLEY, 1931–1942) (WITH HALLIE BURNETT, 1942–1964).
SEXTETTE, NOVELLAS (WITH H.B.) MCKAY, 1951.
STORY IN BOOK FORM, NOS. 1, 2 (WITH H.B.) MCKAY, 1951.
STORY, NOS. 3, 4 (WITH H.B.) A. A. WYN, 1953.
THIS IS MY BEST HUMOR, WORLD CHOICES, ILLUSTRATED, DIAL, 1955.
THE SPIRIT OF ADVENTURE, HENRY HOLT & CO., 1955.
ANIMAL SPIRITS, LIPPINCOTT, 1956.
THIS IS MY PHILOSOPHY, HARPER, 1957; CITADEL, 1967.
THE SPIRIT OF MAN, HAWTHORN BOOKS, INC., 1958.
THE BEST COLLEGE WRITING 1961 (WITH HALLIE BURNETT) RANDOM HOUSE.
FIRSTS OF THE FAMOUS, BALLANTINE BOOKS, 1962.
PRIZE COLLEGE STORIES, 1963 (WITH HALLIE BURNETT) RANDOM HOUSE.
THE STONE SOLDIER, PRIZE COLLEGE STORIES, 1964, (WITH H.B.) FLEET.
THE MODERN SHORT STORY IN THE MAKING, (WITH HALLIE BURNETT) HAWTHORN BOOKS, 1964.
STORY JUBILEE (WITH HALLIE BURNETT) DOUBLEDAY, 1965.
STORY: THE YEARBOOK OF DISCOVERY, STORY AWARDS IN THE COLLEGES, (WITH HALLIE BURNETT), FOUR WINDS PRESS-SCHOLASTIC, 1968, 1969, 1970, 1971.
THAT'S WHAT HAPPENED TO ME, FOUR WINDS PRESS, 1969.
THIS IS MY BEST, IN THE THIRD QUARTER OF THE CENTURY, DOUBLEDAY, 1970.